Entertainment Directory

BRISTOL
GUIDEBOOK
2020

SHOPS, RESTAURANTS, *ATTRACTIONS & NIGHTLIFE*

The Most Positively
Reviewed and Recommended
by Locals and Travelers

BRISTOL
GUIDEBOOK
2020

SHOPS, RESTAURANTS, ATTRACTIONS & NIGHTLIFE

BRISTOL GUIDEBOOK 2020
Shops, Restaurants, Attractions & Nightlife

© Carol W. Bloom, 2020
© E.G.P. Editorial, 2020

ISBN: 9798603041674

Copyright © 2020
All rights reserved.

INDEX

SHOPS
Top 500 Shops - 9

RESTAURANTS
Top 500 Restaurants - 47

ATTRACTIONS
Top 500 Attractions - 85

NIGHTLIFE
Top 500 Nightlife Spots - 119

BRISTOL GUIDEBOOK 2020
Shops, Restaurants, Attractions & Nightlife

*This directory is dedicated to Bristol Business Owners and Managers
who provide the experience that the locals and tourists enjoy.
Thanks you very much for all that you do and thank for being the "People Choice".*

*Thanks to everyone that posts their reviews online and
the amazing reviews sites that make our life easier.*

*The places listed in this book are the most positively reviewed
and recommended by locals and travelers from around the world.*

*You will find in this book 2,000 places to visit organized in four groups
to make your life easier when you decide to go out.*

500 Shops, 500 Restaurants, 500 Attractions and 500 Nightlife Spots.

*Thank you for your time and enjoy the directory that is
designed with locals and tourist in mind!*

TOP 500 SHOPS
Recommended by Locals & Trevelers
(From #1 to #500)

Shops, Restaurants, Attractions & Nightlife/ Bristol Guidebook 2020

#1
Bloom & Curll
Category: Bookstore
Average price: Inexpensive
Address: 74 Colston Street
Bristol BS1 5BB, UK
Phone: +44 7786 960941

#2
Bristol Guild
Category: Department Store
Average price: Expensive
Address: 68 - 70 Park Street
Bristol BS1 5JY, UK
Phone: +44 117 926 5548

#3
The Canteen
Category: Art Gallery
Average price: Modest
Address: 80 Stokes Croft
Bristol BS1 3QY, UK
Phone: +44 117 923 2017

#4
Richer Sounds
Category: Electronics
Average price: Modest
Address: 143 Whiteladies Road
Bristol BS8 2QB, UK
Phone: +44 117 973 4397

#5
Here Gallery
Category: Art Gallery, Bookstore
Average price: Modest
Address: 108 Stokes Croft
Bristol BS1 3RU, UK
Phone: +44 117 942 2222

#6
Stanfords
Category: Bookstore
Average price: Modest
Address: 29 Corn Street
Bristol BS1 1HT, UK
Phone: +44 117 929 9966

#7
Fopp
Category: Music & DVDs
Average price: Inexpensive
Address: 43 Park Street
Bristol BS1 5NL, UK
Phone: +44 117 316 9465

#8
Clifton Hardware
Category: Hardware Store
Average price: Modest
Address: 19 Regent Street
Bristol BS8 4HW, UK
Phone: +44 117 970 6260

#9
Tilly Tomlinson Flowers
Category: Florist
Average price: Expensive
Address: 39 Baldwin Street
Bristol BS1 1RB, UK
Phone: +44 117 904 1141

#10
Molton Brown
Category: Cosmetics & Beauty Supply
Average price: Expensive
Address: Unit SU7 Quakers Friars
Bristol BS1 3BU, UK
Phone: +44 117 929 8359

#11
Cabot Circus
Category: Shopping Centre, Department Store
Average price: Modest
Address: Glass House
Bristol BS2 9AB, UK
Phone: +44 117 952 9360

#12
Les Fleurs
Category: Florist
Average price: Modest
Address: 80 Colston Street
Bristol BS1 5BB, UK
Phone: +44 117 929 8166

#13
Moti
Category: Sporting Goods
Average price: Modest
Address: 49 Whiteladies Road
Bristol BS8 2LS, UK
Phone: +44 117 973 8000

#14
My Yard
Category: Women's Clothing, Men's Clothing
Average price: Modest
Address: 40 Park Street
Bristol BS1 5JG, UK
Phone: +44 117 316 9438

#15
Oxfam Bookshop
Category: Bookstore
Average price: Inexpensive
Address: 56 Cotham Hill
Bristol BS6 6JX, UK
Phone: +44 117 946 7443

#16
Creativity
Category: Arts & Crafts
Average price: Modest
Address: 7-9 Worrall Road
Bristol BS8 2UF, UK
Phone: +44 117 973 1710

#17
Iota Bristol
Category: Flowers & Gifts, Jewelry
Average price: Modest
Address: 167 Gloucester Road
Bristol BS7 8BE, UK
Phone: +44 117 924 4911

#18
Forbidden Planet
Category: Comic Books, Music & DVDs
Average price: Expensive
Address: Triangle Heights
Bristol BS8 1EJ, UK
Phone: +44 117 929 7767

#19
IKEA Bristol
Category: Furniture Store, Mattresses, Kitchen & Bath
Average price: Inexpensive
Address: Eastgate Road
Bristol BS5 6XX, UK
Phone: +44 845 355 2264

#20
Rise Record Shop
Category: Music & DVDs
Average price: Inexpensive
Address: 70 Queens Road
Bristol BS8 1QU, UK
Phone: +44 117 929 7511

#21
RePsycho
Category: Fashion
Average price: Expensive
Address: 85 Gloucester Road
Bristol BS7 8AS, UK
Phone: +44 117 983 0007

#22
Lucy Anna Flowers
Category: Florist
Average price: Modest
Address: 7-8 The Glass Arcade
Bristol BS1 1LA, UK
Phone: +44 7787 478117

#23
The Beat Goes On
Category: Music & DVDs
Average price: Inexpensive
Address: 24 Cotham Hill
Bristol BS6 6LF, UK
Phone: +44 117 974 7241

#24
Bristol City Museum & Art Gallery
Category: Art Gallery, Coffee & Tea
Average price: Inexpensive
Address: Queens Road
Bristol BS8 1RL, UK
Phone: +44 117 922 3571

#25
TK Maxx
Category: Discount Store
Average price: Modest
Address: 32 Castle Gallery
Bristol BS1 3XE, UK
Phone: +44 117 930 4404

#26
Arnolfini Gallery
Category: Art Gallery
Average price: Modest
Address: 16 Narrow Quay
Bristol BS1 4QA, UK
Phone: +44 117 917 2300

#27
Childrens Scrapstore and Artrageous
Category: Art Supplies
Average price: Inexpensive
Address: 21 Sevier Street
Bristol BS2 9LB, UK
Phone: +44 117 908 5644

#28
Shop Vintage Lounge
Category: Vintage & Consignment
Average price: Inexpensive
Address: 19 Christmas Steps
Bristol BS1 5BS, UK
Phone: +44 117 316 9421

Shops, Restaurants, Attractions & Nightlife/ Bristol Guidebook 2020

#29
The Apple Store
Category: Computers
Average price: Expensive
Address: 11 Philadelphia Street
Bristol BS1 3BZ, UK
Phone: +44 117 900 3450

#30
Bamba Beads
Category: Arts & Crafts
Average price: Modest
Address: 7 Gloucester Rd
Bristol BS7 8AA, UK
Phone: +44 117 924 9959

#31
BS8
Category: Fashion
Average price: Modest
Address: 34 Park Street
Bristol BS1 5JG, UK
Phone: +44 117 929 9011

#32
Lion Store
Category: Hardware Store
Average price: Inexpensive
Address: 219 North Street
Bristol BS3 1JJ, UK
Phone: +44 117 966 7233

#33
Aroha
Category: Framing, Cards & Stationery
Average price: Modest
Address: 29 The Arcade
Bristol BS1 3JD, UK
Phone: +44 117 983 8808

#34
Riverside Garden Centre
Category: Nursery, Gardening
Average price: Modest
Address: Clift House Road
Bristol BS3 1RX, UK
Phone: +44 800 037 5796

#35
St Peters Hospice Shop
Category: Thrift Store
Average price: Inexpensive
Address: 147 St Michael's Hill
Bristol BS2 8DB, UK
Phone: +44 117 974 5038

#36
Chaos Cycles
Category: Bikes
Average price: Inexpensive
Address: Corn Street
Bristol BS1 1JQ, UK
Phone: +44 7966 430534

#37
H & M
Category: Men's Clothing,
Women's Clothing
Average price: Modest
Address: Pegasus Road
Bristol BS34 5DG, UK
Phone: +44 117 950 9590

#38
Royal West Of England Academy
Category: Art Gallery, Museum
Average price: Expensive
Address: Queens Road
Bristol BS8 1PX, UK
Phone: +44 117 973 5129

#39
Rooted Records
Category: Music & DVDs
Average price: Modest
Address: 9 Gloucester Road
Bristol BS7 8AA, UK
Phone: +44 117 907 4372

#40
Bernard Hunter
Category: Photography Store
Average price: Inexpensive
Address: 246 North Street
Bristol BS3 1JD, UK
Phone: +44 117 966 6066

#41
Lush Hand Made Cosmetics
Category: Cosmetics & Beauty Supply
Average price: Expensive
Address: 73 Broadmead
Bristol BS1 3DX, UK
Phone: +44 117 925 7582

#42
Nomad Travel Clinic & Store
Category: Health & Medical,
Travel Services, Outdoor Gear
Average price: Expensive
Address: 38 Park Street
Bristol BS1 5JG, UK
Phone: +44 117 922 6567

#43
Urban Outfitters
Category: Fashion
Average price: Expensive
Address: SU38 Concorde Street
Bristol BS1 3BF, UK
Phone: +44 117 929 3221

#44
Chemical Records
Category: Music & DVDs, Electronics
Average price: Modest
Address: Feeder Road
Bristol BS2 0UY, UK
Phone: +44 117 971 4924

#45
Fred Baker Cycles
Category: Bikes
Average price: Modest
Address: 144 Cheltenham Road
Bristol BS6 5RL, UK
Phone: +44 117 924 9610

#46
Maplin Electronics
Category: Electronics
Average price: Modest
Address: 1-3 Gloucester Road
Bristol BS7 8AA, UK
Phone: +44 117 923 2014

#47
Happy Island Jewellers
Category: Jewelry
Average price: Expensive
Address: 43 Gloucester Road
Bristol BS7 8AD, UK
Phone: +44 117 924 5351

#48
Space NK Apothecary
Category: Cosmetics & Beauty Supply
Average price: Exclusive
Address: 81 Queens Road
Bristol BS8 1QP, UK
Phone: +44 117 929 4979

#49
Mud Dock
Category: Bikes
Average price: Modest
Address: 40 The Grove
Bristol BS1 4RB, UK
Phone: +44 117 929 2151

#50
Reclaimers Reclamation
Category: Antiques
Average price: Exclusive
Address: 347A Gloucester Road
Bristol BS7 8TG, UK
Phone: +44 117 924 8000

#51
Fopp
Category: Music & DVDs, Bookstore
Average price: Inexpensive
Address: 27 - 29 College Green
Bristol BS1 5NL, UK
Phone: +44 117 937 7110

#52
Rag Trade
Category: Women's Clothing
Average price: Modest
Address: 2 Upper Maudlin Street
Bristol BS2 8DJ, UK
Phone: +44 117 376 3085

#53
Blackwells
Category: Bookstore
Average price: Modest
Address: 89 Park Street
Bristol BS1 5PW, UK
Phone: +44 117 927 6602

#54
Angry Dave's
Category: Fashion
Average price: Modest
Address: 17 Christmas Steps
Bristol BS1 4, UK
Phone: +44 117 316 9455

#55
The 10 O'clock Shop
Category: Convenience Store
Average price: Modest
Address: 14a Richmond Terrace
Bristol BS8 1AB, UK
Phone: +44 117 973 7320

#56
Marks & Spencer
Category: Department Store
Average price:
Address: The Mall
Bristol BS34 5QT, UK
Phone: +44 117 904 4444

Shops, Restaurants, Attractions & Nightlife/ Bristol Guidebook 2020

#57
Lloyds
Category: Florist
Average price: Modest
Address: 3 Clifton Down Shopping Centre
Bristol BS8 2NN, UK
Phone: +44 117 973 1155

#58
Avon Textiles
Category: Fabric Store
Average price: Inexpensive
Address: 1-2 Market Gate St. Nicholas St
Bristol BS1 1LA, UK
Phone: +44 1454 632279

#59
KitchensCookshop
Category: Kitchen & Bath
Average price: Modest
Address: 167 Whiteladies Road
Bristol BS8 2SQ, UK
Phone: +44 117 973 9614

#60
Playfull Toy Shop
Category: Toy Store
Average price: Modest
Address: 87 Gloucester Rd
Bristol BS7 8AS, UK
Phone: +44 117 944 6767

#61
Marcruss Store
Category: Fashion, Hiking
Average price: Inexpensive
Address: 177-181 Hotwells Road
Bristol BS8 4RY, UK
Phone: +44 117 929 2119

#62
Blaze
Category: Jewelry, Home Decor
Average price: Expensive
Address: 84 Colston Street
Bristol BS1 5BB, UK
Phone: +44 117 904 7067

#63
Allsorts
Category: Antiques, Furniture Store
Average price: Modest
Address: 198A Cheltenham Road
Bristol BS6 5QZ, UK
Phone: +44 117 908 6893

#64
Billie Jean Clothes
Category: Vintage & Consignment
Average price: Expensive
Address: 208 Gloucester Road
Bristol BS7 8NU, UK
Phone: +44 117 944 5353

#65
La Ruca
Category: Latin American,
Home & Garden, Coffee & Tea
Average price: Modest
Address: 89 Gloucester Road
Bristol BS7 8AS, UK
Phone: +44 117 944 6810

#66
Spike Island
Category: Art Gallery
Average price: Inexpensive
Address: 133 Cumberland Road
Bristol BS1 6UX, UK
Phone: +44 117 929 2266

#67
Early Learning Centre
Category: Toy Store
Average price: Modest
Address: 1 The Mall
Bristol BS34 5GF, UK
Phone: +44 117 950 8775

#68
Primark
Category: Women's Clothing
Average price: Inexpensive
Address: 1-27 The Horsefair
Bristol BS1 3BB, UK
Phone: +44 117 922 5657

#69
Birds of Baldwin Street
Category: Tobacco Shop
Average price: Modest
Address: 35 Baldwin Street
Bristol BS1 1RG, UK
Phone: +44 117 927 3676

#70
Books For Amnesty
Category: Bookstore, Thrift Store
Average price: Inexpensive
Address: 103 Gloucester Road
Bristol BS7 8AT, UK
Phone: +44 117 942 2969

#71
Card Factory
Category: Cards & Stationery
Average price: Modest
Address: 19 Broadmead
Bristol BS1 3EA, UK
Phone: +44 117 925 5095

#72
Beware Of The Leopard Books
Category: Bookstore
Average price: Modest
Address: 66-69 & 77 ST. Nicholas Market
Bristol BS1 1LJ, UK
Phone: +44 117 925 7277

#73
Wilkinson
Category: Department Store
Average price: Inexpensive
Address: 15-29 Union Street
Bristol BS1 2DF, UK
Phone: +44 117 929 1667

#74
Christmas Steps Costume Hire and Joke Shop
Category: Costumes
Average price: Modest
Address: 47 Colston Street
Bristol BS1 5AX, UK
Phone: +44 117 926 4703

#75
Cooshti
Category: Men's Clothing, Women's Clothing
Average price: Expensive
Address: 57 Park Street
Bristol BS1 5NU, UK
Phone: +44 117 929 0850

#76
Cath Kidston
Category: Interior Design, Flowers & Gifts, Jewelry
Average price: Expensive
Address: 79 Park Street
Bristol BS1 5PF, UK
Phone: +44 117 930 4722

#77
London Camera Exchange
Category: Photography Store
Average price: Expensive
Address: 3 Alliance House
Bristol BS1 1SA, UK
Phone: +44 117 929 1935

#78
Shop Dutty
Category: Art Supplies, Women's Clothing, Men's Clothing
Average price: Modest
Address: 116 Cheltenham Road
Bristol BS6 5RW, UK
Phone: +44 117 924 9990

#79
Bristol Fine Art
Category: Arts & Crafts
Average price: Modest
Address: 74 Park Row
Bristol BS1 5LE, UK
Phone: +44 117 926 0344

#80
Plastic Wax Records
Category: Music & DVDs
Average price: Inexpensive
Address: 222 Cheltenham Road
Bristol BS6 5QU, UK
Phone: +44 117 942 7368

#81
Better Food Company
Category: Food, Shopping
Average price: Expensive
Address: Proving House Sevier St
Bristol BS2 9QS, UK
Phone: +44 117 935 1725

#82
Fabric Land
Category: Fabric Store, Knitting Supplies
Average price: Modest
Address: 52-56 Bond Street
Bristol BS1 3, UK
Phone: +44 117 922 0500

#83
Soukous
Category: Flowers & Gifts, Jewelry
Average price: Expensive
Address: 44a - 46 Cotham Hill
Bristol BS6 6LA, UK
Phone: +44 117 923 9854

Shops, Restaurants, Attractions & Nightlife/ Bristol Guidebook 2020

#84
Sky
Category: Framing, Art Gallery, Cards & Stationery
Average price: Modest
Address: 27 Waterloo Street
Bristol BS8 4BT, UK
Phone: +44 117 973 4074

#85
Handmade Boots and Shoes
Category: Shoe Store
Average price:
Address: 7 Christmas Steps
Bristol BS1 5BS, UK
Phone: +44 117 921 4247

#86
Cooperative Pharmacy
Category: Drugstore
Average price: Modest
Address: 143 St Michael's Hill
Bristol BS2 8DB, UK
Phone: +44 117 973 1473

#87
Joy
Category: Flowers & Gifts, Fashion
Average price: Expensive
Address: 70-78 Queen's Rd
Bristol BS8 1QU, UK
Phone: +44 117 929 8613

#88
Lunartique
Category: Accessories
Average price: Modest
Address: 47 Exchange Avenue
Bristol BS1 1JQ, UK
Phone: +44 7816 114062

#89
The Mall At Cribbs Causeway
Category: Shopping Centre
Average price: Modest
Address: The Mall
Bristol BS34 5DG, UK
Phone: +44 117 903 0303

#90
Focus On The Past
Category: Antiques, Jewelry, Furniture Store
Average price: Expensive
Address: 25 Waterloo Street
Bristol BS8 4BT, UK
Phone: +44 117 973 8080

#91
Next Retail
Category: Fashion
Average price:
Address: Unit 110 The Mall
Bristol BS34 5UP, UK
Phone: +44 844 844 5094

#92
Sainsbury's Supermarkets
Category: Shopping Centre
Average price: Modest
Address: Winterstoke Road
Bristol BS3 2NS, UK
Phone: +44 117 953 7273

#93
Pink Lemons
Category: Women's Clothing
Average price: Expensive
Address: 41 Gloucester Road
Bristol BS7 8AD, UK
Phone: +44 117 942 2103

#94
Boots Opticians
Category: Eyewear & Opticians, Drugstore
Average price: Modest
Address: 59 Broadmead
Bristol BS1 3EA, UK
Phone: +44 117 927 2418

#95
Game
Category: Computers
Average price: Modest
Address: Cribbs Causeway Regional Shopping Centre Bristol BS34 5GG, UK
Phone: +44 117 950 9292

#96
Nails Gallery
Category: Art Gallery
Average price: Modest
Address: Corn Street
Bristol BS1 1LJ, UK
Phone: +44 117 929 2083

#97
Credit Cruncher
Category: Wholesale Store, Home Decor
Average price: Inexpensive
Address: 163-164 Gloucester Rd
Bristol BS7 8BE, UK
Phone: +44 117 942 8639

#98
BiShopton Books
Category: Bookstore
Average price: Inexpensive
Address: 259 Gloucester Road
Bristol BS7 8NY, UK
Phone: +44 117 944 5303

#99
Gyles Brothers Limited
Category: Sports Wear
Average price: Modest
Address: 188 Whiteladies Road
Bristol BS8 2XU, UK
Phone: +44 117 973 3143

#100
KBK Shoes
Category: Shoe Store
Average price: Expensive
Address: 203A Cheltenham Road
Bristol BS6 5QX, UK
Phone: +44 117 924 3707

#101
Avon Books
Category: Bookstore
Average price: Modest
Address: 4 Waterloo Street
Bristol BS8 4BT, UK
Phone: +44 117 973 9848

#102
Tux & Tails
Category: Wedding Planning, Men's Clothing, Women's Clothing
Average price: Modest
Address: 372 Gloucester Road
Bristol BS7 8TP, UK
Phone: +44 117 942 9966

#103
Bristol Cameras
Category: Photography Store
Average price: Modest
Address: 47 High Street
Bristol BS1 2AZ, UK
Phone: +44 117 914 0089

#104
Leftbank Centre
Category: Bar, Art Gallery, Adult Education
Average price: Modest
Address: 128 Cheltenham Rd
Bristol BS6 5RW, UK
Phone: +44 117 944 4433

#105
Harvey Nichols & Second Floor Bristol
Category: Shopping Centre
Average price: Exclusive
Address: Second Floor Restaurant and Bar - Bristol c/o Harvey Nichols Re
Bristol BS1 3BZ, UK
Phone: +44 117 916 8898

#106
Georgian House Museum
Category: Art Gallery
Average price: Inexpensive
Address: 7 Great George St
Bristol BS1 5RR, UK
Phone: +44 117 921 1362

#107
Oxfam
Category: Thrift Store
Average price: Inexpensive
Address: 62 Cotham Hill
Bristol BS6 6JX, UK
Phone: +44 117 973 5200

#108
Cotham Hardware
Category: Hardware Store
Average price: Modest
Address: 11 Cotham Hill
Bristol BS6 6LD, UK
Phone: +44 117 973 5687

#109
Art At Bristol
Category: Art Supplies
Average price: Modest
Address: 44 Gloucester Road
Bristol BS7 8AR, UK
Phone: +44 117 923 2259

#110
Taunton Leisure
Category: Outdoor Gear
Average price: Modest
Address: 38-42 Bedminster Parade
Bristol BS3 4HS, UK
Phone: +44 117 963 7640

#111
Lime Tree Gallery
Category: Art Gallery
Average price: Expensive
Address: 84 Hotwell Rd
Bristol BS8 4UB, UK
Phone: +44 117 929 2527

#112
Bristol Blue Glass
Category: Arts & Crafts
Average price: Modest
Address: Whitby Road
Bristol BS4 3QZ, UK
Phone: +44 117 972 0818

#113
The Dragons Gallery Fossils & Crystals
Category: Arts & Crafts
Average price: Modest
Address: 13 The Arcade
Bristol BS1 3JA, UK
Phone: +44 7881 853290

#114
Mastershoe
Category: Shoe Store
Average price: Modest
Address: 52 Park Street
Bristol BS1 5JN, UK
Phone: +44 117 929 2020

#115
Mamas & Papas
Category: Baby Gear & Furniture, Maternity Wear, Children's Clothing
Average price: Modest
Address: Eastgate Retail Park
Bristol BS5 6XX, UK
Phone: +44 845 268 2000

#116
Twilight Fashions
Category: Fashion, Cosmetics & Beauty Supply
Average price: Modest
Address: 141-143 ST. Nicholas Market
Bristol BS1 1LJ, UK
Phone: +44 117 922 1951

#117
Make
Category: Women's Clothing
Average price: Modest
Address: 59 Gloucester Road
Bristol BS7 8AD, UK
Phone: +44 117 942 3030

#118
Pod
Category: Flowers & Gifts
Average price: Expensive
Address: 24 The Mall
Bristol BS8 4DS, UK
Phone: +44 117 973 9040

#119
The Flower Shop
Category: Florist
Average price: Expensive
Address: 145 Gloucester Road
Bristol BS7 8BA, UK
Phone: +44 117 942 0050

#120
Get Knitted
Category: Art Supplies
Average price: Modest
Address: 39 Brislington Hill
Bristol BS4 5BE, UK
Phone: +44 117 300 5211

#121
BHS
Category: Department Store
Average price: Modest
Address: 19 The Mall
Bristol BS34 5GF, UK
Phone: +44 845 841 0170

#122
Evolution Bristol
Category: Home Decor, Gift Shop
Average price: Modest
Address: Gallery Shopping Centre
Bristol BS1 3XF, UK
Phone: +44 117 922 5577

#123
The Entertainer
Category: Toy Store
Average price: Modest
Address: 30 Broadmead Gallery
Bristol BS1 3XB, UK
Phone: +44 844 800 5108

#124
The Sofa Project
Category: Thrift Store
Average price: Modest
Address: 48-45 West Street
Bristol BS2 0BL, UK
Phone: +44 117 954 3567

Shops, Restaurants, Attractions & Nightlife/ Bristol Guidebook 2020

#125
Office
Category: Shoe Store
Average price: Expensive
Address: Union Street
Bristol BS1 2D, UK
Phone: +44 117 929 4434

#126
3D Gallery
Category: Art Gallery, Jewelry
Average price: Expensive
Address: 13 Perry Rd
Bristol BS1 5BG, UK
Phone: +44 117 929 1363

#127
Cremona House Violin Shop
Category: Musical Instruments
Average price: Modest
Address: 7 Perry Road
Bristol BS1 5BQ, UK
Phone: +44 117 926 4617

#128
Cartridge Right
Category: Office Equipment, Computers
Average price: Inexpensive
Address: 53 Gloucester Road
Bristol BS7 8AD, UK
Phone: +44 117 924 8888

#129
Art @ Bristol
Category: Arts & Crafts
Average price:
Address: 40 Gloucester Rd
Bristol BS7 8AR, UK
Phone: +44 117 923 2259

#130
Waterstones
Category: Bookstore
Average price:
Address: University Walk
Bristol BS8 1TW, UK
Phone: +44 117 925 4297

#131
Arnolfini Bookshop
Category: Bookstore
Average price: Expensive
Address: 16 Narrow Quay
Bristol BS1 4QA, UK
Phone: +44 117 917 2304

#132
Bike UK
Category: Bikes
Average price: Expensive
Address: Queens Avenue
Bristol BS8 1SB, UK
Phone: +44 117 929 3500

#133
Elsie Riley
Category: Fashion
Average price: Modest
Address: 59 Broad Street
Bristol BS1 2EJ, UK
Phone: +44 117 934 9139

#134
Crystals
Category: Jewelry
Average price: Expensive
Address: 3 Lower Park Row
Bristol BS1 5BJ, UK
Phone: +44 117 926 6729

#135
Jessops
Category: Photography Store
Average price:
Address: 98 Whiteladies Road
Bristol BS8 2QY, UK
Phone: +44 845 458 7049

#136
British Heart Foundation
Category: Thrift Store
Average price: Modest
Address: 57a East Street
Bristol BS3 4HB, UK
Phone: +44 844 248 9144

#137
Clifton Brides
Category: Bridal
Average price: Expensive
Address: 186 Whiteladies Road
Bristol BS8 2XU, UK
Phone: +44 117 923 7928

#138
Motiq
Category: Jewelry, Women's Clothing
Average price: Modest
Address: 8 Boyces Avenue
Bristol BS8 4AA, UK
Phone: +44 117 973 8868

Shops, Restaurants, Attractions & Nightlife/ Bristol Guidebook 2020

#139
Craft Works
Category: Arts & Crafts
Average price: Modest
Address: 355-357 Gloucester Road
Bristol BS7 8TG, UK
Phone: +44 117 942 1644

#140
Carnival Costumes
Category: Costumes
Average price: Modest
Address: 131 Coldharbour Road
Bristol BS6 7SN, UK
Phone: +44 117 924 8429

#141
Bees & Graves
Category: Jewelry
Average price: Modest
Address: Unit 3 Clifton Arcade
Bristol BS8 4BJ, UK
Phone: +44 117 973 8448

#142
Jewellery Lane
Category: Jewelry
Average price: Expensive
Address: 9 All Saints Lane
Bristol BS1 1JH, UK
Phone: +44 117 922 6530

#143
Cotham Antiques
Category: Antiques
Average price: Modest
Address: 39a Cotham Hill
Bristol BS6 6JY, UK
Phone: +44 117 973 3326

#144
Sage
Category: Flowers & Gifts,
Home Decor, Jewelry
Average price: Expensive
Address: 214 Gloucester Road
Bristol BS7 8NU, UK
Phone: +44 117 942 9000

#145
Monsoon
Category: Fashion
Average price:
Address: Unit 157-158 The Cribbs
Causeway Centre
Bristol BS10 7TT, UK
Phone: +44 117 950 4175

#146
Bristol Tools
Category: Hardware Store
Average price: Modest
Address: 166 Gloucester Road
Bristol BS7 8NT, UK
Phone: +44 117 924 7413

#147
Area 51
Category: Hobby Shop
Average price: Modest
Address: 230 Gloucester Rd
Bristol BS7 8NZ, UK
Phone: +44 117 924 4655

#148
British Heart Foundation Books and Music
Category: Bookstore
Average price: Modest
Address: 148 Whiteladies Road
Bristol BS8 2RS, UK
Phone: +44 117 973 9274

#149
Blackboy Hill Cycles
Category: Bikes, Bike Rental
Average price: Modest
Address: 180 Whiteladies Rd
Bristol BS8 2XU, UK
Phone: +44 117 973 1420

#150
Rainbow Wools
Category: Knitting Supplies
Average price: Modest
Address: 405 Gloucester Road
Bristol BS7 8TS, UK
Phone: +44 117 924 8973

#151
Spanish Guitar Centre
Category: Musical Instruments
Average price: Expensive
Address: 103 Coldharbour Road
Bristol BS6 7SD, UK
Phone: +44 117 942 0479

#152
Barry Toogood
Category: Florist, Cards & Stationery
Average price: Modest
Address: 101 Coldharbour Road
Bristol BS6 7SD, UK
Phone: +44 117 942 4104

#153
Diana Porter Contemporary Jewellery
Category: Jewelry
Average price: Expensive
Address: 33 Park Street
Bristol BS1 5NH, UK
Phone: +44 117 909 0225

#154
BiShopton Trading Company
Category: Women's Clothing
Average price: Modest
Address: 193 Gloucester Road
Bristol BS7 8BG, UK
Phone: +44 117 924 5598

#155
Chaplins Of Bristol
Category: Costumes
Average price: Modest
Address: 9 St Augustines Parade
Bristol BS1 4UT, UK
Phone: +44 117 922 7773

#156
Totally Toys
Category: Toy Store
Average price: Modest
Address: 109 Gloucester Road
Bristol BS7 8AT, UK
Phone: +44 117 942 3833

#157
Woolies Indoor Market
Category: Farmers Market
Average price: Modest
Address: 30 Whiteladies Road
Bristol BS8 2LG, UK
Phone: +44 117 317 9423

#158
Inca
Category: Flowers & Gifts, Jewelry
Average price: Modest
Address: 2 Clifton Down Shopping Ctr
Bristol BS8 2NP, UK
Phone: +44 117 317 9758

#159
Natures Genius
Category: Specialty Food
Average price: Expensive
Address: 773 Fishponds Rd
Bristol BS16 3BS, UK
Phone: +44 117 958 4996

#160
House Of Fraser
Category: Department Store, Cosmetics & Beauty Supply
Average price: Expensive
Address: Cabot Circus
Bristol BS1 3BD, UK
Phone: +44 870 160 7228

#161
Avalaan
Category: Sports Wear, Men's Clothing, Women's Clothing
Average price: Modest
Address: 59 Gloucester Road
Bristol BS7 8AD, UK
Phone: +44 117 924 4273

#162
BiShopton Hardware
Category: Hardware Store, Home Decor
Average price: Modest
Address: 211a Gloucester Road
Bristol BS7 8NN, UK
Phone: +44 117 924 5935

#163
Debenhams
Category: Department Store
Average price: Modest
Address: 1 - 5 St. James Barton
Bristol BS1 3LT, UK
Phone: +44 844 800 8884

#164
Niche Frames
Category: Framing, Cards & Stationery
Average price: Modest
Address: 26 Stokes Croft
Bristol BS1 3QD, UK
Phone: +44 117 942 2213

#165
Jigsaw
Category: Women's Clothing
Average price: Expensive
Address: 80 Park Street
Bristol BS1 5LA, UK
Phone: +44 117 926 5775

#166
Sticky Neon
Category: Fashion
Average price: Inexpensive
Address: Gloucester Rd
Bristol BS7 8AL, UK
Phone: +44 117 924 7726

#167
Pink Planet
Category: Music & DVDs
Average price: Inexpensive
Address: 41A East Street
Bristol BS3 4HB, UK
Phone: +44 117 953 1776

#168
Faith Shoes
Category: Shoe Store
Average price: Modest
Address: Cribbs Causeway Regional Shopping Centre Bristol BS34 5DG, UK
Phone: +44 117 950 6749

#169
Wilkinson
Category: Discount Store, Drugstore, Home & Garden
Average price: Inexpensive
Address: 142-146 East St
Bristol BS3 4EW, UK
Phone: +44 117 966 4548

#170
Poundland
Category: Discount Store, Home & Garden
Average price: Inexpensive
Address: 82-92 The Horsefair
Bristol BS1 3JU, UK
Phone: +44 117 930 0113

#171
Urbi et Orbi
Category: Flowers & Gifts
Average price: Modest
Address: 18 Upper Maudlin St
Bristol BS2 8DJ, UK
Phone: +44 117 926 4999

#172
Shirt Tales
Category: Fashion
Average price: Modest
Address: 16 Upper Maudlin Street
Bristol BS2 8DJ, UK
Phone: +44 117 921 4885

#173
Furniture Store
Category: Furniture Store
Average price: Modest
Address: 196 Cheltenham Road
Bristol BS6 5RB, UK
Phone: +44 117 924 8930

#174
Bristol Handmade Glass
Category: Home Decor, Local Flavor
Average price: Modest
Address: 15 Perry Rd
Bristol BS1 5BG, UK
Phone: +44 117 929 8765

#175
Creations Nail Studio
Category: Nail Salons, Skin Care
Average price: Modest
Address: 67a Gloucester Road
Bristol BS7 8AD, UK
Phone: +44 117 924 6602

#176
Pink Planet DVD &Games
Category: Music & DVDs
Average price: Inexpensive
Address: 115 Gloucester Road
Bristol BS7 8AT, UK
Phone: +44 1373 455191

#177
Oskar
Category: Furniture Store, Home Decor
Average price: Expensive
Address: 47 Whiteladies Road
Bristol BS8 2LS, UK
Phone: +44 117 973 4777

#178
The Architecture Centre
Category: Art Gallery
Average price: Inexpensive
Address: Narrow Quay
Bristol BS1 4QA, UK
Phone: +44 117 922 1540

#179
St Peters Hospice
Category: Thrift Store
Average price: Inexpensive
Address: 154 Whiteladies Road
Bristol BS8 2XZ, UK
Phone: +44 117 974 5038

#180
Uncle Sam's American Vintage Clothing
Category: Men's Clothing, Women's Clothing, Vintage & Consignment
Average price: Modest
Address: 54a Park Street
Bristol BS1 5JN, UK
Phone: +44 117 929 8404

#181
T Mobile
Category: Mobile Phones
Average price: Inexpensive
Address: 64 Broadmead
Bristol BS1 3ED, UK
Phone: +44 117 929 9432

#182
H Samuel
Category: Jewelry
Average price: Modest
Address: 85 Broadmead
Bristol BS1 3DT, UK
Phone: +44 117 927 7219

#183
Central Rose
Category: Florist
Average price: Inexpensive
Address: 19 Christmas Street
Bristol BS1 5BT, UK
Phone: +44 117 927 9960

#184
Bristol Design
Category: Hardware Store, Art Supplies
Average price: Inexpensive
Address: 14 Perry Road
Bristol BS1 5BG, UK
Phone: +44 117 929 1740

#185
River Island Clothing Co
Category: Fashion
Average price: Modest
Address: 24-26 Broadmead
Bristol BS1 3HA, UK
Phone: +44 117 927 7913

#186
7G - Seven Generations
Category: Bookstore, Internet Cafe
Average price: Modest
Address: 10-12 Picton St
Bristol BS6 5QA, UK
Phone: +44 117 924 4986

#187
Dulay
Category: Men's Clothing, Women's Clothing
Average price: Modest
Address: 10-16 The Horsefair
Bristol BS1 3HT, UK
Phone: +44 117 933 0933

#188
The Range
Category: Furniture Store, Hobby Shop, Arts & Crafts
Average price: Inexpensive
Address: Unit 7
Bristol BS2 0SP, UK
Phone: +44 117 980 3883

#189
Gimme Shelter!
Category: Vintage & Consignment
Average price: Modest
Address: 22 Nelson St
Bristol BS1 2LE, UK
Phone: +44 117 325 1979

#190
Wanted Records
Category: Vinyl Records
Average price: Inexpensive
Address: Unit 1
Bristol BS1 1HQ, UK
Phone: +44 117 929 0524

#191
Rituals
Category: Kitchen & Bath, Cosmetics & Beauty Supply
Average price: Modest
Address: Cabot Circus
Bristol BS2 9AB, UK
Phone: +44 117 929 9877

#192
The Spokesman Bicycle Shop
Category: Bikes
Average price: Inexpensive
Address: 78 Mina Road
Bristol BS2 9YU, UK
Phone: +44 7929 061145

#193
Enso Martial Arts Supplies
Category: Sporting Goods, Martial Arts
Average price:
Address: 190 Cheltenham Road
Bristol BS6 5RB, UK
Phone: +44 117 942 5832

#194
College Green Bridal
Category: Bridal
Average price: Modest
Address: 44 College Green
Bristol BS1 5SL, UK
Phone: +44 117 316 9132

Shops, Restaurants, Attractions & Nightlife/ Bristol Guidebook 2020

#195
Savers
Category: Discount Store, Drugstore Cosmetics & Beauty Supply
Average price: Inexpensive
Address: 13 Castle Gallery
Bristol BS1 3XE, UK
Phone: +44 117 925 9582

#196
The Florist Ltd
Category: Florist
Average price: Expensive
Address: 1 Broad Quay
Bristol BS1 4DA, UK
Phone: +44 117 945 1820

#197
Bang & Olufsen
Category: Electronics
Average price: Exclusive
Address: 69 Queens Road
Bristol BS8 1QL, UK
Phone: +44 117 922 7522

#198
Easy Runner
Category: Sporting Goods
Average price: Modest
Address: 6 Horfield Road
Bristol BS2 8EA, UK
Phone: +44 117 929 7787

#199
Hobgoblin Music
Category: Musical Instruments
Average price: Modest
Address: 36 Park Street
Bristol BS1 5JG, UK
Phone: +44 117 929 0902

#200
Music Room
Category: Musical Instruments
Average price: Modest
Address: 30 College Green
Bristol BS1 5TB, UK
Phone: +44 117 929 0390

#201
Amphora Aromatics
Category: Discount Store
Average price: Modest
Address: 36 Cotham Hill
Bristol BS6 6LA, UK
Phone: +44 117 904 7212

#202
House Of Flowers
Category: Florist
Average price: Modest
Address: 8 Chandos Road
Bristol BS6 6PE, UK
Phone: +44 117 974 5655

#203
Inspirations Furniture
Category: Furniture Store
Average price: Modest
Address: 111 Whiteladies Road
Bristol BS8 2PB, UK
Phone: +44 117 974 4949

#204
Branches
Category: Furniture Store
Average price: Modest
Address: Temple Gate
Bristol BS1 6PL, UK
Phone: +44 117 934 9200

#205
F C Searle & Co
Category: Home & Garden, Electricians
Average price: Modest
Address: 66 Alma Road
Bristol BS8 2DJ, UK
Phone: +44 117 973 5124

#206
Beast
Category: Men's Clothing, Women's Clothing, Children's Clothing
Average price: Inexpensive
Address: 224 Cheltenham Road
Bristol BS6 5QU, UK
Phone: +44 117 942 8200

#207
Fig
Category: Cards & Stationery, Jewelry
Average price: Modest
Address: 206 Gloucester Road
Bristol BS7 8NU, UK
Phone: +44 117 924 4898

#208
Henleaze Garden Shop
Category: Nursery, Gardening
Average price: Expensive
Address: 146-148 Henleaze Road
Bristol BS9 4NB, UK
Phone: +44 117 962 0418

Shops, Restaurants, Attractions & Nightlife/ Bristol Guidebook 2020

#209
Soma
Category: Art Gallery, Arts & Crafts
Average price: Expensive
Address: 4 Boyces Ave
Bristol BS8 4AA, UK
Phone: +44 117 973 9838

#210
The Clifton Vintage Boutique
Category: Vintage & Consignment, Antiques
Average price: Modest
Address: 5 Clifton Arcade
Bristol BS8 4AA, UK
Phone: +44 7791 671229

#211
Pharmacy Plus
Category: Drugstore
Average price: Inexpensive
Address: 4-6 Cannon Street
Bristol BS3 1BN, UK
Phone: +44 117 985 3388

#212
Sense
Category: Home Decor
Average price: Expensive
Address: 6A Boyces Avenue
Bristol BS8 4AA, UK
Phone: +44 117 974 5347

#213
Kathmandu
Category: Sports Wear, Outdoor Gear
Average price: Expensive
Address: 11-13 Queens Road
Bristol BS7 9, UK
Phone: +44 117 927 7814

#214
Katze
Category: Fashion, Jewelry, Cards & Stationery
Average price: Modest
Address: 55 Gloucester Road
Bristol BS7 8AD, UK
Phone: +44 117 942 5625

#215
Cara
Category: Women's Clothing
Average price: Expensive
Address: 26 Park Street
Bristol BS1 5JA, UK
Phone: +44 117 925 7495

#216
Chandni Chowk
Category: Home & Garden, Fashion
Average price: Modest
Address: 66 Park Street
Bristol BS1 5JN, UK
Phone: +44 117 930 0059

#217
Woolly Thinking
Category: Fabric Store
Average price: Modest
Address: 6 Clifton Arcade
Bristol BS8 4AA, UK
Phone: +44 117 973 4444

#218
Oxfam Bookshop
Category: Books, Mags, Music & Video
Average price: Modest
Address: 26 Princess Victoria Street
Bristol BS8 4BU, UK
Phone: +44 117 946 7926

#219
Rachels Antiques
Category: Antiques
Average price: Modest
Address: 59-61 North Street
Bristol BS3 1ES, UK
Phone: +44 117 966 4747

#220
Fishponds Fruit & Flowers
Category: Fruits & Veggies, Flowers & Gifts
Average price: Inexpensive
Address: 731 Fishponds Rd
Bristol BS16 3UP, UK
Phone: +44 117 965 2500

#221
St Peters Hospice Charity Shop
Category: Thrift Store
Average price: Inexpensive
Address: 43 Sandy Park Road
Bristol BS4 3PH, UK
Phone: +44 117 977 7597

#222
Harveys Cycle Exchange
Category: Bikes
Average price: Expensive
Address: 178 Henleaze Road
Bristol BS9 4NE, UK
Phone: +44 117 962 9520

Shops, Restaurants, Attractions & Nightlife/ Bristol Guidebook 2020

#223
Rajani Superstore
Category: Department Store
Average price: Inexpensive
Address: Maggs Ln
Bristol BS5 7EW, UK
Phone: +44 117 965 5201

#224
John Lewis
Category: Department Store
Average price: Modest
Address: The Mall
Bristol BS34 5QU, UK
Phone: +44 117 959 1100

#225
Gamescene
Category: Books, Mags, Music & Video
Average price: Modest
Address: 723 Fishponds Road
Bristol BS16 3UW, UK
Phone: +44 117 965 2244

#226
H & M
Category: Fashion
Average price: Inexpensive
Address: 1 Odeon Buildings
Bristol BS1 2DS, UK
Phone: +44 117 945 1870

#227
Silver Shop
Category: Jewelry
Average price: Expensive
Address: 72 Colston St
Bristol BS1 5BB, UK
Phone: +44 117 929 4466

#228
The Sale Shop
Category: Furniture Store
Average price: Modest
Address: 203 Cheltenham Road
Bristol BS6 5QP, UK
Phone: +44 117 907 1785

#229
Sweaty Betty
Category: Women's Clothing
Average price: Expensive
Address: 59 Queens Road
Bristol BS8 1QL, UK
Phone: +44 117 929 9179

#230
St Peters Hospice Shop
Category: Thrift Store
Average price: Inexpensive
Address: 231 Lodge Causeway
Bristol BS16 3RA, UK
Phone: +44 117 965 1338

#231
Scope
Category: Thrift Store
Average price: Inexpensive
Address: 85-87 East Street
Bristol BS3 4EX, UK
Phone: +44 117 923 1637

#232
Topshop / Topman
Category: Men's Clothing, Women's Clothing
Average price: Inexpensive
Address: Brigstowe St
Bristol BS1 3BH, UK
Phone: +44 117 929 4991

#233
Cube Gallery
Category: Art Gallery
Average price: Expensive
Address: 12 Perry Road
Bristol BS1 5BG, UK
Phone: +44 117 377 1470

#234
Temple News
Category: Newspapers & Magazines
Average price: Inexpensive
Address: 62 Victoria Street
Bristol BS1 6DE, UK
Phone: +44 117 927 3720

#235
Shark Bite Surf Skate & Snow Centre
Category: Sports Wear, Outdoor Gear
Average price: Expensive
Address: 68 Park Row
Bristol BS1 5LE, UK
Phone: +44 117 929 9211

#236
ClicSargent
Category: Thrift Store
Average price: Inexpensive
Address: 38 Cotham Hill
Bristol BS6 6LA, UK
Phone: +44 117 914 1217

Shops, Restaurants, Attractions & Nightlife/ Bristol Guidebook 2020

#237
Clifton Down Shopping Centre
Category: Shopping Centre
Average price: Modest
Address: Whiteladies Road
Bristol BS8 2NN, UK
Phone: +44 117 973 2518

#238
The Rock Shop
Category: Accessories
Average price: Modest
Address: 63-65 St Nicholas Market
Bristol BS1, UK
Phone: +44 117 927 7300

#239
Rosebud Florist
Category: Florist
Average price: Expensive
Address: 184 Gloucester Road
Bristol BS7 8NU, UK
Phone: +44 117 924 1460

#240
St. Peters Hospice Shop
Category: Thrift Store
Average price: Inexpensive
Address: 221 Church Road
Bristol BS5 9HL, UK
Phone: +44 117 941 4690

#241
PDSA
Category: Thrift Store
Average price: Inexpensive
Address: 120 East St
Bristol BS3 4EY, UK
Phone: +44 117 963 3375

#242
Hotwells Pine
Category: Furniture Store
Average price: Modest
Address: 253 Hotwell Road
Bristol BS8 4SF, UK
Phone: +44 117 927 3700

#243
Cats Protection League
Category: Thrift Store
Average price: Inexpensive
Address: 272 North St
Bristol BS3 1JA, UK
Phone: +44 117 966 5428

#244
Bargain Booze
Category: Discount Store, Beer, Wine & Spirits
Average price: Inexpensive
Address: 137-139 West Street
Bristol BS3 3PD, UK
Phone: +44 117 963 5957

#245
Dolland & Aitchison
Category: Eyewear & Opticians
Average price: Expensive
Address: 8 Broadmead
Bristol BS1 3HH, UK
Phone: +44 117 926 2859

#246
Overburys Specialist Cycles
Category: Bikes
Average price: Expensive
Address: 138 Ashley Road
Bristol BS6 5PA, UK
Phone: +44 117 955 7924

#247
Centrespace Gallery
Category: Art Gallery
Average price: Modest
Address: 6 Leonard Lane
Bristol BS1 1EA, UK
Phone: +44 117 929 1234

#248
Snap
Category: Art Gallery
Average price: Modest
Address: 20-21 Lower Park Row
Bristol BS1 5BN, UK
Phone: +44 117 376 3564

#249
Sainsbury's Local
Category: Grocery
Average price: Modest
Address: 9 Broad Quay
Bristol BS1 4DA, UK
Phone: +44 117 948 5220

#250
Harvey Nichols
Category: Department Store
Average price: Exclusive
Address: 1 Philadelphia St
Bristol BS1 3BZ, UK
Phone: +44 117 916 8888

#251
PK Music Exchange
Category: Electronics,
Musical Instruments
Average price: Expensive
Address: 51 Gloucester Road
Bristol BS7 8AD, UK
Phone: +44 117 924 1658

#252
Hobbs-Style
Category: Hair Salons,
Cosmetics & Beauty Supply
Average price: Expensive
Address: 50 Park Row
Bristol BS1 5LH, UK
Phone: +44 117 929 1635

#253
Futon Company
Category: Home Decor, Furniture Store
Average price: Expensive
Address: 81 Park Street
Bristol BS1 5PF, UK
Phone: +44 117 922 0215

#254
Jacobs
Category: Photography Store
Average price: Modest
Address: 88 Whiteladies Road
Bristol BS8 2QN, UK
Phone: +44 117 973 3610

#255
The Grant Bradley Gallery
Category: Art Gallery, Framing
Average price: Modest
Address: 1 St Peters Court
Bristol BS3 4AQ, UK
Phone: +44 117 963 7673

#256
Clifton Framing
Category: Framing, Cards & Stationery
Average price: Expensive
Address: 110a Whiteladies Road
Bristol BS8 2RP, UK
Phone: +44 117 974 2026

#257
Alexander Gallery
Category: Art Gallery
Average price: Expensive
Address: 122 Whiteladies Road
Bristol BS8 2RP, UK
Phone: +44 117 973 9582

#258
Lisa Elliot Floral Design
Category: Florist
Average price: Expensive
Address: 1 Waterloo St
Bristol BS8 4BT, UK
Phone: +44 117 973 2440

#259
Treblerock
Category: Musical Instruments
Average price: Modest
Address: 37 Princess Victoria Street
Bristol BS8 4BX, UK
Phone: +44 117 9737 6666

#260
St Peters Hospice
Category: Thrift Store
Average price: Inexpensive
Address: 156 East Street
Bristol BS3 4EW, UK
Phone: +44 117 963 9557

#261
Lynne Fernandes
Category: Eyewear & Opticians
Average price: Expensive
Address: 182a Wells Road
Bristol BS4 2AL, UK
Phone: +44 117 977 6330

#262
Food For All Folk Centre and Charity Shop
Category: Thrift Store
Average price: Inexpensive
Address: 75 North St
Bristol BS3 1ES, UK
Phone: +44 117 966 9770

#263
Secka
Category: Jewelry
Average price: Expensive
Address: 225 Church Rd
Bristol BS5 9HL, UK
Phone: +44 117 955 2165

#264
St Peters Hospice
Category: Thrift Store
Average price: Inexpensive
Address: 256 North St
Bristol BS3 1JA, UK
Phone: +44 117 963 4214

Shops, Restaurants, Attractions & Nightlife/ Bristol Guidebook 2020

#265
Glass Designs
Category: Arts & Crafts,
Art Gallery, Home Decor
Average price: Expensive
Address: 261 North St
Bristol BS3 1JN, UK
Phone: +44 117 378 9227

#266
Gardiner Haskins
Category: Home & Garden, Lighting Fixtures & Equipment, Electronics
Average price: Modest
Address: Straight St
Bristol BS2 0JP, UK
Phone: +44 117 929 2288

#267
Henleaze Florist
Category: Florist
Average price: Inexpensive
Address: 57 Henleaze Road
Bristol BS9 4JT, UK
Phone: +44 117 962 2447

#268
Avon Meads Retail Park
Category: Shopping Centre
Average price: Modest
Address: St Philips Causeway
Bristol BS2 0SP, UK
Phone: +44 117 972 8044

#269
Unlock It UK
Category: Electronics, IT Services
Average price: Inexpensive
Address: 70 Stokes Croft
Bristol BS1 3QY, UK
Phone: +44 117 909 4129

#270
Gamestation
Category: Books, Mags, Music & Video
Average price: Modest
Address: 28 Broadmead
Bristol BS1 3HA, UK
Phone: +44 117 922 5995

#271
Claires Accessories
Category: Accessories
Average price: Inexpensive
Address: Castle Gallery
Bristol BS1 3XE, UK
Phone: +44 117 922 6657

#272
Dusk Til Dawn
Category: Furniture Store
Average price: Expensive
Address: 182-186 Cheltenham Road
Bristol BS6 5RB, UK
Phone: +44 117 944 2388

#273
Bike Workshop
Category: Bikes
Average price: Modest
Address: 88 Colston Street
Bristol BS1 5BB, UK
Phone: +44 117 926 8961

#274
Trevor Jones Brass & Woodwind
Category: Musical Instruments
Average price: Expensive
Address: 13 Christmas Steps
Bristol BS1 5BS, UK
Phone: +44 117 922 7402

#275
World Fossils Gems & Minerals
Category: Jewelry, Antiques
Average price: Expensive
Address: Unit 8 Corn Street
Bristol BS1 1HQ, UK
Phone: +44 117 930 0504

#276
Fifty Fifty
Category: Sports Wear, Shoe Store
Average price: Modest
Address: 8 Park Street
Bristol BS1 5HR, UK
Phone: +44 117 930 4990

#277
Stationery World
Category: Cards & Stationery, Art Supplies
Average price: Expensive
Address: 63 Park Street
Bristol BS1 5NU, UK
Phone: +44 117 929 8099

#278
Ablectrics Electrical Wholesalers
Category: Electronics
Average price: Modest
Address: 131 Gloucester Road
Bristol BS7 8AX, UK
Phone: +44 117 942 5355

Shops, Restaurants, Attractions & Nightlife/ Bristol Guidebook 2020

#279
Flying Saucers
Category: Arts & Crafts
Average price: Modest
Address: 9 Byron Pl
Bristol BS8 1JT, UK
Phone: +44 117 927 3666

#280
N E G Nailsea Electrical
Category: Appliances, Electronics
Average price: Modest
Address: 195 Gloucester Road
Bristol BS7 8BG, UK
Phone: +44 117 924 6002

#281
Emmaus
Category: Furniture Store
Average price: Inexpensive
Address: Shaftesbury House Kingsland Road St Philips Bristol BS2 0QW, UK
Phone: +44 117 954 0919

#282
Vision Express UK
Category: Eyewear & Opticians
Average price: Expensive
Address: 9 Broadmead
Bristol BS1 3HF, UK
Phone: +44 117 929 2206

#283
Which Watch
Category: Jewelry
Average price: Modest
Address: 32 The Arcade
Bristol BS1 3JD, UK
Phone: +44 117 921 0070

#284
Luggage & Case Store
Category: Luggage
Average price: Inexpensive
Address: 59 Union Street
Bristol BS1 2DU, UK
Phone: +44 117 922 1916

#285
Excelsior Comics
Category: Books, Music & Video
Average price: Modest
Address: 48 Bond Street
Bristol BS1 3LZ, UK
Phone: +44 7717 711756

#286
Tucks News
Category: Newspapers & Magazines
Average price: Modest
Address: 5 Cotham Road South
Bristol BS6 5TZ, UK
Phone: +44 117 924 9457

#287
The White Company
Category: Women's Clothing, Home Decor, Children's Clothing
Average price: Expensive
Address: 15 Philadelphia St
Bristol BS1 3BZ, UK
Phone: +44 845 678 8150

#288
Bi-Hand
Category: Flowers & Gifts
Average price: Modest
Address: 121 St. George's Rd
Bristol BS1 5UW, UK
Phone: +44 117 921 0053

#289
Timpson
Category: Jewelry, Watches
Average price: Modest
Address: 2 Clifton Down Shopping Centre
Bristol BS8 2NN, UK
Phone: +44 117 973 2455

#290
Kodak Express
Category: Photography Store
Average price: Inexpensive
Address: Whiteladies Rd
Bristol BS8 2NN, UK
Phone: +44 117 974 2862

#291
Romantica
Category: Cards & Stationery
Average price: Inexpensive
Address: 309 Gloucester Road
Bristol BS7 8PE, UK
Phone: +44 117 983 0099

#292
Payback Records
Category: Vinyl Records
Average price: Modest
Address: Unit 35 St Nicholas Street
Bristol BS1 1HQ, UK
Phone: +44 7966 347412

Shops, Restaurants, Attractions & Nightlife/ Bristol Guidebook 2020

#293
Bojo Brownz
Category: Tanning, Cosmetics & Beauty Supply, Hair Salons
Average price: Inexpensive
Address: 10 Park Row
Bristol BS1 5LJ, UK
Phone: +44 117 922 7744

#294
Fox & Feather
Category: Women's Clothing
Average price: Modest
Address: 43 Gloucester Road
Bristol BS7 8AD, UK
Phone: +44 117 329 2575

#295
Calico & Co
Category: Furniture Store
Average price: Modest
Address: 78-82 Bedminster Parade
Bristol BS3 4HL, UK
Phone: +44 117 953 3663

#296
Id Est Bristol
Category: Gift Shop
Average price: Expensive
Address: Glass Walk
Bristol BS1 3BQ, UK
Phone: +44 117 927 2850

#297
Romantica
Category: Cards & Stationery
Average price: Modest
Address: 309 Gloucester Road
Bristol BS7 8PE, UK
Phone: +44 117 983 0099

#298
Superdrug Store
Category: Drugstore
Average price: Inexpensive
Address: 44-46 East Street
Bristol BS3 4HD, UK
Phone: +44 117 966 1676

#299
Paul Roberts Hifi
Category: Electronics, Electricians
Average price: Expensive
Address: 31-33 Gloucester Road
Bristol BS7 8AA, UK
Phone: +44 117 942 9370

#300
Lexies
Category: Convenience Store
Average price: Inexpensive
Address: 88 Park St
Bristol BS1 5LA, UK
Phone: +44 117 929 9267

#301
Save The Children
Category: Thrift Store
Average price: Inexpensive
Address: 24 Regent Street
Bristol BS8 4HG, UK
Phone: +44 117 973 4057

#302
Stationery World
Category: Hobby Shop
Average price: Modest
Address: 63 Park St
Bristol BS1 5NU, UK
Phone: +44 117 929 8099

#303
Beautology
Category: Massage, Hair Removal, Cosmetics & Beauty Supply
Average price: Modest
Address: 107 Coldharbour Road
Bristol BS6 7SD, UK
Phone: +44 117 950 0500

#304
St Peters Hospice
Category: Thrift Store
Average price: Inexpensive
Address: 3 Boyces Avenue
Bristol BS8 4AA, UK
Phone: +44 117 923 8039

#305
Otomi
Category: Cards & Stationery, Ethnic Food, Jewelry
Average price: Modest
Address: 7 Clifton Arcade
Bristol BS8 4AA, UK
Phone: +44 117 973 2906

#306
RJ Media
Category: Electronics
Average price: Exclusive
Address: 348/350 Gloucester Road
Bristol BS7 8TP, UK
Phone: +44 117 942 9400

#307
Avon News
Category: Newspapers & Magazines
Average price: Inexpensive
Address: 38 North Street
Bristol BS3 1HW, UK
Phone: +44 117 966 4370

#308
Tesco Express
Category: Grocery
Average price: Expensive
Address: 171 - 175 Gloucester Road
Bristol BS7 8BE, UK
Phone: +44 845 026 9443

#309
Kellaway Pharmacy
Category: Drugstore
Average price: Modest
Address: 18 Kellaway Avenue
Bristol BS6 7XR, UK
Phone: +44 117 924 6579

#310
Arcadia Antiques & Interiors
Category: Antiques
Average price: Inexpensive
Address: 4 Boyces Avenue
Bristol BS8 4AA, UK
Phone: +44 117 914 4479

#311
Eddys Domestic Aplliances
Category: Appliances
Average price: Modest
Address: 279 North Street
Bristol BS3 1JP, UK
Phone: +44 117 966 5609

#312
The Snowboard Asylum
Category: Sporting Goods
Average price: Expensive
Address: 160A Whiteladies Rd
Bristol BS8 2XZ, UK
Phone: +44 117 974 1157

#313
Ellis Brigham
Category: Sports Wear, Outdoor Gear
Average price: Expensive
Address: 160 Whiteladies Road
Bristol BS8 2XZ, UK
Phone: +44 117 974 1157

#314
Cherri Burrelle
Category: Florist
Average price: Modest
Address: Bath Road
Bristol BS4 3EH, UK
Phone: +44 117 972 1356

#315
Solanki Store
Category: Newspapers & Magazines
Average price: Expensive
Address: 2 Gwilliam Street
Bristol BS3 4LS, UK
Phone: +44 117 966 5865

#316
Fiesta Flowers
Category: Florist
Average price: Modest
Address: 12 Sandy Park Rd
Bristol BS4 3PE, UK
Phone: +44 117 971 2917

#317
Direct Sewing Machine Supply
Category: Arts & Crafts
Average price: Modest
Address: 46 Sandy Park Road
Bristol BS4 3PF, UK
Phone: +44 117 977 8312

#318
Vinegar Hill
Category: Women's Clothing, Home Decor
Average price: Expensive
Address: 46 Queens Rd
Bristol BS8 1RE, UK
Phone: +44 117 929 4224

#319
Cabot Carpets
Category: Home & Garden
Average price: Modest
Address: 281 Southmead Road
Bristol BS10 5EL, UK
Phone: +44 117 959 1485

#320
Matalan
Category: Fashion
Average price: Modest
Address: 1 Abbey Retail Park
Bristol BS34 7JL, UK
Phone: +44 117 974 8000

Shops, Restaurants, Attractions & Nightlife/ Bristol Guidebook 2020

#321
PDSA
Category: Thrift Store, Knitting Supplies
Average price: Inexpensive
Address: 5a Clifton Down
Bristol BS8 4, UK
Phone: +44 117 923 8600

#322
Merilyn At 21
Category: Flowers & Gifts
Average price: Inexpensive
Address: 21 Canford Lane
Bristol BS9 3DQ, UK
Phone: +44 117 950 7060

#323
Edith Wilmot
Category: Florist, Bridal
Average price: Modest
Address: 5 Carlton Ct
Bristol BS9 3DF, UK
Phone: +44 117 950 8589

#324
Westworld
Category: Men's Clothing, Women's Clothing
Average price: Modest
Address: 35-37 Park Street
Bristol BS1 5NH, UK
Phone: +44 117 945 7783

#325
One Hundred
Category: Cards & Stationery
Average price: Expensive
Address: 100 Whiteladies Rd
Bristol BS8 2QY, UK
Phone: +44 117 974 1133

#326
Woodstock
Category: Furniture Store, Home Decor
Average price: Expensive
Address: 103 Stokes Croft
Bristol BS1 3RW, UK
Phone: +44 117 924 6491

#327
Taylor Made Frames
Category: Framing
Average price: Modest
Address: 63 Broad Street
Bristol BS1 2EJ, UK
Phone: +44 117 929 4819

#328
Sage Hair & Beauty
Category: Hair Salons, Cosmetics & Beauty Supply
Average price: Expensive
Address: 194 Cheltenham Road
Bristol BS6 5RB, UK
Phone: +44 117 923 2110

#329
The Gallery
Category: Shopping Centre
Average price: Modest
Address: 25 Union Gallery
Bristol BS1 3XD, UK
Phone: +44 117 929 0569

#330
Potters Antiques & Coins
Category: Antiques
Average price: Modest
Address: 60 Colston St
Bristol BS1 5AZ, UK
Phone: +44 117 926 2551

#331
The Carphone Warehouse
Category: Mobile Phones
Average price: Modest
Address: 2 Zetland Road
Bristol BS6 7AE, UK
Phone: +44 870 168 2751

#332
Bristol Green Store
Category: Fashion, Baby Gear & Furniture
Average price: Expensive
Address: Corn Street
Bristol BS1 1JQ, UK
Phone: +44 7812 472777

#333
Flaming Fireplaces
Category: Home & Garden
Average price: Expensive
Address: 4 The Promenade
Bristol BS7 8AL, UK
Phone: +44 117 924 3450

#334
Kindle Wood Burning Stoves
Category: Appliances
Average price: Modest
Address: 177 Gloucester Rd
Bristol BS7 8BE, UK
Phone: +44 117 924 3898

#335
Ten Tiny Toes
Category: Children's Clothing, Baby Gear & Furniture
Average price: Expensive
Address: 1a Pitville Place
Bristol BS6 6JZ, UK
Phone: +44 117 973 9966

#336
Gulzar Fancy Goods
Category: Gift Shop
Average price: Inexpensive
Address: 85 St Marks Rd
Bristol BS5 6HX, UK
Phone: +44 117 951 0495

#337
Atmosphere Electric Bikes
Category: Bikes
Average price: Expensive
Address: 137 Saint George's Road
Bristol BS1 5UW, UK
Phone: +44 117 908 7153

#338
Littleduck
Category: Baby Gear & Furniture
Average price: Inexpensive
Address: 8 Imperial Archade Street E
Bristol BS3 4HH, UK
Phone: +44 117 963 4123

#339
Pearces Hardware Store
Category: Hardware Store
Average price: Inexpensive
Address: 295 Gloucester Rd
Bristol BS7 8PE, UK
Phone: +44 117 924 5787

#340
Poundstretcher
Category: Discount Store
Average price: Inexpensive
Address: 48-58 East Street
Bristol BS3 4HD, UK
Phone: +44 117 953 8871

#341
Brackenwood Plant & Garden Centre
Category: Nursery, Gardening
Average price: Inexpensive
Address: Pill Road
Bristol BS8 3RA, UK
Phone: +44 1275 375292

#342
Globe Sports & Leisure
Category: Sporting Goods
Average price: Modest
Address: 167/169 Hotwell Road
Bristol BS8 4RY, UK
Phone: +44 117 929 3444

#343
Clifton Arcade Music
Category: Music & DVDs
Average price: Inexpensive
Address: 14-15 Clifton Arcade
Bristol BS8 4AA, UK
Phone: +44 117 946 7106

#344
Tamrakar
Category: Jewelry, Women's Clothing
Average price: Modest
Address: 1 North Street
Bristol BS3 1EN, UK
Phone: +44 117 963 9851

#345
Retro Collectables
Category: Vintage & Consignment
Average price: Modest
Address: 55 North Street
Bristol BS3 1AW, UK
Phone: +44 117 373 9724

#346
Tenovus
Category: Thrift Store
Average price: Inexpensive
Address: 110 Henleaze Rd
Bristol BS9 4JZ, UK
Phone: +44 117 962 8650

#347
St Peters Hospice Shop
Category: Thrift Store
Average price: Inexpensive
Address: 95 Gloucester Road
Bristol BS7 8AT, UK
Phone: +44 117 942 3109

#348
Peoples Republic of Stokes Croft
Category: Art Gallery, Local Flavor
Average price: Modest
Address: 37 Jamaica Street
Bristol BS2 8JP, UK
Phone: +44 7866 627052

Shops, Restaurants, Attractions & Nightlife/ Bristol Guidebook 2020

#349
Salvation Army Charity Shop
Category: Thrift Store
Average price: Inexpensive
Address: 110 Cheltenham Rd
Bristol BS6 6TB, UK
Phone: +44 117 924 5018

#350
The Mall Bristol
Category: Shopping Centre
Average price: Modest
Address: 25 Union Gallery
Bristol BS1 3XD, UK
Phone: +44 117 929 0569

#351
British Heart Foundation
Category: Thrift Store
Average price: Inexpensive
Address: 72 East St
Bristol BS3 4EY, UK
Phone: +44 117 953 5374

#352
Stuff
Category: Home & Garden
Average price: Inexpensive
Address: 231 Church Rd
Bristol BS5 9HL, UK
Phone: +44 117 941 4116

#353
Boots Shoes and More
Category: Shoe Store, Men's Clothing, Women's Clothing
Average price: Exclusive
Address: 106-108 High Street
Bristol BS16 5HH, UK
Phone: +44 117 956 8606

#354
Doug Hillard Sports
Category: Sporting Goods
Average price: Modest
Address: 647 Fishponds Road
Bristol BS16 3BQ, UK
Phone: +44 117 965 2473

#355
Castle Gallery
Category: Art Gallery
Average price: Expensive
Address: Pegasus Road
Bristol BS34 5UR, UK
Phone: +44 117 959 4647

#356
Hazel Holly
Category: Florist
Average price: Modest
Address: 1 Badminton Road
Bristol BS16 6BB, UK
Phone: +44 117 957 0977

#357
Reiss
Category: Fashion
Average price: Expensive
Address: Bond Street
Bristol BS1 3LZ, UK
Phone: +44 117 927 9199

#358
Robert Dyas
Category: Hardware Store, Building Supplies
Average price: Modest
Address: 18-19 Castle Gallery
Bristol BS1 3XE, UK
Phone: +44 117 929 4484

#359
The Handmade Shoe Co
Category: Shoe Store
Average price: Modest
Address: 64 Colston Street
Bristol BS1 5AZ, UK
Phone: +44 117 921 4247

#360
Roud Fabrics
Category: Fabric Store
Average price: Modest
Address: 221 Stapleton Road
Bristol BS5 0PD, UK
Phone: +44 117 951 1672

#361
Genesis Music & Clothing
Category: Music & DVDs, Men's Clothing, Women's Clothing
Average price: Inexpensive
Address: 226 Stapleton Road
Bristol BS5 0NX, UK
Phone: +44 117 935 5764

#362
Wesley Owen
Category: Bookstore
Average price: Modest
Address: 60 Park Street
Bristol BS1 5JN, UK
Phone: +44 117 926 4426

Shops, Restaurants, Attractions & Nightlife/ Bristol Guidebook 2020

#363
F Derbyshire & Partners
Category: Newspapers & Magazines
Average price: Inexpensive
Address: 123 Whiteladies Road
Bristol BS8 2PL, UK
Phone: +44 117 973 9002

#364
Machine Mart
Category: Hardware Store
Average price: Inexpensive
Address: 1-3 Church Road
Bristol BS5 9JJ, UK
Phone: +44 117 935 1060

#365
Hassans Persian Tailoring
Category: Sewing & Seamstress
Average price: Modest
Address: 6 Jacob's Wells Road
Bristol BS8 1EA, UK
Phone: +44 7837 011490

#366
Reeves Jewellers
Category: Jewelry
Average price: Expensive
Address: 19 East Street
Bristol BS3 4HH, UK
Phone: +44 117 966 4931

#367
The Card Factory
Category: Cards & Stationery
Average price: Inexpensive
Address: 84 East Street
Bristol BS3 4EY, UK
Phone: +44 117 966 5867

#368
Olivers Framery
Category: Framing
Average price: Expensive
Address: 111 Coldharbour Road
Bristol BS6 7SD, UK
Phone: +44 117 944 6244

#369
Jan Morrison
Category: Antiques
Average price: Expensive
Address: Clifton Arcade
Bristol BS8 4AA, UK
Phone: +44 117 970 6822

#370
Wyatt & Ackerman
Category: Cards & Stationery
Average price: Inexpensive
Address: 30 North St
Bristol BS3 1HW, UK
Phone: +44 117 966 1675

#371
Pirates & Roses
Category: Women's Clothing, Men's Clothing, Jewelry
Average price: Expensive
Address: 15 Portland St Clifton Village
Bristol BS8 4JA, UK
Phone: +44 117 970 6282

#372
Parkide Picture Framers
Category: Framing
Average price: Expensive
Address: 287 Church Road
Bristol BS5 8AH, UK
Phone: +44 7815 934873

#373
Eileens
Category: Florist
Average price: Modest
Address: 105a West Street
Bristol BS3 3NU, UK
Phone: +44 117 966 5412

#374
Marks & Spencer
Category: Department Store
Average price: Expensive
Address: Pegasus Road
Bristol BS34 5QT, UK
Phone: +44 117 904 4444

#375
Just So
Category: Toy Store
Average price: Modest
Address: 61 Henleaze Rd
Bristol BS9 4JT, UK
Phone: +44 117 962 8205

#376
Pack Of Cards
Category: Cards & Stationery
Average price: Expensive
Address: 77 Henleaze Road
Bristol BS9 4JP, UK
Phone: +44 117 962 3000

#377
Veron Ikon
Category: Home Decor
Average price: Expensive
Address: Top House, Christmas Steps
Bristol BS1 5BS, UK
Phone: +44 117 927 3005

#378
Wessex Reclamation
Category: Antiques, Pawn Shop
Average price: Expensive
Address: St Werburghs Rd
Bristol BS2 9PG, UK
Phone: +44 7881 817372

#379
Jack Wills
Category: Fashion
Average price: Expensive
Address: 65 Queens Road
Bristol BS8 1QL, UK
Phone: +44 117 922 5854

#380
Matalan
Category: Department Store
Average price: Modest
Address: Brislington Retail Park Bath Rd
Bristol BS4 5NG, UK
Phone: +44 117 300 5350

#381
Fired Earth
Category: Interior Design, Home & Garden
Average price: Expensive
Address: 65a Whiteladies Road
Bristol BS8 2LY, UK
Phone: +44 117 973 7400

#382
Tenovus
Category: Thrift Store
Average price: Inexpensive
Address: Unit 7 St James
Bristol BS1 3LT, UK
Phone: +44 117 927 9142

#383
Dance World
Category: School of Dancing
Average price: Modest
Address: 52 Bedminster Parade
Bristol BS3 4HS, UK
Phone: +44 117 953 7941

#384
WHSmiths
Category: Newspapers & Magazines
Average price: Inexpensive
Address: Lower Station Approach Rd
Bristol BS1 6QS, UK
Phone: +44 117 927 3488

#385
Peacocks
Category: Fashion
Average price: Inexpensive
Address: 102-106 E Street
Bristol BS3 4EY, UK
Phone: +44 117 966 2852

#386
Garlands Antiques
Category: Antiques
Average price: Inexpensive
Address: 22 North St
Bristol BS3 1JD, UK
Phone: +44 117 966 3876

#387
Blunts
Category: Shoe Store
Average price: Inexpensive
Address: 127 East Street
Bristol BS3 4ER, UK
Phone: +44 117 963 3816

#388
Old & New
Category: Home & Garden
Average price: Modest
Address: 24 West St
Bristol BS3 3LG, UK
Phone: +44 117 966 3296

#389
Rockwell Signs
Category: Graphic Design
Average price: Modest
Address: 341 Southmead Road
Bristol BS10 5LW, UK
Phone: +44 117 950 4506

#390
Bobbys Newsagents
Category: Grocery
Average price: Inexpensive
Address: 457 Gloucester Road
Bristol BS7 8TS, UK
Phone: +44 117 976 8006

#391
Frenchay Hospital Cardiac Support Group
Category: Thrift Store
Average price: Inexpensive
Address: 252a Lodge Causeway
Bristol BS16 3QS, UK
Phone: +44 117 907 8895

#392
Cardiac
Category: Cards & Stationery
Average price: Modest
Address: 253 N St
Bristol BS3 1JN, UK
Phone: +44 117 378 1485

#393
Jaydene Fashion Shop
Category: Fashion
Average price: Expensive
Address: 83 Henleaze Road
Bristol BS9 4JP, UK
Phone: +44 117 962 4091

#394
Osbornes Stationers
Category: Cards & Stationery, Office Equipment
Average price: Inexpensive
Address: 800 Fishponds Road
Bristol BS16 3TE, UK
Phone: +44 117 958 6061

#395
Shaws The Drapers
Category: Home & Garden
Average price: Modest
Address: 771 Fishponds Road
Bristol BS16 3BS, UK
Phone: +44 117 965 3524

#396
Clic Sargent
Category: Thrift Store
Average price: Modest
Address: 4 Straits Parade
Bristol BS16 2LA, UK
Phone: +44 117 958 3010

#397
Perfect Fit
Category: Lingerie
Average price: Expensive
Address: 50 Temple Street
Bristol BS31 1EH, UK
Phone: +44 117 986 0950

#398
Broadmead Shopping Centre
Category: Shopping Centre
Average price: Modest
Address: The Mall
Bristol BS1 3XD, UK
Phone: +44 117 925 7053

#399
The Works
Category: Bookstore
Average price: Inexpensive
Address: 8 The Horsefair
Bristol BS1 3HT, UK
Phone: +44 117 925 1554

#400
Fancy Dress Fanatics
Category: Costumes, Party & Event Planning
Average price: Modest
Address: 212 Cheltenham Road
Bristol BS6 5QU, UK
Phone: +44 117 329 0093

#401
Parsons Jewlers
Category: Jewelry
Average price: Modest
Address: 42 Castle Gallery
Bristol BS1 3XB, UK
Phone: +44 117 927 3846

#402
Frontline Video
Category: Books, Music & Video
Average price: Modest
Address: 124 Ashley Road
Bristol BS2 8YA, UK
Phone: +44 117 955 4992

#403
Superdrug Store
Category: Drugstore, Cosmetics & Beauty Supply
Average price: Modest
Address: 757-759 Fishponds Road
Bristol BS16 3UP, UK
Phone: +44 117 958 6767

#404
Karen Reilly
Category: Bridal
Average price: Expensive
Address: 16 Christmas Steps
Bristol BS1 5BS, UK
Phone: +44 117 929 2614

Shops, Restaurants, Attractions & Nightlife/ Bristol Guidebook 2020

#405
West Region Stamps
Category: Stamp Dealer
Average price: Modest
Address: 9 Christmas Steps
Bristol BS1 5BS, UK
Phone: +44 117 927 7836

#406
Centre Sewing Machines
Category: Arts & Crafts
Average price: Inexpensive
Address: 14 Castle Gallery
Bristol BS1 3XE, UK
Phone: +44 117 926 4071

#407
**Amelie & Melanie
Japanese Antiques**
Category: Antiques, Jewelry
Average price: Expensive
Address: 10 Perry Rd
Bristol BS1 5BG, UK
Phone: +44 117 330 9090

#408
United Supermarket
Category: Newspapers & Magazines
Average price: Inexpensive
Address: 66-68 Stapleton Road
Bristol BS5 0RB, UK
Phone: +44 117 955 1331

#409
Period Fireplaces
Category: Home & Garden, Antiques
Average price: Expensive
Address: Station Rd
Bristol BS6 5EE, UK
Phone: +44 117 944 4449

#410
Shrinking Violet
Category: Women's Clothing
Average price: Inexpensive
Address: Corn Street
Bristol BS1 1JQ, UK
Phone: +44 117 929 4566

#411
Reiss
Category: Women's Clothing
Average price: Modest
Address: 13 Philadelphia St
Bristol BS1 3BZ, UK
Phone: +44 117 927 9199

#412
Hakuna Matata
Category: Gift Shop
Average price: Inexpensive
Address: 286 Stapleton Road
Bristol BS5 0NW, UK
Phone: +44 117 951 9996

#413
Merchants News
Category: Print Media
Average price: Modest
Address: 62 Prince Street
Bristol BS1 4QD, UK
Phone: +44 117 925 3711

#414
Clifton Colour
Category: Photography Store
Average price: Exclusive
Address: Unit 4 Clifton Down Shopping Centre, Whiteladies Road
Bristol BS8 2NN, UK
Phone: +44 117 974 2862

#415
Sofa Workshop
Category: Furniture Store
Average price: Modest
Address: 76-78 Whiteladies Road
Bristol BS8 2QN, UK
Phone: +44 117 970 6171

#416
Card Bar
Category: Cards & Stationery, Chocolatiers &Shop
Average price: Modest
Address: 6 Clifton Down Shopping Centre
Bristol BS8 2NN, UK
Phone: +44 117 317 9457

#417
Star News & Booze
Category: Newspapers & Magazines
Average price: Inexpensive
Address: 46 Bedminster Parade
Bristol BS3 4HS, UK
Phone: +44 117 963 6883

#418
Crawfords News
Category: Newspapers & Magazines
Average price: Modest
Address: 200 Gloucester Road
Bristol BS7 8NU, UK
Phone: +44 117 924 6969

Shops, Restaurants, Attractions & Nightlife/ Bristol Guidebook 2020

#419
Heron Music
Category: Musical Instruments
Average price: Modest
Address: 158 Whitehall Road
Bristol BS5 9BP, UK
Phone: +44 117 955 3763

#420
George Elworthy & Co
Category: Cards & Stationery
Average price: Modest
Address: 185 Redland Road
Bristol BS6 6XP, UK
Phone: +44 117 973 7252

#421
Innocent Fine Art
Category: Art Gallery
Average price: Exclusive
Address: 7a Boyces Avenue
Bristol BS8 4AA, UK
Phone: +44 117 973 2614

#422
Clifton Arcade
Category: Shopping Centre
Average price: Expensive
Address: Boyces Avenue
Bristol BS8 4AA, UK
Phone: +44 117 974 4348

#423
Lisa Elliott
Category: Florist
Average price: Modest
Address: 1 Waterloo Street
Bristol BS8 4BT, UK
Phone: +44 117 973 2440

#424
Instep
Category: Shoe Store
Average price: Modest
Address: 19 Princess Victoria Street
Bristol BS8 4BX, UK
Phone: +44 117 973 1506

#425
Maze
Category: Women's Clothing, Men's Clothing
Average price: Modest
Address: 26-28 The Mall
Bristol BS8 4DS, UK
Phone: +44 117 974 4459

#426
Garlands
Category: Bikes
Average price: Modest
Address: 11-13 North Street
Bristol BS3 1EN, UK
Phone: +44 117 966 0743

#427
Mr Ben Travel Goods and Handbags
Category: Luggage
Average price: Inexpensive
Address: 128 East Street
Bristol BS3 4ET, UK
Phone: +44 117 953 5484

#428
Pipkins
Category: Drugstore, Hobby Shop
Average price: Inexpensive
Address: 140 East Street
Bristol BS3 4EW, UK
Phone: +44 117 966 3751

#429
Jack & Jill
Category: Toy Store
Average price: Inexpensive
Address: 192 Wells Rd
Bristol BS4 2AX, UK
Phone: +44 117 958 8860

#430
Up & Running Bristol
Category: Sporting Goods
Average price: Expensive
Address: 38 North View
Bristol BS6 7QA, UK
Phone: +44 117 973 9092

#431
Marks & Spencer
Category: Department Store
Average price: Expensive
Address: 78 Broadmead
Bristol BS1 3DS, UK
Phone: +44 117 927 2000

#432
Bon Bon
Category: Newspapers & Magazines
Average price: Inexpensive
Address: 34 Ashton Road
Bristol BS3 2EG, UK
Phone: +44 117 966 7222

Shops, Restaurants, Attractions & Nightlife/ Bristol Guidebook 2020

#433
Step Out Footwear
Category: Shoe Store
Average price: Inexpensive
Address: 161 Gloucester Road
Bristol BS7 8BE, UK
Phone: +44 117 330 1796

#434
St. Peters Hospice
Category: Thrift Store
Average price: Inexpensive
Address: 329 Wells Road
Bristol BS4 2QB, UK
Phone: +44 117 972 0457

#435
Ikon School& Sports
Category: Sports Clothing, Sports Equipment
Average price: Expensive
Address: 190 Henleaze Road
Bristol BS9 4NE, UK
Phone: +44 117 962 0011

#436
Halfords
Category: Automotive, Bikes
Average price: Modest
Address: Bath Road
Bristol BS4 5NG, UK
Phone: +44 117 941 8960

#437
Wet & Windy
Category: Outdoor Gear
Average price: Expensive
Address: 5 Ashton Dr
Bristol BS3 2PN, UK
Phone: +44 117 966 9582

#438
Dwell
Category: Home Decor
Average price: Expensive
Address: Cabot Circus
Bristol BS1 3BQ, UK
Phone: +44 845 678 1004

#439
Reverb
Category: Musical Instruments
Average price: Expensive
Address: 5 Rupert Street
Bristol BS1 2PY, UK
Phone: +44 117 934 9955

#440
Sainsbury's Local
Category: Grocery
Average price: Modest
Address: 255 Gloucester Road
Bristol BS7 8NY, UK
Phone: +44 117 944 6230

#441
Bedminster Parade Post Office & Newsagents
Category: Newspapers & Magazines
Average price: Inexpensive
Address: 7 East Street
Bristol BS3 4HH, UK
Phone: +44 117 963 6248

#442
White Stuff
Category: Women's Clothing
Average price: Modest
Address: 64 Queens Road
Bristol BS8 1RE, UK
Phone: +44 117 929 0100

#443
P S News
Category: Newspapers & Magazines
Average price: Inexpensive
Address: 39 East Street
Bristol BS3 4HB, UK
Phone: +44 117 966 8452

#444
W H Mogford & Son
Category: Hardware Store
Average price: Inexpensive
Address: 2 High Street
Bristol BS9 3DU, UK
Phone: +44 117 950 6801

#445
Smart Set Sports
Category: Sporting Goods
Average price: Expensive
Address: 5 Clifton Down Shopping Centre
Bristol BS8 2NN, UK
Phone: +44 117 974 4272

#446
Multiyork Furniture
Category: Furniture Store
Average price: Expensive
Address: 94c Whiteladies Road
Bristol BS8 2QX, UK
Phone: +44 117 946 7646

Shops, Restaurants, Attractions & Nightlife/ Bristol Guidebook 2020

#447
Bakos Boutique
Category: Women's Clothing
Average price: Expensive
Address: 50 High Street
Bristol BS9 3DZ, UK
Phone: +44 117 950 4909

#448
The Attic
Category: Antiques, Home & Garden
Average price: Inexpensive
Address: 37 North Street
Bristol BS16 5SW, UK
Phone: +44 117 949 7333

#449
Fig 1
Category: Cards & Stationery, Gift Shop
Average price: Modest
Address: 51 St Luke's Road
Bristol BS3 4RX, UK
Phone: +44 117 330 8167

#450
Village
Category: Flowers & Gifts
Average price: Expensive
Address: 2A Boyces Avenue
Bristol BS8 4AA, UK
Phone: +44 117 908 0007

#451
R A Holman
Category: Jewelry
Average price: Modest
Address: 707 Fishponds Road
Bristol BS16 3UH, UK
Phone: +44 117 939 1135

#452
Calas Flowers
Category: Florist
Average price: Inexpensive
Address: 5 Gloucester Road N
Bristol BS7 0SG, UK
Phone: +44 117 969 5000

#453
Budget Boozer
Category: Tobacco Shop
Average price: Inexpensive
Address: 161 East St
Bristol BS3 4EJ, UK
Phone: +44 117 963 5622

#454
Cartridge World
Category: Computers
Average price: Modest
Address: 184 Wells Road
Bristol BS4 2AL, UK
Phone: +44 117 971 9305

#455
Tailor Made Office Supplies
Category: Cards & Stationery
Average price: Modest
Address: Bonville Road
Bristol BS4 5QR, UK
Phone: +44 117 972 1678

#456
Bensons Bed Centres
Category: Home & Garden
Average price: Modest
Address: Unit 4
Bristol BS4 5NG, UK
Phone: +44 117 972 0382

#457
Global Furniture
Category: Furniture Store
Average price: Modest
Address: 329 Two Mile Hill Road
Bristol BS15 1AN, UK
Phone: +44 117 947 8000

#458
Corner News
Category: Newspapers & Magazines
Average price: Inexpensive
Address: 90 Wick Road
Bristol BS4 4HF, UK
Phone: +44 117 977 4953

#459
Vikesh News
Category: Newspapers & Magazines
Average price: Inexpensive
Address: 537 Fishponds Road
Bristol BS16 3AF, UK
Phone: +44 117 965 3576

#460
Good Timez
Category: Flowers & Gifts
Average price: Inexpensive
Address: 18 Regent Street
Bristol BS15 8JS, UK
Phone: +44 117 967 5105

#461
Hooked On Crafts
Category: Arts & Crafts
Average price: Modest
Address: 1a Regent Street
Bristol BS15 8JX, UK
Phone: +44 117 947 8333

#462
Poundstretcher
Category: Discount Store
Average price: Inexpensive
Address: 707a Fishponds Rd
Bristol BS16 3UH, UK
Phone: +44 117 965 9734

#463
Kingswood Kards
Category: Cards & Stationery
Average price: Inexpensive
Address: 105 Regent Street
Bristol BS15 8LJ, UK
Phone: +44 117 967 3828

#464
Theatek
Category: Electronics
Average price: Inexpensive
Address: Unit 1 95 Church Road
Bristol BS13 8JU, UK
Phone: +44 117 978 2360

#465
Shoe Zone
Category: Shoe Store
Average price: Inexpensive
Address: 741 Fishponds Road
Bristol BS16 3UP, UK
Phone: +44 117 958 6370

#466
Knitting Well
Category: Fabric Store, Knitting Supplies
Average price: Inexpensive
Address: 105 High Street
Bristol BS16 5HF, UK
Phone: +44 117 970 1740

#467
Churchs Newsagents
Category: Newspapers & Magazines
Average price: Modest
Address: 60 High Street
Bristol BS31 1DX, UK
Phone: +44 117 986 2418

#468
St. Peters Hospice
Category: Thrift Store
Average price: Inexpensive
Address: 148 Gloucester Road North
Bristol BS34 7AA, UK
Phone: +44 117 969 7295

#469
Norville Opticians
Category: Eyewear & Opticians
Average price: Modest
Address: 16 Downend Road
Bristol BS16 5UJ, UK
Phone: +44 117 956 0939

#470
St. Peters Hospice
Category: Thrift Store
Average price: Inexpensive
Address: 3 Badminton Road
Bristol BS16 6BB, UK
Phone: +44 117 956 0383

#471
20th Century Flicks
Category: Videos & Game Rental
Average price: Modest
Address: 3 Richmond Terrace
Bristol BS8 1AB, UK
Phone: +44 117 974 2570

#472
@MOSS
Category: Collectables, Gift Shop
Average price: Expensive
Address: The Mall
Bristol BS1 3XD, UK
Phone: +44 117 908 2308

#473
WH Smith
Category: Books, Music & Video
Average price: Inexpensive
Address: Pegasus Road
Bristol BS34 5GG, UK
Phone: +44 117 950 9525

#474
Bargainland
Category: Women's Clothing
Average price: Inexpensive
Address: 15-17 East St
Bristol BS3 4HH, UK
Phone: +44 117 966 3033

Shops, Restaurants, Attractions & Nightlife/ Bristol Guidebook 2020

#475
London Camera Exchange
Category: Photography Store
Average price: Modest
Address: 53 The Horsefair
Bristol BS1 3JP, UK
Phone: +44 117 927 6185

#476
High & Mighty
Category: Men's Clothing
Average price: Expensive
Address: 29 Penn Street
Bristol BS1 3AU, UK
Phone: +44 117 926 2697

#477
5 Pointz
Category: Fashion
Average price: Modest
Address: 18 Nelson St
Bristol BS1 2LE, UK
Phone: +44 117 945 0555

#478
Exclusive Tile Studio
Category: Kitchen & Bath
Average price: Expensive
Address: 15-17 Zetland Road
Bristol BS6 7AH, UK
Phone: +44 117 942 8599

#479
Sood Chemists
Category: Drugstore
Average price: Modest
Address: 23-25 Gloucester Rd
Bristol BS7 8AA, UK
Phone: +44 117 949 1143

#480
Thomas Sabo
Category: Jewelry
Average price: Expensive
Address: Unit K5 Brigstowe St
Bristol BS1 3BH, UK
Phone: +44 117 927 9336

#481
Ripples
Category: Kitchen & Bath
Average price: Modest
Address: 88 Whiteladies Road
Bristol BS8 2QN, UK
Phone: +44 117 973 1144

#482
The Orange Shop
Category: Mobile Phones
Average price: Modest
Address: 18 Clifton Down Shopping Centre
Bristol BS8 2NN, UK
Phone: +44 117 980 4930

#483
Images
Category: Engraving Specialist
Average price: Modest
Address: 7 Nelson Parade
Bristol BS3 4JA, UK
Phone: +44 117 963 6662

#484
Electrofix
Category: Musical Instruments
Average price: Inexpensive
Address: 34 Alma Vale Road
Bristol BS8 2HY, UK
Phone: +44 117 923 9119

#485
Robert Mills Architectural Antiques
Category: Antiques, Home & Garden
Average price: Expensive
Address: Narroways Rd
Bristol BS2 9XB, UK
Phone: +44 117 955 6542

#486
The Art Warehouse & Framing Factory
Category: Art Gallery
Average price: Modest
Address: Wapping Wharf
Bristol BS1 6JP, UK
Phone: +44 117 929 8089

#487
Ashgrove Pharmacy
Category: Drugstore
Average price: Modest
Address: 97-99 Ashley Down Road
Bristol BS7 9JT, UK
Phone: +44 117 924 8510

#488
East Street News
Category: Newspapers & Magazines
Average price: Inexpensive
Address: 98 East Street
Bristol BS3 4EY, UK
Phone: +44 117 963 1377

#489
Creative Glass Guild
Category: Art Supplies
Average price: Modest
Address: Albert Road
Bristol BS2 0XJ, UK
Phone: +44 117 958 8820

#490
Atlas Interiors
Category: Furniture Store
Average price: Exclusive
Address: 16 Clifton Down Rd
Bristol BS8 4AD, UK
Phone: +44 117 923 7917

#491
About Face
Category: Flowers & Gifts
Average price: Expensive
Address: 22 Princess Victoria Street
Bristol BS8 4BU, UK
Phone: +44 117 923 7405

#492
G L Jones
Category: Furniture Store
Average price: Expensive
Address: 16 Vivian Street
Bristol BS3 4LW, UK
Phone: +44 117 966 9446

#493
Maze
Category: Fashion
Average price: Expensive
Address: 26-28 The Mall
Bristol BS8 4DS, UK
Phone: +44 117 974 4459

#494
Digital Village
Category: Musical Instruments
Average price: Expensive
Address: 21 The Mall
Bristol BS8 4JG, UK
Phone: +44 117 946 7700

#495
Bristol Flooring Bargains
Category: Home & Garden
Average price: Modest
Address: 144 North Street
Bristol BS3 1HA, UK
Phone: +44 117 966 2506

#496
RSPCA
Category: Thrift Store
Average price: Modest
Address: 78 Gloucester Rd
Bristol BS7 8BN, UK
Phone: +44 117 924 3147

#497
G Williams Fitted Carpets
Category: Home & Garden
Average price: Modest
Address: 169-171 West Street
Bristol BS3 3PX, UK
Phone: +44 117 963 1580

#498
Safran Office Supplies
Category: Office Equipment
Average price: Modest
Address: 41 Sandy Park Road
Bristol BS4 3PH, UK
Phone: +44 117 971 9834

#499
Mastelevision Television Video & Radio Shop
Category: Electronics
Average price: Modest
Address: 13 Redcatch Road
Bristol BS4 2EP, UK
Phone: +44 117 972 1447

#500
Don Gays
Category: Florist
Average price: Inexpensive
Address: 5 Redcatch Road
Bristol BS4 2EP, UK
Phone: +44 117 977 6964

TOP 500 RESTAURANTS

Recommended by Locals & Trevelers
(From #1 to #500)

#1
Bells Diner
Cuisines: French, European
Average price: 26-45
Address: 1-3 York Road
Bristol BS6 5QB, UK
Phone: +44 117 924 0357

#2
Pieminister @ St Nicks Market
Cuisines: British, Specialty Food
Average price: Under 10
Address: Corn Street
Bristol BS1 1JQ, UK
Phone: +44 117 302 0070

#3
Pieminister
Cuisines: Food, British
Average price: Under 10
Address: 24 Stokes Croft
Bristol BS1 3PR, UK
Phone: +44 117 942 3322

#4
The Bristol Sausage Shop
Cuisines: Fast Food
Average price: Under 10
Address: 28-30 The Glass Arcade
Bristol BS1, UK
Phone: +44 7817 478302

#5
Glass Boat Restaurant
Cuisines: European
Average price: 26-45
Address: Welsh Back
Bristol BS1 4SB, UK
Phone: +44 117 929 0704

#6
The Apple
Cuisines: Pub, British
Average price: 11-25
Address: The Apple
Bristol BS1 4SB, UK
Phone: +44 117 925 3500

#7
Cedars Express
Cuisines: Middle Eastern, Fast Food, Pizza
Average price: Under 10
Address: 60 Park Row
Bristol BS1 5LE, UK
Phone: +44 117 925 6085

#8
Riverstation
Cuisines: British
Average price: 26-45
Address: The Grove
Bristol BS6 5UQ, UK
Phone: +44 117 914 4434

#9
The Louisiana
Cuisines: Pub, Music Venues, British
Average price: 11-25
Address: Bathurst Terrace
Bristol BS1 6UA, UK
Phone: +44 117 936 3615

#10
Watershed
Cuisines: Venues & Event Space, Cinema, Brasserie
Average price: 11-25
Address: 1 Canons Road
Bristol BS1 5TX, UK
Phone: +44 117 927 2082

#11
Thali Cafe
Cuisines: Indian, Fast Food, Gluten-Free
Average price: Under 10
Address: 12a York Road
Bristol BS6 5QE, UK
Phone: +44 117 942 6687

#12
San Carlo Restaurant
Cuisines: Italian, Wineries
Average price: 26-45
Address: 44 Corn Street
Bristol BS1 1HQ, UK
Phone: +44 117 922 6586

#13
Grain Barge
Cuisines: Bar, European
Average price: 11-25
Address: Hotwells Road
Bristol BS8 4RU, UK
Phone: +44 117 929 9347

#14
Las Iguanas
Cuisines: Mexican, Latin American
Average price: 11-25
Address: 113 Whiteladies Road
Bristol BS8 2PB, UK
Phone: +44 117 973 0730

#15
Lido
Cuisines: European
Average price: Above 46
Address: Oakfield Place
Bristol BS8 2BJ, UK
Phone: +44 117 933 9530

#16
The Cowshed
Cuisines: British, Steakhouse
Average price: 26-45
Address: 46 Whiteladies Rd
Bristol BS8 2NH, UK
Phone: +44 117 973 3550

#17
Gourmet Burger Kitchen
Cuisines: American, Burgers
Average price: 11-25
Address: 74 Park Street
Bristol BS1 5JX, UK
Phone: +44 117 316 9162

#18
Renatos
Cuisines: Pizza, Bar
Average price: Under 10
Address: 19 King Street
Bristol BS1 4EF, UK
Phone: +44 117 929 7712

#19
Clifton Sausage
Cuisines: Pub, British
Average price: 26-45
Address: 7-9 Portland Street
Bristol BS8 4JA, UK
Phone: +44 117 973 1192

#20
Maitreya Social
Cuisines: Vegetarian, Vegan
Average price: 26-45
Address: 89 St Marks Road
Bristol BS5 6HY, UK
Phone: +44 117 951 0100

#21
Maximillions Deli
Cuisines: British, Sandwiches
Average price: Under 10
Address: 43 Broad Street
Bristol BS1 2EP, UK
Phone: +44 845 409 3542

#22
A Cappella
Cuisines: Pizza, Italian
Average price: 11-25
Address: 184c Wells Road
Bristol BS4 2AL, UK
Phone: +44 117 971 3377

#23
C & T Licata & Son
Cuisines: Deli, Grocery
Average price: 11-25
Address: 30-36 Picton Street
Bristol BS6 5QA, UK
Phone: +44 117 924 7725

#24
Hope & Anchor
Cuisines: Pub, British
Average price: 11-25
Address: 38 Jacobs Wells Road
Bristol BS8 1DR, UK
Phone: +44 117 929 2987

#25
Tobacco Factory
Cuisines: Mediterranean
Average price: 11-25
Address: Raleigh Road
Bristol BS3 1TF, UK
Phone: +44 117 902 0344

#26
The Olive Shed
Cuisines: Greek, Mediterranean
Average price: 11-25
Address: Floating Harbour
Bristol BS1 4RN, UK
Phone: +44 117 929 1960

#27
Cafe Kino
Cuisines: Coffee & Tea, Vegetarian
Average price: Under 10
Address: 108 Stokes Croft
Bristol BS1 3RU, UK
Phone: +44 117 924 9200

#28
The Lanes
Cuisines: British, Bowling
Average price: 11-25
Address: 22 Nelson Street
Bristol BS1 2LE, UK
Phone: +44 117 325 1979

Shops, Restaurants, Attractions & Nightlife/ Bristol Guidebook 2020

#29
Chickpea
Cuisines: Vegetarian
Average price: Under 10
Address: 1B Pitville Place
Bristol BS6 6JZ, UK
Phone: +44 117 923 8230

#30
El Puerto
Cuisines: Spanish, Basque, Tapas
Average price: 26-45
Address: 57 Prince Street
Bristol BS1 4QH, UK
Phone: +44 117 925 6014

#31
The Clifton
Cuisines: British Pub
Average price: 26-45
Address: 16 Regent Street
Bristol BS8 4HG, UK
Phone: +44 117 974 1967

#32
Lounge
Cuisines: European
Average price: Under 10
Address: 227 - 231 North Street
Bristol BS3 1JJ, UK
Phone: +44 117 963 7340

#33
The Magnet
Cuisines: Fish & Chips, Fast Food
Average price: Under 10
Address: 55 Dean Lane
Bristol BS3 1BS, UK
Phone: +44 117 963 6444

#34
Brunels Buttery
Cuisines: Fast Food, British
Average price: Under 10
Address: Wapping Wharf
Bristol BS1 6RS, UK
Phone: +44 117 929 1696

#35
Marks Bread
Cuisines: Bakery, Cafe
Average price: 11-25
Address: 291 N Street
Bristol BS3 1JU, UK
Phone: +44 7910 979384

#36
Arches Fish Bar
Cuisines: Fish & Chips, Pizza, Halal
Average price: 11-25
Address: 226 Cheltenham Road
Bristol BS6 5QU, UK
Phone: +44 117 924 8996

#37
Tai Pan Oriental Noodle Bistro
Cuisines: Thai
Average price: 11-25
Address: 39 Gloucester Road
Bristol BS7 8AD, UK
Phone: +44 117 924 6786

#38
Boston Tea Party
Cuisines: Coffee & Tea, British, Breakfast & Brunch
Average price: 11-25
Address: 75 Park Street
Bristol BS1 5PF, UK
Phone: +44 117 929 3939

#39
Myristica
Cuisines: Indian
Average price: 26-45
Address: 51 Welshback
Bristol BS1 4AN, UK
Phone: +44 117 927 2277

#40
Dynasty
Cuisines: Chinese
Average price: 26-45
Address: 16a St Thomas Street
Bristol BS1 6JJ, UK
Phone: +44 117 925 0888

#41
Zerodegrees
Cuisines: Italian, Brewery, Bar
Average price: 11-25
Address: 53 Colston Street
Bristol BS1 5BA, UK
Phone: +44 117 925 2706

#42
Redland Tandoori
Cuisines: Indian, Pakistani
Average price: Under 10
Address: 20 Chandos Road
Bristol BS6 6PF, UK
Phone: +44 117 946 6388

#43
The Bristolian
Cuisines: Breakfast & Brunch, Bistro
Average price: Under 10
Address: 2 Picton Street
Bristol BS6 5QA, UK
Phone: +44 117 919 2808

#44
The Big Chill Bar
Cuisines: Lounge, Pub, Tapas Bar
Average price: 11-25
Address: 15 Small Street
Bristol BS1 1DE, UK
Phone: +44 117 930 4217

#45
Rocotillos
Cuisines: Breakfast & Brunch, American
Average price: Under 10
Address: 1 Queen's Row
Bristol BS8 1EZ, UK
Phone: +44 117 929 7207

#46
Cibo Continentals
Cuisines: Deli, Food, Italian
Average price: 11-25
Address: 289 Gloucester Road
Bristol BS7 8NY, UK
Phone: +44 117 942 9475

#47
Flinty Red
Cuisines: European
Average price: 26-45
Address: 34 Cotham Hill
Bristol BS6 6LA, UK
Phone: +44 117 923 8755

#48
Tampopo
Cuisines: Thai, Chinese, Japanese
Average price: 11-25
Address: Glasshouse
Bristol BS1 3BX, UK
Phone: +44 117 927 7008

#49
Zazus Kitchen
Cuisines: European, Coffee & Tea
Average price: 11-25
Address: 45 Jamaica Street
Bristol BS2 8JP, UK
Phone: +44 117 944 5500

#50
Hare On The Hill
Cuisines: Pub, British
Average price: 11-25
Address: 41 Thomas Street North
Bristol BS2 8LX, UK
Phone: +44 117 908 1982

#51
Casa Mexicana
Cuisines: Mexican
Average price: 11-25
Address: 31 Zetland Rd
Bristol BS6 7AH, UK
Phone: +44 117 924 3901

#52
Juniper
Cuisines: French, British
Average price: 26-45
Address: 21 Cotham Road South
Bristol BS6 5TZ, UK
Phone: +44 117 942 1744

#53
Sheesh Mahal
Cuisines: Indian, Pakistani
Average price: 11-25
Address: 13 Gloucester Road
Bristol BS7 8AA, UK
Phone: +44 117 942 2942

#54
Las Iguanas
Cuisines: Latin American
Average price: 11-25
Address: Anchors Square
Bristol BS1 5UH, UK
Phone: +44 117 927 6233

#55
Bangkok House
Cuisines: Thai
Average price: 11-25
Address: 70 Whiteladies Road
Bristol BS8 2QA, UK
Phone: +44 117 937 0409

#56
Wagamama
Cuisines: Japanese, Asian Fusion
Average price: 11-25
Address: 63-65 Queens Road
Bristol BS8 1QL, UK
Phone: +44 117 922 1188

#57
Beijing Bistro
Cuisines: Chinese
Average price: 26-45
Address: 72 Park Street
Bristol BS1 5JX, UK
Phone: +44 117 373 2706

#58
Yoyo Burger
Cuisines: Fast Food, Burgers
Average price: Under 10
Address: 6 Byron Pl
Bristol BS8 1JT, UK
Phone: +44 117 930 4353

#59
Sergios
Cuisines: Italian
Average price: 11-25
Address: 1-3 Frogmore Street
Bristol BS1 5NA, UK
Phone: +44 117 929 1413

#60
Spyglass
Cuisines: Mediterranean, Barbeque
Average price: 11-25
Address: Welsh Back
Bristol BS1 4SB, UK
Phone: +44 117 927 7050

#61
Real Olive Co
Cuisines: Deli, Food
Average price: Under 10
Address: 40-43 St Nicholas Market
Bristol BS1 1LJ, UK
Phone: +44 117 909 9587

#62
Old India
Cuisines: Indian, Pakistani
Average price: 11-25
Address: 34 St Nicholas Street
Bristol BS1 1TG, UK
Phone: +44 117 922 1136

#63
The White Bear
Cuisines: Pub, British
Average price: 11-25
Address: 133 St Michaels Hill
Bristol BS2 8BS, UK
Phone: +44 117 904 9054

#64
Bordeaux Quay
Cuisines: European, Brasserie
Average price: 26-45
Address: V-Shed Canons Way
Bristol BS1 5UH, UK
Phone: +44 117 943 1200

#65
Colston Yard Bristol
Cuisines: British, GastroPub
Average price: 11-25
Address: Colston Street
Bristol BS1 5BD, UK
Phone: +44 117 376 3232

#66
Cosies Wine Bar
Cuisines: British, Wine Bar
Average price: 11-25
Address: 34 Portland Square
Bristol BS2 8RG, UK
Phone: +44 117 942 4110

#67
Plantation
Cuisines: Caribbean
Average price: 11-25
Address: 221-223 Cheltenham Rd
Bristol BS6 5QP, UK
Phone: +44 117 907 7932

#68
Kathmandu
Cuisines: Indian, Asian Fusion, Himalayan/Nepalese
Average price: 11-25
Address: Colston Street
Bristol BS1 4XE, UK
Phone: +44 7738 282383

#69
Jamies Italian
Cuisines: Italian
Average price: 26-45
Address: 87/89 Park Street
Bristol BS1 5PW, UK
Phone: +44 117 370 0265

#70
Papadeli Delicatessens
Cuisines: Deli, European
Average price: 26-45
Address: 84 Alma Road
Bristol BS8 2DJ, UK
Phone: +44 117 973 6569

#71
Curry House
Cuisines: Fast Food, Asian Fusion
Average price: 26-45
Address: 393 Bath Road
Bristol BS4 3EU, UK
Phone: +44 117 977 9090

#72
Gourmet Burger Kitchen
Cuisines: Burgers, Fast Food
Average price: 26-45
Address: Glass Walk
Bristol BS1 3BQ, UK
Phone: +44 117 927 9997

#73
Prosecco Restaurant
Cuisines: Italian
Average price: 26-45
Address: 25 The Mall
Bristol BS8 4JG, UK
Phone: +44 117 973 4499

#74
Blue Juice
Cuisines: Juice Bar& Smoothies, Breakfast & Brunch, Sandwiches
Average price: Under 10
Address: 39 Cotham Hill
Bristol BS6 6JY, UK
Phone: +44 117 973 4800

#75

Bristol Flyer
Cuisines: British, Pub
Average price: 26-45
Address: 96 Gloucester Road
Bristol BS7 8BN, UK
Phone: +44 117 944 1658

#76
Piccolino
Cuisines: Italian
Average price: 26-45
Address: Broad Weir
Bristol BS1 3BZ, UK
Phone: +44 117 929 3255

#77
Simply Thai
Cuisines: Thai, Fast Food
Average price: 11-25
Address: 67 Gloucester Road
Bristol BS7 8AD, UK
Phone: +44 117 924 4117

#78
Tart
Cuisines: Breakfast & Brunch
Average price: 11-25
Address: 16 Gloucester Road
Bristol BS7 8AE, UK
Phone: +44 117 924 7628

#79
Planet Pizza
Cuisines: Pizza
Average price: 11-25
Address: 187 Gloucester Road
Bristol BS7 8BG, UK
Phone: +44 117 944 4717

#80
Watersky
Cuisines: Chinese
Average price: 11-25
Address: 1 Eastgate Oriental City
Bristol BS5 6XY, UK
Phone: +44 117 951 2888

#81
Thali Cafe
Cuisines: Indian, Fast Food
Average price: 11-25
Address: 1 William Street
Bristol BS3 4TU, UK
Phone: +44 117 933 2955

#82
Greens Dining Room
Cuisines: British, European
Average price: Above 46
Address: 25 Zetland Road
Bristol BS6 7AH, UK
Phone: +44 117 924 6437

#83
La Campagnuola
Cuisines: Italian, Pizza
Average price: 11-25
Address: 9 Zetland Road
Bristol BS6 7AG, UK
Phone: +44 117 924 8102

#84
Ciao Burger
Cuisines: Fast Food, Burgers, Do-It-Yourself Food
Average price: 11-25
Address: 207a Gloucester Road
Bristol BS7 8NN, UK
Phone: +44 117 942 6228

#85
Cafe Du Jour
Cuisines: Coffee & Tea, French
Average price: Under 10
Address: 72 Whiteladies Road
Bristol BS8 2QA, UK
Phone: +44 117 973 1563

#86
El Rincon
Cuisines: Spanish, Tapas
Average price: 11-25
Address: 298 North Street
Bristol BS3 1JU, UK
Phone: +44 117 939 3457

#87
Lockside
Cuisines: European
Average price: 26-45
Address: Brunel Lock Road
Bristol BS1 6XS, UK
Phone: +44 117 925 5800

#88
Casamia
Cuisines: European, Italian
Average price: 26-45
Address: 38 High Street
Bristol BS9 3DZ, UK
Phone: +44 117 959 2884

#89
Kuvuka
Cuisines: Coffee & Tea, Sandwiches
Average price: Under 10
Address: 13 Stokes Croft
Bristol BS1 3RW, UK
Phone: +44 117 924 7180

#90
Carluccios
Cuisines: Italian, Coffee & Tea
Average price: 11-25
Address: 11 Quaker's Friars
Bristol BS1 3BU, UK
Phone: +44 117 933 8538

#91
Halo
Cuisines: British, Bar
Average price: 11-25
Address: 141 Gloucester Road
Bristol BS7 8BA, UK
Phone: +44 117 944 2504

#92
Nando's
Cuisines: Portuguese, Fast Food
Average price: 11-25
Address: 49 Park Street
Bristol BS1 5NT, UK
Phone: +44 117 929 9263

#93
Browns
Cuisines: Wine Bar, British, Lounge
Average price: 11-25
Address: 38 Queens Road
Bristol BS8 1RE, UK
Phone: +44 117 930 4777

#94
Goldbrick House
Cuisines: British, Champagne Bar
Average price: 26-45
Address: 69 Park St
Bristol BS1 5PB, UK
Phone: +44 117 945 1950

#95
Bauhinia
Cuisines: Asian Fusion
Average price: 11-25
Address: 5 Boyces Avenue
Bristol BS8 4AA, UK
Phone: +44 117 973 3138

#96
Zizzi
Cuisines: Italian
Average price: 11-25
Address: 29 Princess Victoria Street
Bristol BS8 4BX, UK
Phone: +44 117 317 9842

#97
Fishminster
Cuisines: Fish & Chips
Average price: Under 10
Address: 267 North Street
Bristol BS3 1JN, UK
Phone: +44 117 966 2226

#98
Hatters
Cuisines: Breakfast & Brunch
Average price: 11-25
Address: 97 Gloucester Road
Bristol BS7 8AT, UK
Phone: +44 117 330 5740

Shops, Restaurants, Attractions & Nightlife/ Bristol Guidebook 2020

#99
Thali Cafe
Cuisines: Indian, Fast Food
Average price: Under 10
Address: 1 Regent Street
Bristol BS8 4HW, UK
Phone: +44 117 974 3793

#100
Ganesha
Cuisines: Indian, Fast Food
Average price: 11-25
Address: 54-56 Bedminster Parade
Bristol BS3 4HS, UK
Phone: +44 117 953 3990

#101
Farrows Fish and Chips
Cuisines: Fast Food, Fish & Chips
Average price: Under 10
Address: 146 Wells Road
Bristol BS4 2AG, UK
Phone: +44 117 908 5511

#102
Fishers Restaurant
Cuisines: Seafood
Average price: 26-45
Address: 35 Princess Victoria St
Bristol BS8 4BX, UK
Phone: +44 117 974 7044

#103
Joy Raj Restaurant
Cuisines: Indian, Food
Average price: 11-25
Address: 31 Regent Street
Bristol BS8 4HR, UK
Phone: +44 117 923 8892

#104
Yia Mass
Cuisines: Bar, Mediterranean
Average price: 26-45
Address: 67 Park Street
Bristol BS1 5PB, UK
Phone: +44 117 929 9530

#105
The Kebab House
Cuisines: Greek, Fast Food
Average price: Under 10
Address: 6 St Michaels Hill
Bristol BS2 8DT, UK
Phone: +44 117 921 1958

#106
Delmonico Restaurant
Cuisines: Italian, British
Average price: 26-45
Address: 217a Gloucester Road
Bristol BS7 8NN, UK
Phone: +44 117 944 5673

#107
Renatos Numero Uno
Cuisines: Italian
Average price: 11-25
Address: 203 Whiteladies Road
Bristol BS8 2XT, UK
Phone: +44 117 974 4484

#108
Thai Pepper
Cuisines: Fast Food, Thai
Average price: 11-25
Address: 215 Cheltenham Road
Bristol BS6 5QP, UK
Phone: +44 117 924 9402

#109
Harvest
Cuisines: Deli
Average price: 11-25
Address: 11 Gloucester Road
Bristol BS7 8AA, UK
Phone: +44 117 942 5997

#110
Arnolfini Cafe Bar
Cuisines: Cafe
Average price: 11-25
Address: 16 Narrow Quay
Bristol BS1 4QA, UK
Phone: +44 117 917 2305

#111
The Kensington Arms
Cuisines: Pub, British
Average price: 26-45
Address: 35-37 Stanley Road
Bristol BS6 6NP, UK
Phone: +44 117 944 6444

#112
Poco
Cuisines: Latin American, Spanish
Average price: 11-25
Address: 45 Jamaica Street
Bristol BS2 8JP, UK
Phone: +44 117 923 2233

Shops, Restaurants, Attractions & Nightlife/ Bristol Guidebook 2020

#113
The Square
Cuisines: British
Average price: 26-45
Address: 15 Berkeley Square
Bristol BS8 1HB, UK
Phone: +44 117 921 0455

#114
The Cafe On The Square
Cuisines: Breakfast & Brunch
Average price: Under 10
Address: Queen Square
Bristol BS1 4QS, UK
Phone: +44 117 925 0435

#115
Obento
Cuisines: Japanese, Sushi Bar
Average price: 11-25
Address: 67 Baldwin St
Bristol BS1 1QZ, UK
Phone: +44 117 929 7392

#116
Rosemarino
Cuisines: Italian
Average price: 11-25
Address: 1 York Pl
Bristol BS8 1AH, UK
Phone: +44 117 973 6677

#117
McDonalds Restaurant
Cuisines: Fast Food, Burgers
Average price: 11-25
Address: St Philips Causeway
Bristol BS2 0SP, UK
Phone: +44 870 241 3300

#118
Indian Food Centre
Cuisines: Fast Food
Average price: 11-25
Address: 366 Gloucester Road
Bristol BS7 8TP, UK
Phone: +44 117 942 3532

#119
Chans Chow
Cuisines: Fast Food
Average price: 11-25
Address: 4A Kellaway Avenue
Bristol BS6 7XR, UK
Phone: +44 117 923 2868

#120
The New Emperor Court
Cuisines: Chinese
Average price: 11-25
Address: Portland Street
Bristol BS8 4JB, UK
Phone: +44 117 973 1522

#121
Loch Fyne
Cuisines: Seafood
Average price: 11-25
Address: Queen Charlotte Street
Bristol BS1 4HQ, UK
Phone: +44 117 930 7160

#122
Old Market Tavern
Cuisines: Pub, Gay Bar, British
Average price: Under 10
Address: 29-30 Old Market Street
Bristol BS2 0HB, UK
Phone: +44 117 922 6123

#123
Pellegrinos Fish & Chip Shop
Cuisines: Fish & Chips
Average price: Under 10
Address: 17 Christmas Steps
Bristol BS1 5BT, UK
Phone: +44 117 927 0580

#124
Friska
Cuisines: Breakfast & Brunch
Average price: 11-25
Address: 32 Victoria Street
Bristol BS1 6BX, UK
Phone: +44 7886 659057

#125
Spice Up Your Life
Cuisines: Indian
Average price: Under 10
Address: 7 Exchange Avenue
Bristol BS1 1JP, UK
Phone: +44 117 914 4448

#126
Mad About Sarnies
Cuisines: Sandwiches
Average price: 11-25
Address: 307a Gloucester Road
Bristol BS7 8PE, UK
Phone: +44 117 942 5963

Shops, Restaurants, Attractions & Nightlife/ Bristol Guidebook 2020

#127
Chandos Deli
Cuisines: British, Specialty Food
Average price: 26-45
Address: Quakers Friars
Bristol BS1 3DX, UK
Phone: +44 117 934 9611

#128
Posh Spice
Cuisines: Indian, Pakistani
Average price: Under 10
Address: 9 The Mall
Bristol BS8 4DP, UK
Phone: +44 117 973 0144

#129
Promenade
Cuisines: Deli, Meat Shop
Average price: Under 10
Address: 18 Gloucester Rd
Bristol BS7 8AL, UK
Phone: +44 117 944 3266

#130
Graze Bar and Chophouse
Cuisines: Lounge, British
Average price: 11-25
Address: 63 Queen Square
Bristol BS1 4JZ, UK
Phone: +44 117 927 6706

#131
Cottage Inn
Cuisines: Pub, British, Fish & Chips
Average price: 11-25
Address: Cumberland Road
Bristol BS1 6XG, UK
Phone: +44 117 921 5256

#132
Tasty Stop
Cuisines: Diner
Average price: Under 10
Address: 202 North St
Bristol BS3 1JF, UK
Phone: +44 117 953 7648

#133
Boulangerie
Cuisines: Bakery, Sandwiches
Average price: Under 10
Address: 3 Queens Rd
Bristol BS8 1QE, UK
Phone: +44 117 929 3983

#134
Orchid Restaurant
Cuisines: Singaporean, Chinese, Thai
Average price: 11-25
Address: 81 Whiteladies Road
Bristol BS8 2NT, UK
Phone: +44 117 973 2198

#135
Havana Coffee
Cuisines: Breakfast & Brunch
Average price: Under 10
Address: 37A Cotham Hill
Bristol BS6 6JY, UK
Phone: +44 117 973 3020

#136
Frankie and Bennys
Cuisines: American, Italian
Average price: 26-45
Address: The Venue Merlin Road
Bristol BS10 7SR, UK
Phone: +44 117 959 1180

#137
The Star & Dove
Cuisines: Pub, British
Average price: 11-25
Address: 75-78 St Lukes Road
Bristol BS3 4RY, UK
Phone: +44 117 933 2892

#138
Willow Garden
Cuisines: Fast Food, Chinese
Average price: Under 10
Address: 283 North Street
Bristol BS3 1JP, UK
Phone: +44 117 966 3308

#139
Headley Fish Bar
Cuisines: Fish & Chips
Average price: Under 10
Address: A 1 ST. Peters Rise
Bristol BS13 7LU, UK
Phone: +44 117 964 0698

#140
Amano Cafe
Cuisines: Cafe
Average price: 11-25
Address: Unit Ko3 Concorde Street
Bristol BS1 3BF, UK
Phone: +44 117 927 3747

Shops, Restaurants, Attractions & Nightlife/ Bristol Guidebook 2020

#141
Bridge Café
Cuisines: European, Cafe
Average price: 11-25
Address: Avon Gorge Hotel
Bristol BS8 4LD, UK
Phone: +44 117 973 8955

#142
Hole in the Wall
Cuisines: British, Pub
Average price: 11-25
Address: 2 The Grove
Bristol BS1 4QZ, UK
Phone: +44 117 926 5967

#143
BrewDog
Cuisines: Burgers, Pub
Average price: 26-45
Address: 58 Baldwin Street
Bristol BS1 1QW, UK
Phone: +44 117 927 9258

#144
Caffe Gusto
Cuisines: Coffee & Tea, Sandwiches
Average price: 11-25
Address: 120 St Michaels Hill
Bristol BS2 8BU, UK
Phone: +44 117 929 8113

#145
Racks Bar & Kitchen
Cuisines: Wine Bar, British
Average price: 11-25
Address: St Pauls Road
Bristol BS8 1LX, UK
Phone: +44 117 974 1626

#146
All In One Restaurant
Cuisines: British
Average price: Under 10
Address: 46 Park Street
Bristol BS1 5JG, UK
Phone: +44 117 926 5622

#147
Coal Bar and Grill
Cuisines: European
Average price: 11-25
Address: Unit SU84D
Bristol BS1 3BX, UK
Phone: +44 117 954 4624

#148
Grecian Kebab House
Cuisines: Fast Food
Average price: Under 10
Address: 2 Cromwell Road
Bristol BS6 5AA, UK
Phone: +44 117 942 3456

#149
The Scotchman & His Pack
Cuisines: Pub, British
Average price: 11-25
Address: 20 St Michaels Hill
Bristol BS2 8DX, UK
Phone: +44 117 373 0138

#150
Bar Humbug
Cuisines: Pub, British, Lounge
Average price: 11-25
Address: 89 Whiteladies Road
Bristol BS8 2NT, UK
Phone: +44 117 904 0061

#151
The Green Man
Cuisines: Pub, British
Average price: 26-45
Address: 21 Alfred Place
Bristol BS2 8HD, UK
Phone: +44 117 930 4824

#152
Argus Fish Bar
Cuisines: Fish & Chips
Average price: 11-25
Address: 114 West Street
Bristol BS3 3LR, UK
Phone: +44 117 966 4850

#153
Coffee#1
Cuisines: Coffee & Tea, Sandwiches
Average price: 11-25
Address: 157 Gloucester Road
Bristol BS7 8BA, UK
Phone: +44 117 942 9909

#154
The Love Inn
Cuisines: Bar, Burgers
Average price: 11-25
Address: 84 Stokes Croft
Bristol BS1 3QY, UK
Phone: +44 117 923 2565

Shops, Restaurants, Attractions & Nightlife/ Bristol Guidebook 2020

#155
The Mayflower Chinese Restaurant
Cuisines: Chinese
Average price: 11-25
Address: 3a-5 Haymarket Walk
Bristol BS1 3LN, UK
Phone: +44 117 925 0555

#156
Tiffins
Cuisines: Indian
Average price: Under 10
Address: 151 St Michael's Hill
Bristol BS2 8DB, UK
Phone: +44 117 973 4834

#157
Beerd
Cuisines: Bar, Tapas Bar
Average price: 11-25
Address: 155 St Michael's Hill
Bristol BS2 8DB, UK
Phone: +44 845 202 5837

#158
Jasmine
Cuisines: Fast Food, Chinese
Average price: 11-25
Address: 235 Cheltenham Road
Bristol BS6 5QP, UK
Phone: +44 117 924 3870

#159
Farrows Fish & Chips
Cuisines: Fish & Chips
Average price: 11-25
Address: Unit 8 224 Kingsway
Bristol BS5 8NS, UK
Phone: +44 117 961 6626

#160
Zen Restaurants
Cuisines: Chinese
Average price: 11-25
Address: Explore Lane
Bristol BS1 5TY, UK
Phone: +44 117 920 9370

#161
Rice & Things
Cuisines: Caribbean
Average price: 11-25
Address: 120 Cheltenham Road
Bristol BS6 5RW, UK
Phone: +44 117 924 4832

#162
Ahmeds Masala Cafe
Cuisines: Indian, Fast Food
Average price: 11-25
Address: 2 Jacob Wells Road
Bristol BS8 1EA, UK
Phone: +44 117 930 4194

#163
Jeffersons Patisserie & Sandwich Bar
Cuisines: Fast Food, Coffee & Tea
Average price: Under 10
Address: 5-7 Bridewell Street
Bristol BS1 2QD, UK
Phone: +44 117 927 7799

#164
Domino's
Cuisines: Pizza
Average price: 11-25
Address: 119 Whiteladies Road
Bristol BS8 2PL, UK
Phone: +44 117 973 3400

#165
Strada
Cuisines: Italian
Average price: 11-25
Address: 34 Princess Victoria Street
Bristol BS8 4BZ, UK
Phone: +44 117 923 7224

#166
Number 10
Cuisines: Breakfast & Brunch, Bar
Average price: 11-25
Address: 10 Zetland Road
Bristol BS6 7AD, UK
Phone: +44 117 924 1301

#167
Raj Bari Bristol
Cuisines: Indian
Average price: 11-25
Address: 183 Hotwell Road
Bristol BS8 4SA, UK
Phone: +44 117 922 7617

#168
Grainhouse Cafe
Cuisines: Coffee & Tea, Sandwiches
Average price: 11-25
Address: 14 Narrow Quay
Bristol BS1 4QA, UK
Phone: +44 117 922 1659

Shops, Restaurants, Attractions & Nightlife/ Bristol Guidebook 2020

#169
The Hobgoblin
Cuisines: Pub, Burgers, American
Average price: 11-25
Address: 69-71 Gloucester Road
Bristol BS7 8AS, UK
Phone: +44 117 942 9534

#170
Don Giovannis Restaurant
Cuisines: Italian
Average price: 11-25
Address: Temple Gate
Bristol BS1 6PW, UK
Phone: +44 117 926 0614

#171
Royce Rolls Cafe
Cuisines: Vegetarian, Coffee & Tea
Average price: Under 10
Address: Corn Street
Bristol BS1 1JQ, UK
Phone: +44 7967 211870

#172
The Rockfish Grill & Seafood
Cuisines: Food, Fish & Chips
Average price: 11-25
Address: 128 Whiteladies Road
Bristol BS8 2RS, UK
Phone: +44 117 973 7384

#173
Bristol Ram
Cuisines: Pub, GastroPub
Average price: 11-25
Address: 32 Park Street
Bristol BS1 5JA, UK
Phone: +44 117 926 8654

#174
Yum Yum Thai
Cuisines: Thai, Asian Fusion
Average price: 11-25
Address: 50 Park St
Bristol BS1 5JN, UK
Phone: +44 117 929 0987

#175
La Boheme
Cuisines: Coffee & Tea, Sandwiches
Average price: 11-25
Address: 22 Cotham Hill
Bristol BS6 6LF, UK
Phone: +44 117 946 7567

#176
Nazar Meze Restaurant
Cuisines: Mediterranean, Turkish
Average price: 11-25
Address: 599 Fishponds Road
Bristol BS16 3AA, UK
Phone: +44 117 378 9379

#177
Marhaba Bistro
Cuisines: Moroccan
Average price: 11-25
Address: 611 Fishponds Road
Bristol BS16 3AA, UK
Phone: +44 117 965 0752

#178
Tamarind
Cuisines: Indian
Average price: 26-45
Address: 5 Badminton Road
Bristol BS16 6BB, UK
Phone: +44 117 957 3030

#179
Princes Traditional Fish & Chips
Cuisines: Fish & Chips
Average price: Under 10
Address: 721 Fishponds Road
Bristol BS16 3UW, UK
Phone: +44 117 939 9393

#180
Castellanos
Cuisines: Deli
Average price: 26-45
Address: 802 Fishponds Road
Bristol BS16 3TE, UK
Phone: +44 117 965 2792

#181
Bocabar
Cuisines: Pub, Pizza, Burgers
Average price: 11-25
Address: Unit 3 1 Paintworks
Bristol BS4 3EH, UK
Phone: +44 117 972 8838

#182
Snuff Mill Harvester
Cuisines: British, Pub
Average price: 26-45
Address: 207 Frenchay Park Road
Bristol BS16 1LF, UK
Phone: +44 117 956 6560

#183
Rendezvous Restaurant & Take-Away
Cuisines: Fish & Chips
Average price: Under 10
Address: 9 Denmark Street
Bristol BS1 5DQ, UK
Phone: +44 117 929 8683

#184
Papa Costa
Cuisines: Deli, Breakfast & Brunch
Average price: Under 10
Address: 67 Queens Road
Bristol BS8 1QL, UK
Phone: +44 117 929 1600

#185
Thali Cafe
Cuisines: Indian, Fast Food
Average price: Under 10
Address: 64-66 St Marks Road
Bristol BS5 6JH, UK
Phone: +44 117 951 4979

#186
La Casbah
Cuisines: Mediterranean, Moroccan
Average price: 11-25
Address: 96 St. Marks Road
Bristol BS5 6JD, UK
Phone: +44 117 939 8804

#187
Porto Lounge
Cuisines: GastroPub, Coffee & Tea
Average price: 11-25
Address: 765 Fishponds Road
Bristol BS16 3BS, UK
Phone: +44 117 902 4567

#188
Bosphorus Restaurant
Cuisines: Turkish
Average price: 11-25
Address: 45 Baldwin Street
Bristol BS1 1RA, UK
Phone: +44 117 922 1333

#189
The Stable
Cuisines: Pizza
Average price: 11-25
Address: The Harbourside
Bristol BS1 5TX, UK
Phone: +44 117 927 9999

#190
Penfolds
Cuisines: Wine Bar, Tapas Bar
Average price: 11-25
Address: 85 Whiteladies Road
Bristol BS8 2NT, UK
Phone: +44 117 909 4383

#191
Fungs Noodle Bar
Cuisines: Chinese
Average price: Under 10
Address: 330 Gloucester Road
Bristol BS7 8TJ, UK
Phone: +44 117 923 2020

#192
Take 5 Cafe
Cuisines: Asian Fusion
Average price: 11-25
Address: 72 Stokes Croft
Bristol BS1 3QY, UK
Phone: +44 117 907 7502

#193
Zizzi
Cuisines: Italian
Average price: 11-25
Address: 84B Glass House Cabot Circus
Bristol BS1 3BX, UK
Phone: +44 117 929 1066

#194
New Happy Garden
Cuisines: Fast Food
Average price: 11-25
Address: 200 Cheltenham Road
Bristol BS6 5QZ, UK
Phone: +44 117 904 9345

#195
Q.E.D.
Cuisines: Sandwiches
Average price: Under 10
Address: 122 St Michael's Hill
Bristol BS2 8BU, UK
Phone: +44 117 929 3803

#196
The Birdcage
Cuisines: Breakfast & Brunch, British
Average price: 11-25
Address: 28 Clare Street
Bristol BS1 1YE, UK
Phone: +44 117 929 1130

Shops, Restaurants, Attractions & Nightlife/ Bristol Guidebook 2020

#197
Caribbean Wrap
Cuisines: Caribbean
Average price: 11-25
Address: Unit 33 St Nicholas Market
Bristol BS1 1JQ, UK
Phone: +44 7989 745944

#198
The Whole Baked Cafe
Cuisines: Coffee & Tea, Cafe
Average price: Under 10
Address: 7-10 Lawford Street
Bristol BS2 0DH, UK
Phone: +44 117 908 2266

#199
Spicer + Cole
Cuisines: Cafe, Coffee & Tea
Average price: 11-25
Address: 1 Queen Square Avenue
Bristol BS1 4JA, UK
Phone: +44 117 922 0513

#200
City Cafe
Cuisines: British, Coffee & Tea
Average price: 11-25
Address: Temple Way
Bristol BS1 6BF, UK
Phone: +44 117 925 1001

#201
The Berkeley Square Hotel
Cuisines: British
Average price: 26-45
Address: 15 Berkeley Square
Bristol BS8 1HB, UK
Phone: +44 117 925 4000

#202
Yo! Sushi
Cuisines: Sushi Bar
Average price: 11-25
Address: Glass Walk
Bristol BS1 3BQ, UK
Phone: +44 117 321 3161

#203
HK Diner
Cuisines: Chinese
Average price: Under 10
Address: 58 Park Street
Bristol BS1 5JN, UK
Phone: +44 117 927 2628

#204
Vincenzos Pizza House
Cuisines: Pizza, Italian
Average price: 11-25
Address: 71a Park Street
Bristol BS1 5PB, UK
Phone: +44 117 926 0908

#205
The Brunel
Cuisines: British, Pub
Average price: 11-25
Address: 315 St John's Lane
Bristol BS3 5AZ, UK
Phone: +44 117 966 3339

#206
The Botanist
Cuisines: British
Average price: 11-25
Address: Berkeley Square
Bristol BS8 1HP, UK
Phone: +44 117 927 7333

#207
Starbucks Coffee
Cuisines: Coffee & Tea, Cafe
Average price: 26-45
Address: Queens Road
Bristol BS8 1RE, UK
Phone: +44 117 922 6959

#208
Old Cheese Shop
Cuisines: Sandwiches
Average price: Under 10
Address: 1 Worrall Road
Bristol BS8 2UF, UK
Phone: +44 117 946 6940

#209
Soho Coffee Co.
Cuisines: Coffee & Tea, Sandwiches
Average price: Under 10
Address: Unit SU32 Concorde St
Bristol BS1 3BF, UK
Phone: +44 117 376 3224

#210
Happy Rendezvous
Cuisines: Chinese
Average price: Under 10
Address: 287 Gloucester Rd
Bristol BS7 8NY, UK
Phone: +44 117 924 6627

Shops, Restaurants, Attractions & Nightlife/ Bristol Guidebook 2020

#211
The Walrus & Carpenter
Cuisines: British
Average price: 11-25
Address: 1 Regent Street
Bristol BS8 4HW, UK
Phone: +44 117 974 3793

#212
Rupsha
Cuisines: Indian
Average price: 11-25
Address: 3A Regent Street
Bristol BS8 4HW, UK
Phone: +44 117 973 9937

#213
No.4 Clifton Village
Cuisines: British, European
Average price: 11-25
Address: 4 Rodney Place
Bristol BS8 4HY, UK
Phone: +44 117 970 6869

#214
Old Lock & Weir
Cuisines: Pub, British
Average price: 11-25
Address: Hanham Mills
Bristol BS15 3NU, UK
Phone: +44 117 967 3793

#215
Chi Chinese Restaurant
Cuisines: Chinese, Fast Food
Average price: 11-25
Address: 21 Regent Street
Bristol BS8 4HW, UK
Phone: +44 117 907 7840

#216
Ha Ha Bar & Canteen
Cuisines: British
Average price: 26-45
Address: 20 Berkeley Square
Bristol BS8 1HP, UK
Phone: +44 117 927 7333

#217
Mud Dock Cafe
Cuisines: Cafe
Average price: 26-45
Address: 40 The Grove
Bristol BS1 4RB, UK
Phone: +44 117 934 9734

#218
The Kellaway
Cuisines: British, Pub
Average price: 11-25
Address: 138-140 Kellaway Avenue
Bristol BS6 7YQ, UK
Phone: +44 117 942 6210

#219
Souk Kitchen
Cuisines: Middle Eastern
Average price: 11-25
Address: 277 North Street
Bristol BS3 1JP, UK
Phone: +44 117 966 6880

#220
The Curry Centre
Cuisines: Fast Food
Average price: Under 10
Address: 43 West Street
Bristol BS3 3NS, UK
Phone: +44 117 953 2637

#221
The Assilah Bistro
Cuisines: Moroccan
Average price: 11-25
Address: 194 -196 Wells Road
Bristol BS4 2, UK
Phone: +44 7816 202827

#222
Thai Garden
Cuisines: Thai, Fast Food
Average price: Under 10
Address: 100 West Street
Bristol BS3 3LR, UK
Phone: +44 117 963 6113

#223
Savana Coffee
Cuisines: Coffee & Tea, Mediterranean
Average price: 11-25
Address: 273 North Street
Bristol BS3 1JN, UK
Phone: +44 117 966 0088

#224
Kondi Brasserie
Cuisines: Breakfast & Brunch
Average price: 11-25
Address: 105 Henleaze Road
Bristol BS9 4JP, UK
Phone: +44 117 962 8230

Shops, Restaurants, Attractions & Nightlife/ Bristol Guidebook 2020

#225
New Oriental Kitchen
Cuisines: Fast Food, Chinese
Average price: 11-25
Address: 660 Fishponds Road
Bristol BS16 3HJ, UK
Phone: +44 117 965 5050

#226
Horts City Tavern
Cuisines: Pub, British
Average price: 11-25
Address: 49 Broad Street
Bristol BS1 2EP, UK
Phone: +44 117 925 2520

#227
Cafe A Roma
Cuisines: Coffee & Tea, Italian
Average price: Under 10
Address: 234 Cheltenham Road
Bristol BS6 5QU, UK
Phone: +44 117 904 7302

#228
Red Lion
Cuisines: Pub, British
Average price: 11-25
Address: 26 Worrall Road
Bristol BS8 2UE, UK
Phone: +44 117 903 0773

#229
Bottelino
Cuisines: Italian
Average price: 11-25
Address: 22 Bond Street
Bristol BS1 3LU, UK
Phone: +44 117 926 8054

#230
Jolly Fryer
Cuisines: Fish & Chips, Burgers
Average price: Under 10
Address: 557A Filton Avenue
Bristol BS7 0QH, UK
Phone: +44 117 969 2376

#231
Henleaze Fish Bar
Cuisines: Fish & Chips
Average price: 11-25
Address: 150 Henleaze Road
Bristol BS9 4NB, UK
Phone: +44 117 907 3383

#232
Johns York Cafe
Cuisines: Breakfast & Brunch, British
Average price: Under 10
Address: 46 Bond St
Bristol BS1, UK
Phone: +44 117 929 0101

#233
La Grotta
Cuisines: Italian
Average price: 11-25
Address: 9 Union Street
Bristol BS1 2DD, UK
Phone: +44 117 929 0466

#234
The H Bar
Cuisines: Mediterranean, Spanish
Average price: 11-25
Address: Colston Street
Bristol BS1 5AR, UK
Phone: +44 117 204 7130

#235
Za Za Bazaar
Cuisines: Diner
Average price: 11-25
Address: Canons Road
Bristol BS1, UK
Phone: +44 117 922 0330

#236
Dragon Grill
Cuisines: Asian Fusion
Average price: 26-45
Address: 1-2 Frogmore St
Bristol BS1 5NA, UK
Phone: +44 117 929 3288

#237
TGI Fridays UK
Cuisines: American
Average price: 11-25
Address: Lysander Road
Bristol BS10 7UB, UK
Phone: +44 117 959 1987

#238
Bottelinos
Cuisines: Italian
Average price: 11-25
Address: The Old Police Station
Bristol BS3 4HS, UK
Phone: +44 117 966 6676

Shops, Restaurants, Attractions & Nightlife/ Bristol Guidebook 2020

#239
Bombay Spice
Cuisines: Indian, Pakistani
Average price: Above 46
Address: 10 The Mall
Bristol BS8 4DR, UK
Phone: +44 117 970 6066

#240
Undercroft Cafe
Cuisines: Coffee & Tea, British
Average price: Under 10
Address: St Mary Redcliffe Church
Bristol BS1 6RA, UK
Phone: +44 117 933 8644

#241
Spice Express
Cuisines: Fast Food
Average price: 11-25
Address: 224 Church Rd
Bristol BS5 8AD, UK
Phone: +44 117 955 4763

#242
ONeills
Cuisines: Irish, Bar
Average price: Under 10
Address: 16-24 Baldwin Street
Bristol BS1 1SE, UK
Phone: +44 117 945 8891

#243
Manor Kitchen
Cuisines: Deli
Average price: 11-25
Address: 3 Soundwell Road
Bristol BS16 4QG, UK
Phone: +44 117 956 9291

#244
Pizza Provencale
Cuisines: Pizza, French
Average price: 11-25
Address: 29 Regent Street
Bristol BS8 4HR, UK
Phone: +44 117 974 1175

#245
Piazza Di Roma
Cuisines: Pizza
Average price: 11-25
Address: 178 Whiteladies Road
Bristol BS8 2XU, UK
Phone: +44 117 973 4183

#246
Bella Italia
Cuisines: Italian
Average price: 11-25
Address: Unit SU57
Bristol BS1 3BX, UK
Phone: +44 117 927 7230

#247
NHG Takeaway
Cuisines: Malaysian, Fast Food, Asian Fusion
Average price: 11-25
Address: 200 Cheltenham Road
Bristol BS6 5QZ, UK
Phone: +44 117 904 9345

#248
Mission Burrito
Cuisines: Mexican
Average price: Under 10
Address: 65 Park St
Bristol BS1 5JN, UK
Phone: +44 117 927 3339

#249
Caffe Gusto
Cuisines: Bakery, Sandwiches
Average price: 11-25
Address: 5 Queens Rd
Bristol BS8 1QE, UK
Phone: +44 117 925 0868

#250
Spice Route
Cuisines: Persian/Iranian, Mediterranean
Average price: 11-25
Address: 61 Gloucester Rd
Bristol BS7 8AD, UK
Phone: +44 117 904 0040

#251
Oz Restaurant
Cuisines: Turkish
Average price: 11-25
Address: 3 - 4 Triangle South
Bristol BS8 1EY, UK
Phone: +44 117 927 3097

#252
Caffe Gusto
Cuisines: Coffee & Tea, Cafe
Average price: 11-25
Address: Whiteladies Road
Bristol BS8 2NN, UK
Phone: +44 117 974 7277

Shops, Restaurants, Attractions & Nightlife/ Bristol Guidebook 2020

#253
Willow Curry Bar
Cuisines: Fast Food
Average price: Under 10
Address: 86 St Johns Ln
Bristol BS3 5AQ, UK
Phone: +44 117 977 8910

#254
Allspice
Cuisines: Indian, Fast Food
Average price: 11-25
Address: 389 Bath Road
Bristol BS4 3EU, UK
Phone: +44 117 971 5551

#255
Clarks Pies
Cuisines: Bakery, Deli, Fast Food
Average price: Under 10
Address: 259 N Street
Bristol BS3 1JN, UK
Phone: +44 117 966 3894

#256
Pitcher & Piano
Cuisines: British, Bar
Average price: 11-25
Address: Cannon's Road
Bristol BS1 5UH, UK
Phone: +44 117 929 9652

#257
Lucs Chinese Takeaway
Cuisines: Fast Food
Average price: 11-25
Address: 21 Midland Road
Bristol BS2 0JT, UK
Phone: +44 117 955 7691

#258
Chiquito
Cuisines: Mexican, Tex-Mex
Average price: 11-25
Address: Merlin Road
Bristol BS10 7SR, UK
Phone: +44 117 959 1459

#259
Subway
Cuisines: Coffee & Tea, Sandwiches
Average price: 11-25
Address: 103 Whiteladies Road
Bristol BS8 2PB, UK
Phone: +44 117 973 4500

#260
Atomic Burger
Cuisines: Burgers, Fast Food
Average price: 11-25
Address: 189 Gloucester Road
Bristol BS7 8BG, UK
Phone: +44 117 942 8600

#261
Phoenix Restaurant and Bar
Cuisines: British, Bar
Average price: 11-25
Address: The Mercure Hotel
Bristol BS1 6SQ, UK
Phone: +44 117 968 9900

#262
Johns Cafe Bar
Cuisines: Taiwanese, British
Average price: 11-25
Address: 27-29 Midland Road
Bristol BS2 0JT, UK
Phone: +44 117 955 0333

#263
Teppan
Cuisines: Asian Fusion
Average price: 11-25
Address: 13a Small St
Bristol BS1 1DE, UK
Phone: +44 117 929 3516

#264
Hotline Pizza
Cuisines: Pizza
Average price: 11-25
Address: 72 Stapleton Road
Bristol BS5 0RB, UK
Phone: +44 117 908 8338

#265
Sandwich Sandwich
Cuisines: Sandwiches, Cafe
Average price: Under 10
Address: 52 Baldwin Street
Bristol BS1 1QQ, UK
Phone: +44 117 929 2330

#266
St. Michaels Cafe
Cuisines: Cafe, Bed & Breakfast
Average price: 11-25
Address: 145 St Michaels Hill
Bristol BS2 8DB, UK
Phone: +44 117 907 7820

#267
My Burrito
Cuisines: Mexican
Average price: 11-25
Address: 7 Broad Quay
Bristol BS1 4DA, UK
Phone: +44 117 929 7239

#268
Redbones Carribean Canteen
Cuisines: Caribbean
Average price: 11-25
Address: 4 Haymarket Walk
Bristol BS1 3LN, UK
Phone: +44 117 930 4221

#269
Cathay Rendezvous
Cuisines: Chinese
Average price: 11-25
Address: 30 King Street
Bristol BS1 4DZ, UK
Phone: +44 117 934 9345

#270
The Social
Cuisines: Bar, British
Average price: 11-25
Address: 130 Cheltenham Road
Bristol BS6 5RW, UK
Phone: +44 117 924 4500

#271
Bravas
Cuisines: Tapas
Average price: 11-25
Address: 7 Cotham Hill
Bristol BS6, UK
Phone: +44 117 329 6887

#272
Zulu
Cuisines: African, Burgers
Average price: 11-25
Address: 27A Gloucester Road
Bristol BS7 8AA, UK
Phone: +44 117 973 3404

#273
Chandos Delicatessen
Cuisines: Deli, Food
Average price: 26-45
Address: 6 Princess Victoria Street
Bristol BS8 4BP, UK
Phone: +44 117 974 3275

#274
Shore Cafe Bar
Cuisines: Burgers, Pub
Average price: 11-25
Address: Prince Street
Bristol BS1 4QF, UK
Phone: +44 117 923 0333

#275
Kebele Cafe
Cuisines: Cafe
Average price: 11-25
Address: 14 Robertson Road
Bristol BS5 6JY, UK
Phone: +44 117 939 9469

#276
New Taj
Cuisines: Fast Food
Average price: 11-25
Address: 404 Gloucester Road
Bristol BS7 8TR, UK
Phone: +44 117 942 1992

#277
The Marmalade Cafe
Cuisines: Cafe
Average price: 11-25
Address: 3 Worrall Rd
Bristol BS8 2UF, UK
Phone: +44 117 329 3474

#278
Smiley's Plaice
Cuisines: Fish & Chips
Average price: 11-25
Address: 73 East Street
Bristol BS3 4HB, UK
Phone: +44 117 953 2792

#279
Rising Sun Chinese Takeaway
Cuisines: Fast Food
Average price: 11-25
Address: 91 Ashley Down Road
Bristol BS7 9JT, UK
Phone: +44 117 942 0083

#280
Beijing Express
Cuisines: Fast Food
Average price: 11-25
Address: 230 ST. Johns Lane
Bristol BS3 5AU, UK
Phone: +44 117 963 9888

#281
Enids Fish Bar
Cuisines: Fish & Chips, Chinese
Average price: 11-25
Address: 181 North Street
Bristol BS3 1JQ, UK
Phone: +44 117 966 1505

#282
The Hungry Caterpillar
Cuisines: Cafe
Average price: 11-25
Address: 30 Cannon Street
Bristol BS3 1BN, UK
Phone: +44 117 953 0235

#283
Cordial & Grace
Cuisines: Cafe
Average price: 11-25
Address: 9 The Mall
Bristol BS8 4DP, UK
Phone: +44 117 970 6259

#284
Zazus Kitchen
Cuisines: British, European
Average price: 11-25
Address: 220 North Street
Bristol BS3 1JD, UK
Phone: +44 117 963 9044

#285
Ganges
Cuisines: Indian, Pakistani
Average price: 11-25
Address: 368 Gloucester Road
Bristol BS7 8TP, UK
Phone: +44 117 924 5234

#286
Subway
Cuisines: Fast Food, Sandwiches
Average price: Under 10
Address: 80-82 East Street
Bristol BS3 4EY, UK
Phone: +44 117 963 7616

#287
Shanghai Express
Cuisines: Fish & Chips, Chinese
Average price: 11-25
Address: 365 Gloucester Road
Bristol BS7 8TN, UK
Phone: +44 117 908 2226

#288
Clifton Kitchen
Cuisines: British
Average price: 11-25
Address: 112 Princess Victoria St
Bristol BS8 4DB, UK
Phone: +44 117 946 7870

#289
Falafel King
Cuisines: Middle Eastern, Vegetarian
Average price: Under 10
Address: 6 Cotham Hill
Bristol BS6 6LF, UK
Phone: +44 117 329 4476

#290
Bristol Fryer
Cuisines: Fish & Chips, Coffee & Tea
Average price: Under 10
Address: 431 Gloucester Road
Bristol BS7 8TZ, UK
Phone: +44 117 951 5415

#291
Chandos Deli
Cuisines: Deli
Average price: 11-25
Address: 97 Henleaze Road
Bristol BS9 4JP, UK
Phone: +44 117 907 4391

#292
Jade Palace Restaurant
Cuisines: Chinese
Average price: 11-25
Address: 277 Two Mile Hill Road
Bristol BS15 1AX, UK
Phone: +44 117 967 3851

#293
Als Tikka Grill
Cuisines: Indian
Average price: 11-25
Address: 33 Ashton Road
Bristol BS3 2EG, UK
Phone: +44 117 985 3016

#294
Mange Tout
Cuisines: Fast Food, Coffee & Tea
Average price: Under 10
Address: 58 Corn Street
Bristol BS1 1JG, UK
Phone: +44 117 927 7927

Shops, Restaurants, Attractions & Nightlife/ Bristol Guidebook 2020

#295
Dominos Pizza
Cuisines: Pizza, Fast Food, Food Delivery Services
Average price: 26-45
Address: 119 Whiteladies Road
Bristol BS8 2PL, UK
Phone: +44 117 973 3400

#296
MeSushi
Cuisines: Sushi Bar, Fast Food, Food Delivery Services
Average price: 11-25
Address: Bristol, UK
Phone: +44 7825 787358

#297
Raj Pavillions
Cuisines: Indian
Average price: 11-25
Address: 14 Filton Road
Bristol BS7 0PA, UK
Phone: +44 117 951 3310

#298
Siam Harbourside Thai Restaurant
Cuisines: Thai
Average price: 26-45
Address: 129 Hotwell Rd
Bristol BS8 4RU, UK
Phone: +44 117 330 6476

#299
The Grand Hotel
Cuisines: British
Average price: 26-45
Address: Broad St
Bristol BS1 2EL, UK
Phone: +44 871 376 9042

#300
China House Take Away
Cuisines: Fish & Chips
Average price: 11-25
Address: 50 Bristol Hill
Bristol BS4 5AB, UK
Phone: +44 117 977 0868

#301
Mumtaz Restaurant
Cuisines: Indian, Pakistani
Average price: 11-25
Address: 61 High Street
Bristol BS9 3ED, UK
Phone: +44 117 950 7771

#302
Wai Sing Fish Bar
Cuisines: Fast Food, Chinese
Average price: 11-25
Address: 101 BiShopworth Road
Bristol BS13 7JR, UK
Phone: +44 117 966 9718

#303
Tikka Flame
Cuisines: Wine Bar, Indian
Average price: 11-25
Address: Anchor Road
Bristol BS1 5DB, UK
Phone: +44 117 316 9393

#304
Lock Keeper
Cuisines: Pub, British
Average price: 11-25
Address: Keynsham Road
Bristol BS31 2DD, UK
Phone: +44 117 986 2383

#305
Roccos Pasta and Pizza
Cuisines: Italian, Pizza
Average price: 11-25
Address: 3-4 The Promenade
Bristol BS7 8AL, UK
Phone: +44 117 942 5829

#306
Tesco Metro
Cuisines: British, Fast Food
Average price: 11-25
Address: 314 Lodge Causeway
Bristol BS16 3RA, UK
Phone: +44 117 965 5222

#307
China Capital
Cuisines: Fast Food, Chinese
Average price: 11-25
Address: 10 Gloucester Road N
Bristol BS7 0SF, UK
Phone: +44 117 969 5486

#308
Brasserie Blanc
Cuisines: Brasserie, French
Average price: 26-45
Address: Bakers & Cutlers Hall
Bristol BS1 3DF, UK
Phone: +44 117 910 2410

Shops, Restaurants, Attractions & Nightlife/ Bristol Guidebook 2020

#309
Pizza King
Cuisines: Fast Food, Pizza
Average price: 11-25
Address: 107 Stokes Croft
Bristol BS1 3, UK
Phone: +44 117 944 5290

#310
One30
Cuisines: Spanish
Average price: 11-25
Address: 130 Cheltenham Rd
Bristol BS6 5RW, UK
Phone: +44 117 944 2442

#311
Baowow
Cuisines: Vietnamese, Japanese, Thai
Average price: 11-25
Address: 53 Baldwin Street
Bristol BS1, UK
Phone: +44 117 329 0581

#312
Fresh Takeaway
Cuisines: Fast Food, Chinese
Average price: 11-25
Address: 124 St Michael's Hill
Bristol BS2 8BU, UK
Phone: +44 117 926 5959

#313
Kalahari Moon
Cuisines: Deli, Grocery
Average price: 11-25
Address: 88-91 The Covered Market
Bristol BS1 1JQ, UK
Phone: +44 117 929 9879

#314
New Ki Lee Fish Bar
Cuisines: Fish & Chips, Chinese
Average price: 11-25
Address: 90 Mina Road
Bristol BS2 9XW, UK
Phone: +44 117 955 1044

#315
The Burger Joint
Cuisines: Burgers
Average price: 11-25
Address: 83 Whiteladies Road
Bristol BS8 2NT, UK
Phone: +44 117 329 0887

#316
Paprika Indian Restaurant
Cuisines: Indian, Pakistani
Average price: 11-25
Address: 16 Gilda Parade
Bristol BS14 9HY, UK
Phone: +44 1275 830014

#317
Monte Carlo Cafe
Cuisines: Breakfast & Brunch
Average price: Under 10
Address: 458 Stapleton Road
Bristol BS5 6, UK
Phone: +44 117 951 0199

#318
The Assembly
Cuisines: Pub, British
Average price: 11-25
Address: 110-112 East Street
Bristol BS3 4EY, UK
Phone: +44 117 966 6506

#319
Baguette Express
Cuisines: Sandwiches, Fast Food
Average price: Under 10
Address: 107 East Street
Bristol BS3 4EX, UK
Phone: +44 117 953 3499

#320
Melanies Kitchen
Cuisines: Deli
Average price: 11-25
Address: 2 Downend Rd
Bristol BS16 5UJ, UK
Phone: +44 117 957 2662

#321
Karachi Karahi
Cuisines: Fast Food
Average price: Under 10
Address: 234 St John's Lane
Bristol BS3 5AU, UK
Phone: +44 117 953 8000

#322
Kebab King
Cuisines: Fast Food
Average price: 11-25
Address: 288 Church Road
Bristol BS5 8AH, UK
Phone: +44 117 955 6523

Shops, Restaurants, Attractions & Nightlife/ Bristol Guidebook 2020

#323
Bagel Boy
Cuisines: Breakfast & Brunch
Average price: 11-25
Address: 39-41 Saint Nicholas Street
Bristol BS1 1TP, UK
Phone: +44 117 922 0417

#324
Lin-Seng
Cuisines: Fast Food
Average price: 11-25
Address: 175-177 Conygre Grove
Bristol BS34 7HZ, UK
Phone: +44 117 969 3260

#325
Greggs
Cuisines: Bakery, Donuts, Fast Food
Average price: Under 10
Address: 55 Union Street
Bristol BS1 2DU, UK
Phone: +44 117 925 2863

#326
TGI Fridays
Cuisines: American
Average price: 26-45
Address: Merlin Road
Bristol BS34 5DG, UK
Phone: +44 117 959 1987

#327
Miss Millies Fried Chicken
Cuisines: Fast Food
Average price: Under 10
Address: 79 East Street
Bristol BS3 4EX, UK
Phone: +44 117 966 2583

#328
Boston Tea Party
Cuisines: Breakfast & Brunch
Average price: 11-25
Address: 97 Whieladies Road
Bristol BS8 2NT, UK
Phone: +44 117 317 9736

#329
Valentino
Cuisines: Italian
Average price: 11-25
Address: 124 Stoke Lane
Bristol BS9 3RJ, UK
Phone: +44 117 962 3222

#330
Pimm's Pizza
Cuisines: Pizza
Average price: 11-25
Address: 257 North Street
Bristol BS3 1JN, UK
Phone: +44 117 378 7878

#331
Lal Jomi Pavillion Restaurant
Cuisines: Indian, Pakistani
Average price: 11-25
Address: 2 Harcourt Road
Bristol BS6 7RG, UK
Phone: +44 117 942 1640

#332
Shadin Indian & Balti Takeaway
Cuisines: Indian
Average price: 11-25
Address: 70 Broad Street
Bristol BS16 5NL, UK
Phone: +44 117 957 5786

#333
Golden Palace
Cuisines: Fast Food
Average price: 11-25
Address: 92 Broad Street
Bristol BS16 5NJ, UK
Phone: +44 117 957 4898

#334
Four Seasons
Cuisines: Fast Food
Average price: 11-25
Address: 23 Cleeve Wd Road
Bristol BS16 2SF, UK
Phone: +44 117 970 1134

#335
Tikka Raaz Restaurant
Cuisines: Indian, Pakistani
Average price: 26-45
Address: 36 Downend Road
Bristol BS16 5UJ, UK
Phone: +44 117 956 4013

#336
Pepenero
Cuisines: Pizza, Italian, Vegan
Average price: 11-25
Address: 22 Bond Street
Bristol BS2 3LU, UK
Phone: +44 117 926 8057

#337
Shalimar Balti
Cuisines: Indian
Average price: 11-25
Address: 126 Cheltenham Road
Bristol BS6 5RW, UK
Phone: +44 117 942 3808

#338
The Pear Cafe
Cuisines: Sandwiches, Coffee & Tea
Average price: Under 10
Address: 2 Upper York St
Bristol BS2 8QN, UK
Phone: +44 117 942 8392

#339
Roccos Restaurant & Takeaway
Cuisines: Italian
Average price: 11-25
Address: 4a The Promenade
Bristol BS2 8BU, UK
Phone: +44 117 942 5829

#340
British Raj Lar
Cuisines: Ethiopian, Indian
Average price: 26-45
Address: 1-3 Passage Road
Bristol BS9 3HN, UK
Phone: +44 117 950 7149

#341
Turtle Bay
Cuisines: Caribbean
Average price: 11-25
Address: 8 Broad Quay
Bristol BS1 4DA, UK
Phone: +44 117 929 0209

#342
Wongs
Cuisines: Chinese
Average price: 11-25
Address: 12 Denmark Street
Bristol BS1 5DQ, UK
Phone: +44 117 925 8883

#343
Magic Roll
Cuisines: British
Average price: 11-25
Address: Redcliff St
Bristol BS1 6JG, UK
Phone: +44 7851 760939

#344
Natraj Tandoori
Cuisines: Chinese, Himalayan/Nepalese
Average price: 11-25
Address: 185 Gloucester Road
Bristol BS7 8BG, UK
Phone: +44 117 924 8145

#345
Jack's Brasserie
Cuisines: Bar, British
Average price: 11-25
Address: 1 Hannover Quay
Bristol BS1 5JE, UK
Phone: +44 117 945 3990

#346
The Black Bear
Cuisines: Pub, Cafe
Average price: 11-25
Address: 168 Whiteladies Road
Bristol BS8 2XZ, UK
Phone: +44 117 973 3993

#347
Gert Lush
Cuisines: Sandwiches
Average price: Under 10
Address: 9A Regent Street
Bristol BS8 4HW, UK
Phone: +44 117 973 1003

#348
Best Spice
Cuisines: Indian, Fast Food
Average price: Under 10
Address: 180 Wells Road
Bristol BS4 2AL, UK
Phone: +44 117 971 7758

#349
Domino's Pizza
Cuisines: Pizza
Average price: 11-25
Address: 439 Gloucester Road
Bristol BS7 8TZ, UK
Phone: +44 117 951 2777

#350
Yo! Sushi - Cribbs Causeway
Cuisines: Sushi
Average price: 11-25
Address: The Avenue
Bristol BS34 5DG, UK
Phone: +44 117 321 3170

#351
Blue Rhubarb
Cuisines: European
Average price: 11-25
Address: 50 Priness Victoria Street
Bristol BS8 4BZ, UK
Phone: +44 117 973 7673

#352
Full Court Press
Cuisines: Cafe
Average price: Under 10
Address: 59 Broad Street
Bristol BS1 2EJ, UK
Phone: +44 7794 808552

#353
Hotel Du Vin
Cuisines: European, French
Average price: 26-45
Address: The Sugar House
Bristol BS1 2NU, UK
Phone: +44 117 925 5577

#354
McDonalds Restaurant
Cuisines: American, Fast Food
Average price: 11-25
Address: 101-105 The Horsefair
Bristol BS1 3JR, UK
Phone: +44 870 241 3300

#355
Vanoosh
Cuisines: Fast Food
Average price: 11-25
Address: 3 West Street
Bristol BS2 0DF, UK
Phone: +44 117 330 6879

#356
Bombay Boulevard
Cuisines: Indian
Average price: Under 10
Address: 4 Denmark St
Bristol BS1 5DQ, UK
Phone: +44 117 927 3544

#357
Bristol Kebab & Burger House
Cuisines: Fast Food
Average price: Under 10
Address: 3 St. Augustines Parade
Bristol BS1 4XG, UK
Phone: +44 117 926 0858

#358
M & M Kebabs
Cuisines: Fast Food
Average price: 11-25
Address: 63 Whiteladies Road
Bristol BS8 2LY, UK
Phone: +44 117 974 7070

#359
All In Flavour
Cuisines: Fast Food, Coffee & Tea
Average price: 11-25
Address: 3 Ashton Drive
Bristol BS3 2PN, UK
Phone: +44 117 966 5063

#360
River Cottage Canteen
Cuisines: British, GastroPub
Average price: 26-45
Address: St John's Court
Bristol BS8 2QY, UK
Phone: +44 117 973 2458

#361
International Cafe
Cuisines: Breakfast & Brunch
Average price: 11-25
Address: 33a East St
Bristol BS3 4HH, UK
Phone: +44 117 963 5241

#362
Bedminster Kebab House
Cuisines: Indian
Average price: Under 10
Address: 29A East Street
Bristol BS3 4HH, UK
Phone: +44 117 953 3339

#363
McDonald's
Cuisines: Fast Food, Burgers
Average price: 11-25
Address: East Street
Bristol BS3 4JY, UK
Phone: +44 117 963 1710

#364
Alma Tavern
Cuisines: Pub, British
Average price: 11-25
Address: 18-20 Alma Vale Road
Bristol BS8 2HY, UK
Phone: +44 117 973 5171

#365
Taste Of Orient
Cuisines: Fast Food
Average price: 11-25
Address: 246 Lodge Causeway
Bristol BS16 3QS, UK
Phone: +44 117 965 3388

#366
Mr Crispins
Cuisines: Fish & Chips
Average price: Under 10
Address: 280 Wells Road
Bristol BS4 2PU, UK
Phone: +44 117 987 9333

#367
Magic Roll
Cuisines: Sandwiches
Average price: Under 10
Address: 9 New Station Rd
Bristol BS16 3RP, UK
Phone: +44 117 329 4393

#368
Cinnamon
Cuisines: Indian, Pakistani
Average price: 11-25
Address: 68 High Street
Bristol BS31 1EA, UK
Phone: +44 117 986 8090

#369
Philpotts
Cuisines: Bakery, Sandwiches
Average price: 11-25
Address: Victoria St
Bristol BS1 6AH, UK
Phone: +44 117 930 4422

#370
The Knights Templar
Cuisines: British, Pub
Average price: Under 10
Address: 1 The Square
Bristol BS1 6DG, UK
Phone: +44 117 925 4439

#371
Taste of China
Cuisines: Thai, Chinese, Fast Food
Average price: 11-25
Address: 596 Fishponds Road
Bristol BS16 3, UK
Phone: +44 117 958 3304

#372
Walkabout
Cuisines: Sports Bar, British
Average price: 11-25
Address: 40 Corn Street
Bristol BS1 1HQ, UK
Phone: +44 117 930 0181

#373
The Hawthorns
Cuisines: Breakfast & Brunch
Average price: Under 10
Address: Woodland Road
Bristol BS8 1UQ, UK
Phone: +44 117 954 5555

#374
Hotcha
Cuisines: Chinese
Average price: 11-25
Address: 44A Temple Street
Bristol BS31 1EH, UK
Phone: +44 871 288 2282

#375
Jessicas Sandwich Bar
Cuisines: Coffee & Tea, Cafe
Average price: Under 10
Address: 176 Kings Head Lane
Bristol BS13 7BW, UK
Phone: +44 117 946 5919

#376
Raj Mahal
Cuisines: Indian, Bangladeshi
Average price: 11-25
Address: 8-10 Frome Valley Road
Bristol BS16 1HD, UK
Phone: +44 117 958 6382

#377
Miss Millies Fried Chicken
Cuisines: Fast Food
Average price: 11-25
Address: 91 Gloucester Road
Bristol BS7 8AT, UK
Phone: +44 117 924 0043

#378
Biblos
Cuisines: Mediterranean
Average price: 11-25
Address: 62a Stokes Croft
Bristol BS1 3QU, UK
Phone: +44 117 923 2737

#379
Burger King
Cuisines: American, Fast Food
Average price: 11-25
Address: 40-42 The Horsefair
Bristol BS1 3JE, UK
Phone: +44 117 929 1211

#380
Kalabash
Cuisines: African, Indian
Average price: 11-25
Address: 120 Cheltenham Road
Bristol BS6 5RW, UK
Phone: +44 117 330 9991

#381
Johns
Cuisines: Thai
Average price: 11-25
Address: 27-29 Midland Road
Bristol BS2 0JT, UK
Phone: +44 117 955 0333

#382
CafeZest
Cuisines: Breakfast & Brunch
Average price: 11-25
Address: 20 Christmas Steps
Bristol BS1 5BS, UK
Phone: +44 117 930 0258

#383
Giuseppes Italian Restaurant
Cuisines: Italian
Average price: 11-25
Address: 59 Baldwin Street
Bristol BS1 1QZ, UK
Phone: +44 117 926 4869

#384
Playground Coffee House
Cuisines: Cafe
Average price: 11-25
Address: 45 St Nicholas Street
Bristol BS1 1LJ, UK
Phone: +44 7510 155709

#385
Brigstow Cafe & Tapas
Cuisines: British, Tapas
Average price: 11-25
Address: 9 Clare Street
Bristol BS1 1XH, UK
Phone: +44 117 929 3876

#386
Yurt Lush
Cuisines: European
Average price: 11-25
Address: Creative Common Isambard Walk Temple quay
Bristol BS1 6DZ, UK
Phone: +44 7582 048090

#387
4500 Miles From Dehli
Cuisines: Indian
Average price: 11-25
Address: 8 Colston Avenue
Bristol BS1 4ST, UK
Phone: +44 117 929 2224

#388
New World
Cuisines: Asian Fusion
Average price: 11-25
Address: 1-2 Frogmore Street
Bristol BS1 5NA, UK
Phone: +44 117 929 3288

#389
Pizza Palace
Cuisines: Pizza
Average price: Under 10
Address: 6 St Augustines Parade
Bristol BS1 4XG, UK
Phone: +44 117 929 2740

#390
Oppo Harmonic Fusion
Cuisines: British, Bar
Average price: 11-25
Address: 72 Park Street
Bristol BS1 5JX, UK
Phone: +44 117 929 1166

#391
Yips Chinese
Cuisines: Chinese
Average price: 11-25
Address: 44 Gloucester Road
Bristol BS7 8, UK
Phone: +44 117 951 9349

#392
Subway
Cuisines: Sandwiches
Average price: 11-25
Address: 15-19 Queens Road
Bristol BS8 1QE, UK
Phone: +44 117 925 6164

#393
Mc Avoys
Cuisines: British, Coffee & Tea
Average price: 11-25
Address: Redcliffe Street
Bristol BS1 2HF, UK
Phone: +44 117 929 8477

#394
Harts Bakery
Cuisines: Breakfast & Brunch, Bakery
Average price: 11-25
Address: Arch 35 Lower Approach Road
Bristol BS1 6QS, UK
Phone: +44 7968 220260

#395
Le Monde
Cuisines: Seafood
Average price: Above 46
Address: Triangle West
Bristol BS8 1ES, UK
Phone: +44 117 934 0999

#396
Dragon Fountain
Cuisines: Chinese, Asian Fusion
Average price: 11-25
Address: 4 Cotham Hill
Bristol BS6 6LF, UK
Phone: +44 117 973 7749

#397
Tantric Jazz
Cuisines: Bar, Jazz & Blues, Mediterranean
Average price: 11-25
Address: 39-41 ST Nicholas St
Bristol BS1 1TP, UK
Phone: +44 117 940 2304

#398
The Big Bang
Cuisines: British
Average price: 11-25
Address: 46 Whiteladies Rd
Bristol BS8 2NH, UK
Phone: +44 117 923 9212

#399
Steak Of The Art
Cuisines: Steakhouse
Average price: 26-45
Address: Cathedral Walk
Bristol BS1 5TT, UK
Phone: +44 117 929 7967

#400
Hunger Hatch
Cuisines: Fast Food
Average price: 11-25
Address: 17 Queens Row
Bristol BS8 1EZ, UK
Phone: +44 117 908 9798

#401
The Bakehouse & Deli
Cuisines: Fast Food, Coffee & Tea
Average price: 11-25
Address: Queens Avenue
Bristol BS8 1SB, UK
Phone: +44 117 926 2730

#402
Sahra Restaurant
Cuisines: Middle Eastern
Average price: 11-25
Address: 95 Queens Road
Bristol BS8 1LW, UK
Phone: +44 117 973 9734

#403
Caffe Gusto
Cuisines: Coffee & Tea, Sandwiches
Average price: 11-25
Address: 3 Hanover Quay
Bristol BS5 9, UK
Phone: +44 117 929 8113

#404
Cibo Restaurante
Cuisines: Italian
Average price: 11-25
Address: 289 Gloucester Road
Bristol BS7 8NY, UK
Phone: +44 117 942 9475

#405
Fishworks Seafood Cafe
Cuisines: Seafood
Average price: 26-45
Address: 128 Whiteladies Road
Bristol BS8 2RS, UK
Phone: +44 117 974 4433

#406
Kohi Noor
Cuisines: Asian Fusion, Indian
Average price: 11-25
Address: 211 Whiteladies Road
Bristol BS8 2XS, UK
Phone: +44 117 973 1313

#407
Hot Wok Xpress
Cuisines: Fast Food
Average price: 11-25
Address: 268 Gloucester Road
Bristol BS7 8PB, UK
Phone: +44 117 924 7373

#408
Thaiphoon
Cuisines: Thai, Deli
Average price: Under 10
Address: 12 Kings Road
Bristol BS8 4AB, UK
Phone: +44 9466 0028

#409
Clifton Bistro
Cuisines: Coffee & Tea, Greek
Average price: 11-25
Address: 6 Clifton Down Rd
Bristol BS8 4AD, UK
Phone: +44 844 249 8930

#410
Di Meo
Cuisines: Italian
Average price: 11-25
Address: 314 Gloucester Road
Bristol BS7 8, UK
Phone: +44 117 924 5676

#411
Joe Kebub
Cuisines: Fast Food, Greek, Mediterranean
Average price: 11-25
Address: 26 Cannon Street
Bristol BS3 1BN, UK
Phone: +44 117 904 0019

#412
New Shang Hai
Cuisines: Chinese
Average price: 11-25
Address: 4 Windmill Hill
Bristol BS3 4LU, UK
Phone: +44 117 966 5177

#413
Oriental Chef
Cuisines: Fast Food
Average price: Under 10
Address: 64 North Street
Bristol BS3 1HJ, UK
Phone: +44 117 966 9166

#414
Shiraz
Cuisines: Persian/Iranian
Average price: 11-25
Address: 275 Hotwells Rd
Bristol BS8 4SF, UK
Phone: +44 117 925 5668

#415
Yee Wah
Cuisines: Fast Food
Average price: Under 10
Address: 27 Raymend Road
Bristol BS3 4QR, UK
Phone: +44 117 966 2898

#416
Gordons
Cuisines: Caribbean, Fast Food
Average price: 11-25
Address: 333 Church Road
Bristol BS5 8, UK
Phone: +44 117 902 1474

#417
Kam Ming House
Cuisines: Fast Food
Average price: 11-25
Address: 17 Harrowdene Road
Bristol BS4 2JL, UK
Phone: +44 117 977 7881

#418
Effes Kebab House
Cuisines: Fast Food
Average price: 11-25
Address: 213 Cheltenham Rd
Bristol BS6 5PQ, UK
Phone: +44 117 924 8015

#419
M & M Kebab & Pizza
Cuisines: Middle Eastern, Greek
Average price: Under 10
Address: 1 Marsh Street
Bristol BS1 1RT, UK
Phone: +44 117 929 1906

#420
Warrens Gourmet Burger Co
Cuisines: Burgers
Average price: 11-25
Address: 8 Wootton Road
Bristol BS4 4AL, UK
Phone: +44 117 370 0625

Shops, Restaurants, Attractions & Nightlife/ Bristol Guidebook 2020

#421
Avenue Cafe
Cuisines: Cafe
Average price: 11-25
Address: 96 Henleaze Road
Bristol BS9 4JZ, UK
Phone: +44 117 904 0064

#422
Wong Tai Sin
Cuisines: Chinese, Fish & Chips
Average price: Under 10
Address: 144 Wells Road
Bristol BS4 2AT, UK
Phone: +44 117 971 9513

#423
The Best Kebab In Town
Cuisines: Fast Food
Average price: 11-25
Address: 210 West Street
Bristol BS3 3NE, UK
Phone: +44 117 953 1480

#424
Golden Gate
Cuisines: Chinese
Average price: 11-25
Address: 172 Henleaze Rd
Bristol BS9 4NE, UK
Phone: +44 117 962 1081

#425
Baileys Court Pub
Cuisines: Pub
Average price: 11-25
Address: Baileys Court Road
Bristol BS32 8BH, UK
Phone: +44 117 923 6486

#426
Ashyana Indian Cuisine
Cuisines: Indian
Average price: 11-25
Address: 238 Henleaze Road
Bristol BS9 4NG, UK
Phone: +44 117 962 4001

#427
Chans
Cuisines: Fast Food, Chinese
Average price: 11-25
Address: 205 Wellington Hill W
Bristol BS9 4QL, UK
Phone: +44 117 962 3078

#428
Spice Out
Cuisines: Fast Food
Average price: 11-25
Address: 211 Wellington Hill West
Bristol BS9 4QL, UK
Phone: +44 117 962 2445

#429
Sandwich Box
Cuisines: Coffee & Tea, Sandwiches
Average price: Under 10
Address: 31 Victoria Street
Bristol BS1 6AA, UK
Phone: +44 117 927 3311

#430
Marling Fish Bar
Cuisines: Fish & Chips
Average price: 11-25
Address: Marling Road
Bristol BS5 7LL, UK
Phone: +44 117 955 6719

#431
New Moon
Cuisines: Fast Food, Chinese
Average price: Under 10
Address: 7 Cotham Rd
Bristol BS6 5TZ, UK
Phone: +44 117 924 4070

#432
The Fantastic Sandwich
Cuisines: Fast Food, Sandwiches
Average price: Under 10
Address: 63 North Road
Bristol BS6 5AD, UK
Phone: +44 117 942 0470

#433
Nando's
Cuisines: Portuguese
Average price: 11-25
Address: Unit SU82
Bristol BS1 3BX, UK
Phone: +44 117 376 3876

#434
Portwall Tavern
Cuisines: Pub, British
Average price: Under 10
Address: Portwall Lane
Bristol BS1 6NB, UK
Phone: +44 117 922 0442

#435
Kingsdown Fish and Chips
Cuisines: Fish & Chips
Average price: Under 10
Address: 2 Kingsdown Parade
Bristol BS6 5UD, UK
Phone: +44 117 921 4627

#436
Caffe Sazz
Cuisines: Coffee & Tea, Turkish
Average price: 11-25
Address: 232 North Street
Bristol BS3 1JD, UK
Phone: +44 117 963 3334

#437
Horfield Fish Bar
Cuisines: Fish & Chips
Average price: 11-25
Address: 66 Filton Road
Bristol BS7 0PB, UK
Phone: +44 117 969 3648

#438
Mint Casino
Cuisines: Casino, British
Average price: 11-25
Address: 1-2 Portwall Ln
Bristol BS1 6NB, UK
Phone: +44 117 926 2753

#439
Daily Bite
Cuisines: Coffee & Tea, Desserts
Average price: 11-25
Address: Victoria Street
Bristol BS1 6AH, UK
Phone: +44 117 925 3507

#440
The Townhouse Bar & Restaurant
Cuisines: European, British, Pub
Average price: 11-25
Address: 85 Whiteladies Road
Bristol BS8 2NT, UK
Phone: +44 117 973 9302

#441
Gala Casino
Cuisines: Casino, Steakhouse
Average price: 11-25
Address: Explore Lane
Bristol BS1 5TY, UK
Phone: +44 117 906 9970

#442
Bristol Grill
Cuisines: Fast Food
Average price: Under 10
Address: 40 Cannon Street
Bristol BS3 1BN, UK
Phone: +44 117 966 2694

#443
Miss Millie's Fried Chicken
Cuisines: Fast Food
Average price: 11-25
Address: 157 Church Rd
Bristol BS5 9LA, UK
Phone: +44 117 955 4909

#444
Pizza Top
Cuisines: Pizza, Fast Food
Average price: 11-25
Address: 110 B Church Road
Bristol BS5 9JL, UK
Phone: +44 117 955 8833

#445
Snax
Cuisines: Breakfast & Brunch
Average price: Under 10
Address: 118 E Street
Bristol BS3 4EY, UK
Phone: +44 117 953 3957

#446
Boston Tea Party
Cuisines: Breakfast & Brunch, British
Average price: 11-25
Address: 164 Cheltenham Road
Bristol BS6, UK
Phone: +44 117 329 1454

#447
Rainbow Cafe
Cuisines: Coffee & Tea, British
Average price: 11-25
Address: 10 Waterloo Street
Bristol BS8 4BT, UK
Phone: +44 117 973 8937

#448
Spice Of Nepal
Cuisines: Fast Food
Average price: 11-25
Address: 245 Lodge Causeway
Bristol BS16 3RA, UK
Phone: +44 117 965 0664

Shops, Restaurants, Attractions & Nightlife/ Bristol Guidebook 2020

#449
Alwaha
Cuisines: Fast Food
Average price: 11-25
Address: 147 Wells Road
Bristol BS4 2BU, UK
Phone: +44 117 300 3600

#450
The Crown Inn Harvester
Cuisines: British, Pub
Average price: Under 10
Address: 126 Bath Road
Bristol BS30 9DE, UK
Phone: +44 117 932 2846

#451
Subway
Cuisines: Fast Food
Average price: 11-25
Address: 790 Fishponds Road
Bristol BS16 3TE, UK
Phone: +44 117 965 7640

#452
Raj Restaurant
Cuisines: Indian, Pakistani
Average price: 11-25
Address: 35 King Street
Bristol BS1 4DZ, UK
Phone: +44 117 929 1132

#453
Dim Sum Oriental Take Away
Cuisines: Fast Food
Average price: 11-25
Address: 263 North Street
Bristol BS3 1JN, UK
Phone: +44 117 953 0606

#454
Als Hot & Spicy
Cuisines: Indian
Average price: 11-25
Address: 223 North Street
Bristol BS3 1JJ, UK
Phone: +44 117 966 9008

#455
Turmeric
Cuisines: Indian
Average price: 11-25
Address: 775 Fishponds Road
Bristol BS16 3, UK
Phone: +44 117 965 0022

#456
Pizza Bella
Cuisines: Fast Food
Average price: 11-25
Address: 104 West Street
Bristol BS3 3LR, UK
Phone: +44 117 963 3882

#457
Pearl City
Cuisines: Fast Food
Average price: 11-25
Address: 5 Straits Parade
Bristol BS16 2LA, UK
Phone: +44 117 965 8889

#458
Lashings Coffee House
Cuisines: Coffee & Tea, Cafe, Bagels
Average price: 11-25
Address: 260 Gloucester Road
Bristol BS7 8PB, UK
Phone: +44 117 329 4252

#459
Blossom Sandwich Bar
Cuisines: Fast Food
Average price: 11-25
Address: A2 Saint Peters Rise
Bristol BS13 7LU, UK
Phone: +44 7799 648388

#460
Happy House
Cuisines: Fast Food
Average price: Under 10
Address: 3 Redcatch Road
Bristol BS4 2EP, UK
Phone: +44 117 977 8709

#461
The Royal Kitchen
Cuisines: Fast Food, Chinese
Average price: 11-25
Address: 117 Coldharbour Rd
Bristol BS6 7SD, UK
Phone: +44 117 944 4495

#462
Perfect Pizza
Cuisines: Pizza, Italian
Average price: 11-25
Address: 13 Straits Parade
Bristol BS16 2LE, UK
Phone: +44 117 958 4848

Shops, Restaurants, Attractions & Nightlife/ Bristol Guidebook 2020

#463
Top Chef
Cuisines: Fish & Chips
Average price: 11-25
Address: 61 Sandy Park Rd
Bristol BS4 3PQ, UK
Phone: +44 117 972 8118

#464
Best Takeaway Kebabs & Burgers
Cuisines: Fast Food
Average price: Under 10
Address: 210 West Street
Bristol BS3 3NE, UK
Phone: +44 117 953 1480

#465
Deco Lounge
Cuisines: Lounge, European
Average price: 11-25
Address: 50 Cotham Hill
Bristol BS6 6JX, UK
Phone: +44 117 373 2688

#466
Ciao
Cuisines: Italian
Average price: 11-25
Address: 203 Wellington Hill West
Bristol BS9 4QL, UK
Phone: +44 117 962 2643

#467
Dominos Pizza
Cuisines: Fast Food
Average price: 11-25
Address: 10 Regent Street
Bristol BS15 8JS, UK
Phone: +44 117 961 6111

#468
Juice Hub
Cuisines: Juice Bar& Smoothies
Average price: 11-25
Address: Wine Street
Bristol BS1 2PH, UK
Phone: +44 870 626 0344

#469
Masa Japanese Restaurant
Cuisines: Japanese
Average price: 11-25
Address: 42-46 Baldwin St
Bristol BS1 1PN, UK
Phone: +44 117 929 3888

#470
McDonald's
Cuisines: American, Fast Food
Average price: Under 10
Address: Sheene Road
Bristol BS3 4EG, UK
Phone: +44 117 953 3755

#471
Bristol Sweet Mart
Cuisines: Ethnic Food, Deli
Average price: 11-25
Address: 71 St Marks Road
Bristol BS5 6HX, UK
Phone: +44 117 951 2257

#472
T & P A Murray
Cuisines: Deli
Average price: 11-25
Address: 153 Gloucester Road
Bristol BS7 8BA, UK
Phone: +44 117 942 4025

#473
Studio One
Cuisines: Italian
Average price: 11-25
Address: Cinema de Lux
Bristol BS1 3BX, UK
Phone: +44 871 220 1000

#474
Benny's Chicken
Cuisines: Fast Food
Average price: Under 10
Address: 15 Gloucester Rd
Bristol BS7 8AA, UK
Phone: +44 117 924 8588

#475
Quigleys
Cuisines: Fast Food
Average price: 11-25
Address: 4A St. Augustines Parade
Bristol BS1 4XG, UK
Phone: +44 117 925 0619

#476
Mickey Lavins Irish Steak House
Cuisines: Irish
Average price: 11-25
Address: 10-11 Denmark Street
Bristol BS1 5DQ, UK
Phone: +44 117 914 3731

#477
Brace & Browns
Cuisines: Tapas Bar
Average price: 11-25
Address: 43 Whiteladies Road
Bristol BS5 2LS, UK
Phone: +44 117 973 7800

#478
Chungs Fish & Chips
Cuisines: Fish & Chips
Average price: 11-25
Address: 13 Station Road
Bristol BS11 9TU, UK
Phone: +44 117 982 5183

#479
Cafe Giardino
Cuisines: Cafe
Average price: 11-25
Address: Merlin Road
Bristol BS34 5DG, UK
Phone: +44 117 904 4438

#480
The Clove Indian Restaurant
Cuisines: Indian, Fast Food
Average price: Above 46
Address: 5 Luckwell Road
Bristol BS3 3EL, UK
Phone: +44 117 963 9635

#481
Bella Pizza
Cuisines: Pizza
Average price: 11-25
Address: 2 Silver Street
Bristol BS1 2DU, UK
Phone: +44 117 929 8014

#482
KFC
Cuisines: Fast Food
Average price: 11-25
Address: Cribbs Causeway Regional Shopping Centre
Bristol BS34 5DG, UK
Phone: +44 117 950 5205

#483
Shazzs
Cuisines: Fast Food
Average price: Above 46
Address: 170 Lawrence Hill
Bristol BS5 0DN, UK
Phone: +44 117 909 0546

#484
La Tasca
Cuisines: Tapas Bar
Average price: 11-25
Address: 8-10 Colston Ave
Bristol BS1 4ST, UK
Phone: +44 845 129 7623

#485
Pizza Express
Cuisines: Pizza
Average price: 11-25
Address: 35 Corn Street
Bristol BS1 1HT, UK
Phone: +44 117 930 0239

#486
Asia Garden
Cuisines: Chinese, Buffet
Average price: 11-25
Address: 29 Oxford St
Bristol BS3 4RJ, UK
Phone: +44 117 971 1835

#487
The Hop House
Cuisines: Pub, British
Average price: 11-25
Address: 16 King's Rd
Bristol BS8 4AB, UK
Phone: +44 117 923 7390

#488
Mezzaluna
Cuisines: Mediterranean
Average price: 11-25
Address: 81 West St
Bristol BS3 3NU, UK
Phone: +44 117 953 2069

#489
Viens Palace
Cuisines: Fast Food, Chinese
Average price: 11-25
Address: 166 Kellaway Avenue
Bristol BS6 7YQ, UK
Phone: +44 117 924 8792

#490
Quba Ice
Cuisines: Caribbean
Average price: 11-25
Address: 220 North Street
Bristol BS3 1JD, UK
Phone: +44 117 963 9222

#491
Teohs Oriental Supermarket & Restaurant
Cuisines: Grocery, Japanese, Asian Fusion,
Average price: Under 10
Address: 28-34 Lower Ashley Rd
Bristol BS2 9NP, UK
Phone: +44 117 907 1191

#492
Coco Coffee Deli
Cuisines: Coffee & Tea, Cafe
Average price: 11-25
Address: 2 Haymarket Walk
Bristol BS1 3LN, UK
Phone: +44 117 929 4859

#493
Costa Coffee
Cuisines: Coffee & Tea, Sandwiches
Average price: 11-25
Address: 32 The Arcade
Bristol BS1 3JD, UK
Phone: +44 117 922 0289

#494
Kings 2 Cantonese
Cuisines: Chinese
Average price: 11-25
Address: 7 Cotham Rd S
Bristol BS6 5TZ, UK
Phone: +44 117 907 6699

#495
Anthem
Cuisines: British, Thai, Asian Fusion
Average price: 11-25
Address: 27-29 St Michael's Hill
Bristol BS2 8DZ, UK
Phone: +44 117 929 2834

#496
That Mexican Place
Cuisines: Mexican, Tex-Mex
Average price: 11-25
Address: 37-39 Corn Street
Bristol BS1 1HT, UK
Phone: +44 117 933 8699

#497
Credo
Cuisines: Sandwiches
Average price: 11-25
Address: 53-55 Baldwin St
Bristol BS1 1, UK
Phone: +44 117 927 9909

#498
Pizza Hut
Cuisines: Pizza, Fast Food
Average price: 26-45
Address: 228 Cheltenham Road
Bristol BS6 5QU, UK
Phone: +44 117 942 2200

#499
Courtyard Restaurant The English Continental
Cuisines: British
Average price: 11-25
Address: Lower Park Row
Bristol BS1 5BN, UK
Phone: +44 117 929 7817

#500
Cathay Rendevous
Cuisines: Chinese
Average price: 11-25
Address: 30 King Street
Bristol BS1 4DZ, UK
Phone: +44 117 922 6161

TOP 500 ATTRACTIONS
Recommended by Locals & Trevelers
(From #1 to #500)

Shops, Restaurants, Attractions & Nightlife/ Bristol Guidebook 2020

#1
Cube Cinema
Category: Cinema
Address: 4 Princess Row
Bristol BS2 8NQ, UK
Phone: +44 117 907 4190

#2
Brandon Hill
Category: Park
Address: Off Park Street
Bristol BS1, UK
Phone: +44 117 962 4577

#3
Brunel's SS Great Britain
Category: Landmark, Museum
Address: Gas Ferry Road
Bristol BS1, UK
Phone: +44 117 926 0680

#4
Ashton Court Estate
Category: Golf, Park
Address: Long Ashton
Bristol BS41 9JN, UK
Phone: +44 117 973 8508

#5
The Old Duke
Category: Music Venues, Jazz & Blues
Address: 45 King Street
Bristol BS1 4ER, UK
Phone: +44 117 927 7137

#6
Bristol Folk House
Category: Performing Arts, Local Flavor, Music Venues
Address: 40a Park Street
Bristol BS1 5JG, UK
Phone: +44 117 926 2987

#7
Undercover Rock
Category: Sports Club, Climbing
Address: St Werburghs Church Mina Road
Bristol BS2 9YH, UK
Phone: +44 117 941 3489

#8
Bristol City Museum & Art Gallery
Category: Museum, Art Gallery
Address: Queens Road
Bristol BS8 1RL, UK
Phone: +44 117 922 3571

#9
Castle Park
Category: Park, Historical Building
Address: Newgate Bristol BS1 3, UK
Phone: +44 117 922 3719

#10
The Farm
Category: Pub, Music Venues
Address: Hopetoun Road
Bristol BS2 9YL, UK
Phone: +44 117 944 2384

#11
Circomedia
Category: Performing Arts, Fitness & Instruction
Address: Portland Sq
Bristol BS2 8SJ, UK
Phone: +44 117 924 7615

#12
The Louisiana
Category: Pub, Music Venues, British
Address: Bathurst Terrace
Bristol BS1 6UA, UK
Phone: +44 117 936 3615

#13
Watershed
Category: Venues & Event Space, Cinema, Brasseries
Address: 1 Canons Road
Bristol BS1 5TX, UK
Phone: +44 117 927 2082

#14
Queen Square
Category: Park
Address: Old City
Bristol BS1 4LH, UK
Phone: +44 117 922 3719

Shops, Restaurants, Attractions & Nightlife/ Bristol Guidebook 2020

#15
Weapon Of Choice
Category: Art Gallery, Fashion
Address: 8B Park Street
Bristol BS1 5HR, UK
Phone: +44 117 929 1865

#16
Bristol Zoo Gardens
Category: Zoo
Address: Bristol Zoo Gardens
Bristol BS8 3HA, UK
Phone: +44 117 973 8951

#17
San Carlo Restaurant
Category: Italian, Wineries
Address: 44 Corn Street
Bristol BS1 1HQ, UK
Phone: +44 117 922 6586

#18
Bristol Harbour Festival
Category: Festival
Address: Waterfront Square
Bristol BS1 5LL, UK
Phone: +44 117 922 3287

#19
Grain Barge
Category: Bar, Music Venues
Address: Hotwells Road
Bristol BS8 4RU, UK
Phone: +44 117 929 9347

#20
Bristol Guild
Category: Art Gallery
Address: 68 - 70 Park Street
Bristol BS1 5JY, UK
Phone: +44 117 926 5548

#21
Coronation Tap
Category: Pub, Music Venues
Address: 8 Sion Place
Bristol BS8 4AX, UK
Phone: +44 117 973 9617

#22
Marcruss Store
Category: Fashion, Hiking
Address: 177-181 Hotwells Road
Bristol BS8 4RY, UK
Phone: +44 117 929 2119

#23
Alma Theatre
Category: Cinema
Address: 18-20 Alma Vale Road
Bristol BS8 2HY, UK
Phone: +44 117 973 5171

#24
The Canteen
Category: Music Venues, Art Gallery
Address: 80 Stokes Croft
Bristol BS1 3QY, UK
Phone: +44 117 923 2017

#25
Bristol Ice Rink
Category: Skating Rink
Address: Frogmore St
Bristol BS1 5NA, UK
Phone: +44 117 929 2148

#26
Here Gallery
Category: Art Gallery, Bookstore
Address: 108 Stokes Croft
Bristol BS1 3RU, UK
Phone: +44 117 942 2222

#27
Tobacco Factory
Category: Music Venues, Mediterranean, Performing Arts
Address: Raleigh Road
Bristol BS3 1TF, UK
Phone: +44 117 902 0344

#28
Cafe Kino
Category: Music Venues
Address: 108 Stokes Croft
Bristol BS1 3RU, UK
Phone: +44 117 924 9200

#29
Fitness 4 Less
Category: Gym
Address: All Saints St
Bristol BS1 2LZ, UK
Phone: +44 117 929 7311

#30
Orpheus Cinema
Category: Cinema
Address: 51 Northumbria Drive
Bristol BS9 4HN, UK
Phone: +44 871 230 3200

#31
The Lanes
Category: Bowling
Address: 22 Nelson Street
Bristol BS1 2LE, UK
Phone: +44 117 325 1979

#32
The Golden Lion
Category: Pub, Music Venues
Address: 244 Gloucester Road
Bristol BS7 8NZ, UK
Phone: +44 117 924 6449

#33
Trinity
Category: Performing Arts
Address: Trinity Road
Bristol BS2 0NW, UK
Phone: +44 117 935 1200

#34
Bristol Old Vic
Category: Performing Arts
Address: King Street
Bristol BS1 4ED, UK
Phone: +44 117 987 7877

#35
The Bristol Climbing Centre
Category: Leisure Centre
Address: Mina Road
Bristol BS2 9YH, UK
Phone: +44 117 941 3489

#36
Watershed Media Centre
Category: Performing Arts
Address: 1 Canons Road
Bristol BS1 5TX, UK
Phone: +44 117 927 6444

#37
Blaise Castle House Museum and Estate
Category: Museum, Park
Address: Henbury Road
Bristol BS10 7QS, UK
Phone: +44 117 353 2268

#38
Bristol Old Vic
Category: Performing Arts
Address: 36 King Street
Bristol BS1 4DZ, UK
Phone: +44 117 987 7877

#39
Aardman Animations
Category: Mass Media
Address: Gas Ferry Road
Bristol BS1 6UN, UK
Phone: +44 117 984 8485

#40
Windmill Hill City Farm
Category: Zoo
Address: Philip St
Bristol BS3 4EA, UK
Phone: +44 117 963 3252

#41
Bristol Balloon Fiesta
Category: Local Flavor, Festival
Address: St. Johns Street
Bristol BS3 4NH, UK
Phone: +44 117 953 5884

#42
Blackboy Hill Cycles
Category: Bikes, Bike Rental
Address: 180 Whiteladies Rd
Bristol BS8 2XU, UK
Phone: +44 117 973 1420

#43
St George's Bristol
Category: Music Venues, Church
Address: 5 Great George Street
Bristol BS1 5RR, UK
Phone: +44 845 402 4001

#44
Horfield Leisure Centre
Category: Gym, Swimming Pool
Address: Dorian Rd
Bristol BS7 0XW, UK
Phone: +44 117 903 1643

#45
The Bristol Hippodrome
Category: Performing Arts, Venues & Event Space
Address: 10 St Augustines Parade
Bristol BS1 4UZ, UK
Phone: +44 117 302 3310

#46
Castaways
Category: Leisure Centre, Kids Activities
Address: Waters Road Bourne Chapel
Bristol BS15 8BE, UK
Phone: +44 117 961 5115

#47
Mr Wolfs
Category: Music Venues
Address: 33 St Stephens Street
Bristol BS1 1JX, UK
Phone: +44 117 927 3221

#48
Easton Leisure Centre
Category: Leisure Centre, Swimming Pool, Gym
Address: Thrissell Street
Bristol BS5 0SW, UK
Phone: +44 117 955 8840

#49
Bristol Harbour Train Rides
Category: Local Flavor, Museum
Address: Bristol Harbourside Bristol, UK
Phone: +44 117 922 3571

#50
Sustrans
Category: Transportation
Address: 2 Cathedral Sq
Bristol BS1 5DD, UK
Phone: +44 117 926 8893

#51
Bristol Cider Festival
Category: Festival
Address: Brunel Passenger Shed
Bristol BS1 6QH, UK
Phone: +44 1225 330304

#52
Enso Martial Arts Supplies
Category: Sporting Goods, Martial Arts
Address: 190 Cheltenham Road
Bristol BS6 5RB, UK
Phone: +44 117 942 5832

#53
Showcase Cinema de Lux
Category: Cinema, Lounge
Address: Glass House
Bristol BS1 3BX, UK
Phone: +44 871 220 1000

#54
Pulse Gym
Category: Sports Club
Address: Tyndall Avenue
Bristol BS8 1TP, UK
Phone: +44 117 928 8810

#55
The Fleece
Category: Pub, Music Venues
Address: 12 St Thomas Street
Bristol BS1 6JJ, UK
Phone: +44 117 945 0996

#56
The Bierkeller
Category: Music Venues
Address: All Saints Street
Bristol BS1 2NA, UK
Phone: +44 117 926 8514

#57
Fitness First
Category: Gym, Yoga
Address: Explore Lane
Bristol BS1 5TY, UK
Phone: +44 844 571 2827

#58
Mr Wolfs
Category: Music Venues, Pub
Address: 33 Saint Stephens Street
Bristol BS1 1JX, UK
Phone: +44 117 927 3221

#59
County Cricket Ground
Category: Stadium
Address: Nevil Road
Bristol BS7 9EJ, UK
Phone: +44 117 910 8000

#60
Bamba Beads
Category: Arts & Crafts, Social Club
Address: 7 Gloucester Rd
Bristol BS7 8AA, UK
Phone: +44 117 924 9959

#61
Mind Body Studio
Category: Day Spa, Massage
Address: 6 Kellaway Avenue
Bristol BS6 7XR, UK
Phone: +44 117 944 1114

Shops, Restaurants, Attractions & Nightlife/ Bristol Guidebook 2020

#62
Colston Hall
Category: Performing Arts, Music Venues
Address: Colston Street
Bristol BS1 5AR, UK
Phone: +44 117 922 3686

#63
Bristol Aquarium
Category: Aquarium, Cinema
Address: Anchor Road
Bristol BS1 5TT, UK
Phone: +44 117 929 8929

#64
Tantric Jazz
Category: Bar, Jazz & Blues, Mediterranean
Address: 39-41 ST Nicholas St
Bristol BS1 1TP, UK
Phone: +44 117 940 2304

#65
Black Swan
Category: Pub, Music Venues
Address: 438 Stapleton Road
Bristol BS5 6NR, UK
Phone: +44 117 902 9984

#66
Bristol Flyer
Category: Pub, British, Music Venues
Address: 96 Gloucester Road
Bristol BS7 8BN, UK
Phone: +44 117 944 1658

#67
Kwik-Fit
Category: Gym
Address: 544 Fishponds Road
Bristol BS16 3DD, UK
Phone: +44 870 999 7375

#68
Royal West Of England Academy
Category: Art Gallery, Museum
Address: Queens Road
Bristol BS8 1PX, UK
Phone: +44 117 973 5129

#69
At Bristol
Category: Museum, Cultural Centre
Address: Harbourside
Bristol BS1 5UH, UK
Phone: +44 117 915 8000

#70
Next Generation Club
Category: Gym
Address: Greystoke Avenue
Bristol BS10 6AZ, UK
Phone: +44 117 959 7140

#71
Circomedia
Category: Specialty School
Address: Old School House Britannia Road
Bristol BS15 8DB, UK
Phone: +44 117 947 7288

#72
Colston Hall Foyer
Category: Bar, Performing Arts
Address: 13 Colston Street
Bristol BS1 5AR, UK
Phone: +44 117 922 3682

#73
Ashton Gate Stadium
Category: Stadium, Soccer
Address: Bristol BS3 2EJ, UK
Phone: +44 871 222 6666

#74
Peoples Republic of Stokes Croft
Category: Local Flavor, Art Gallery
Address: 37 Jamaica Street
Bristol BS2 8JP, UK
Phone: +44 7866 627052

#75
Paintworks
Category: Event Space
Address: Bath Road
Bristol BS4 3EH, UK
Phone: +44 7976 963967

#76
Bristol Buddhist Centre
Category: Yoga
Address: 162 Gloucester Rd
Bristol BS7 8NT, UK
Phone: +44 117 924 9991

#77
Bristol Ticket Shop
Category: Music Venues
Address: 26 Union Street
Bristol BS1 2DP, UK
Phone: +44 117 929 9008

#78
Hollywood Bowl
Category: Bowling
Address: Cribbs Causeway Centre
Bristol BS10 7TT, UK
Phone: +44 117 959 2100

#79
Watershed Cinema
Category: Cinema
Address: 1 Canons Road
Bristol BS1 5TX, UK
Phone: +44 117 927 5100

#80
Gloucestershire County Cricket Club
Category: Sports Club
Address: Nevil Rd
Bristol BS7 9EJ, UK
Phone: +44 117 910 8000

#81
Lab
Category: Music Venues
Address: 27 Broad Street
Bristol BS1 2HG, UK
Phone: +44 117 922 6456

#82
Beach Shack
Category: Outdoor Gear, Diving
Address: 16 Kellaway Avenue
Bristol BS6 7XR, UK
Phone: +44 117 923 2255

#83
The Full Moon
Category: Pub, Music Venues
Address: Stokes Croft
Bristol BS1 3PR, UK
Phone: +44 117 924 5007

#84
David Lloyd Leisure
Category: Leisure Centre, Tennis
Address: Ashton Road
Bristol BS3 2HB, UK
Phone: +44 117 953 1010

#85
Cotham Gardens
Category: Park, Tennis
Address: Redland Grove
Bristol BS6 6QP, UK
Phone: +44 117 974 1044

#86
Room 212
Category: Art Gallery
Address: 212 Gloucester Road
Bristol BS7 8NU, UK
Phone: +44 7855 268922

#87
Dainese Pro Shop
Category: Automotive
Address: 31 Old Market Street
Bristol BS2 0HB, UK
Phone: +44 117 925 2366

#88
Blaze
Category: Art Gallery
Address: 84 Colston Street
Bristol BS1 5BB, UK
Phone: +44 117 904 7067

#89
Red Lodge
Category: Museum, Art Gallery
Address: Park Row
Bristol BS1 5LJ, UK
Phone: +44 117 921 1360

#90
Spike Island
Category: Art School, Art Gallery
Address: 133 Cumberland Road
Bristol BS1 6UX, UK
Phone: +44 117 929 2266

#91
Redwood Lodge Hotel
Category:, Leisure Centre
Address: Beggar Bush Lane
Bristol BS8 3QD, UK
Phone: +44 870 609 6144

#92
Showcase Cinema
Category: Cinema
Address: Avon Meads
Bristol BS2 0SP, UK
Phone: +44 871 220 1000

#93
Fitness Evolution
Category: Fitness Centre
Address: Southfield Road
Bristol BS6 6AX, UK
Phone: +44 7515 827898

#94
The Junction
Category: Music Venues, Pub
Address: 51 Stokes Croft
Bristol BS1 3QP, UK
Phone: +44 117 942 4470

#95
Lush Longboards
Category: Skating & Skateboarding
Address: Kings House 14 Orchard Street
Bristol BS1 5EH, UK
Phone: +44 845 108 7300

#96
Sky
Category: Art Gallery
Address: 27 Waterloo Street
Bristol BS8 4BT, UK
Phone: +44 117 973 4074

#97
At-Bristol
Category: Museum
Address: Anchor Road
Bristol BS1 5DB, UK
Phone: +44 845 345 1235

#98
Playspace
Category: Kids Activities
Address: 85 Barrow Road
Bristol BS5 0AE, UK
Phone: +44 117 955 0070

#99
Helicon Magazine
Category: Print Media
Address: Tyndall Avenue
Bristol BS2 8, UK
Phone: +44 117 928 9000

#100
Spin CIty Pole Fitness
Category: Health & Medical, Gym
Address: The Workshop Hampton Lane
Bristol BS6 6LE, UK
Phone: +44 7866 490876

#101
Fiddlers
Category: Social Club, Music Venues
Address: Willway Street
Bristol BS3 4BG, UK
Phone: +44 117 987 3403

#102
The Blue Lagoon Cafe & Bar
Category: Pub, Music Venues
Address: 20 Gloucester Road
Bristol BS7 8AE, UK
Phone: +44 117 942 7471

#103
Bristol Union Swiming Pool
Category: Swimming Pool
Address: Queens Road
Bristol BS8 1LN, UK
Phone: +44 117 954 5803

#104
The Seven Stars
Category: Music Venues, Pub
Address: Thomas Lane
Bristol BS1 6JG, UK
Phone: +44 117 927 2845

#105
Fit Firm
Category: Gym
Address: 184 Hotwell Road
Bristol BS8 4RP, UK
Phone: +44 117 910 2880

#106
Nails Gallery
Category: Art Gallery
Address: Corn Street
Bristol BS1 1LJ, UK
Phone: +44 117 929 2083

#107
Leftbank Centre
Category: Bar, Art Gallery
Address: 128 Cheltenham Rd
Bristol BS6 5RW, UK
Phone: +44 117 944 4433

#108
CrossFit Avon
Category: Gym
Address: Merton Road
Bristol BS7, UK
Phone: +44 7795 361797

#109
Georgian House Museum
Category: Museum, Art Gallery
Address: 7 Great George St
Bristol BS1 5RR, UK
Phone: +44 117 921 1362

#110
Hollywood Bowl
Category: Sports Club, Bowling
Address: Avonmead Retail Park
Bristol BS2 0UG, UK
Phone: +44 117 977 1777

#111
O2 Academy
Category: Bar, Music Venues
Address: Frogmore Street
Bristol BS1 5NA, UK
Phone: +44 117 927 9227

#112
Lockleaze Adventure Playground
Category: Playground
Address: Romney Avenue
Bristol BS7 9TD, UK
Phone: +44 117 979 8311

#113
Lime Tree Gallery
Category: Art Gallery
Address: 84 Hotwell Rd
Bristol BS8 4UB, UK
Phone: +44 117 929 2527

#114
Freddies Funhouse
Category: Amusement Park
Address: Winterstoke Road
Bristol BS3 2NW, UK
Phone: +44 117 953 1959

#115
Mbargo
Category: Bar, Music Venues
Address: 38-40 Triangle West
Bristol BS8 1ER, UK
Phone: +44 117 925 3256

#116
Memorial Stadium
Category: Sports Club, Stadium
Address: Filton Avenue
Bristol BS7 0BF, UK
Phone: +44 117 909 6648

#117
Ashton Court Mansion
Category: Music Venues
Address: Ashton Court
Bristol BS41 9JN, UK
Phone: +44 117 963 3438

#118
Westbury Trym & Tone
Category: Gym
Address: Carlton Court
Bristol BS9 3DF, UK
Phone: +44 870 120 1999

#119
Pierian Centre
Category: Community Centre
Address: 27 Portland Square
Bristol BS2 8RZ, UK
Phone: +44 117 924 4512

#120
Jungle Rumble Adventure Golf
Category: Mini Golf, Golf
Address: Cabot's Circus
Bristol BS1 3BQ, UK
Phone: +44 117 929 7771

#121
Illusions Magic Bar
Category: Bar, Music Venues
Address: 2 Byron Place
Bristol BS8 1JT, UK
Phone: +44 117 909 3405

#122
Nuffield Health Fitness and Wellbeing Centre
Category: Gym, Swimming Pool
Address: 83 Queen's Road
Bristol BS8 1QS, UK
Phone: +44 117 925 2538

#123
The Poetry Can
Category: Performing Arts, Local Flavor
Address: 12 Great George Street
Bristol BS1 5RH, UK
Phone: +44 117 933 0900

#124
Horseworld
Category: Zoo
Address: Sleep Ln
Bristol BS14 0QJ, UK
Phone: +44 1275 540173

#125
Good Vibrations
Category: Gym
Address: 22 Kellaway Avenue
Bristol BS6 7XR, UK
Phone: +44 117 944 6650

Shops, Restaurants, Attractions & Nightlife/ Bristol Guidebook 2020

#126
The Love Inn
Category: Bar, Music Venues
Address: 84 Stokes Croft
Bristol BS1 3QY, UK
Phone: +44 117 923 2565

#127
Jubilee Swimming Pool
Category: Swimming Pool
Address: Jubilee Road
Bristol BS4 2LP, UK
Phone: +44 117 977 7900

#128
Odeon Cinemas
Category: Cinema
Address: Union Street
Bristol BS1 2DS, UK
Phone: +44 871 224 4007

#129
3D Gallery
Category: Art Gallery
Address: 13 Perry Rd
Bristol BS1 5BG, UK
Phone: +44 117 929 1363

#130
Otium
Category: Gym
Address: 53-58 Broad Street
Bristol BS1 2EL, UK
Phone: +44 117 927 6335

#131
The Tunnels
Category: Music Venues, Bar
Address: Arches 31-32 Lower Approach Road Bristol BS1 6QS, UK
Phone: +44 845 605 0255

#132
University Of Bristol Swimming Pool
Category: Leisure Centre
Address: Queens Road
Bristol BS8 1LN, UK
Phone: +44 117 954 5803

#133
The Thunderbolt
Category: Pub, Music Venues
Address: 124 Bath Road
Bristol BS4 3ED, UK
Phone: +44 117 373 8947

#134
Route One
Category: Sporting Goods
Address: Cribbs Csewy Regional Shopping, Bristol BS34 5DG, UK
Phone: +44 117 959 2696

#135
Metropolis
Category: Comedy Club, Music Venues
Address: 135 - 137 Cheltenham Road
Bristol BS6 5RR, UK
Phone: +44 117 909 6655

#136
University Of Bristol
Category: University
Address: Tyndall Avenue
Bristol BS8 1TH, UK
Phone: +44 117 928 9000

#137
Laser Quest
Category: Leisure Centre, Park
Address: Silver St
Bristol BS1 2PY, UK
Phone: +44 117 929 3699

#138
Loose-Fit Surf Shop
Category: Sporting Goods
Address: 138 Whiteladies Road
Bristol BS8 2RS, UK
Phone: +44 117 973 1255

#139
Basement 45
Category: Music Venues
Address: 8 Frogmore Street
Bristol BS1 5NA, UK
Phone: +44 117 929 3554

#140
Bristol South Swimming Pool
Category: Swimming Pool
Address: Dean Lane
Bristol BS3 1BS, UK
Phone: +44 117 966 3131

#141
Cat & Wheel
Category: Pub, Music Venues
Address: 207 Cheltenham Rd
Bristol BS6 5QX, UK
Phone: +44 117 942 7862

Shops, Restaurants, Attractions & Nightlife/ Bristol Guidebook 2020

#142
Bristol Rovers Football Club
Category: Sports Club
Address: Filton Avenue
Bristol BS7 0BF, UK
Phone: +44 117 909 5659

#143
The Cooler
Category: Music Venues, Bar
Address: 48 Park Street
Bristol BS1 5JG, UK
Phone: +44 117 945 0999

#144
Bristol City Football Club
Category: Sports Club, Soccer
Address: Ashton Gate
Bristol BS3 2EJ, UK
Phone: +44 871 222 6666

#145
Day + Night
Category: Bar, Music Venues
Address: 10 St Nicholas Street
Bristol BS1 1UQ, UK
Phone: +44 7765 208690

#146
Keynsham Leisure Centre
Category: Leisure Centre
Address: River Terrace
Bristol BS31 1HE, UK
Phone: +44 1225 395161

#147
The Architecture Centre
Category: Event Space, Art Gallery
Address: Narrow Quay
Bristol BS1 4QA, UK
Phone: +44 117 922 1540

#148
The Gym Bristol
Category: Gym, Trainers
Address: Quakers Friars Cabot Circus
Bristol BS1 3BU, UK
Phone: +44 844 384 3174

#149
Openbatch Theatre
Category: Performing Arts
Address: Oxford Street
Bristol BS2 0, UK
Phone: +44 7762 722183

#150
Harrys Amusements
Category: Amusement Park
Address: All Saints Street
Bristol BS1 2LZ, UK
Phone: +44 117 927 7671

#151
Bristol City Mueseum & Art Gallery
Category: Museum
Address: 1 Queen's Road
Bristol BS8 1QE, UK
Phone: +44 117 922 3571

#152
Bannatynes Health Club
Category: Gym
Address: 80 Redland Rd
Bristol BS6 6AG, UK
Phone: +44 117 942 5805

#153
Everyday Yoga
Category: Yoga
Address: 23 Belmont Road
Bristol BS6 5AW, UK
Phone: +44 7855 941166

#154
Polish Ex Servicemens Club
Category: Social Club, Music Venues
Address: 50 St Pauls Road
Bristol BS8 1LP, UK
Phone: +44 117 973 6244

#155
The Gym
Category: Gym, Leisure Centre
Address: Unit LS4A LS4B
Bristol BS1 3BU, UK
Phone: +44 844 384 3174

#156
City of Bristol Rowing Club
Category: Rafting/Kayaking
Address: Albion Dockside Estate Hanover Place, Bristol BS1 6, UK
Phone: +44 117 954 4621

#157
Soma
Category: Art Gallery
Address: 4 Boyces Ave
Bristol BS8 4AA, UK
Phone: +44 117 973 9838

Shops, Restaurants, Attractions & Nightlife/ Bristol Guidebook 2020

#158
**Welsh Back Squash
& Health Club**
Category: Gym
Address: Welsh Back
Bristol BS1 4SB, UK
Phone: +44 117 937 8020

#159
Lakota
Category: Dance Club, Music Venues
Address: 6 Upper York Street
Bristol BS2 8QN, UK
Phone: +44 117 942 6208

#160
Bristol Yoga Space
Category: Yoga
Address: 10 Park Row
Bristol BS1 5LJ, UK
Phone: +44 7530 053543

#161
Pure Gym Bristol Harbourside
Category: Leisure Centre
Address: Explore Lane
Bristol BS1 5TY, UK
Phone: +44 845 217 0676

#162
Bristol Shoguns & Rovers
Category: Stadium
Address: Filton Avenue
Bristol BS7 0AG, UK
Phone: +44 117 311 1461

#163
Pro Fitness Personal Training
Category: Trainers
Address: 26 Oakfield Road
Bristol BS8 2AT, UK
Phone: +44 117 973 9253

#164
**University Of Bristol
Student Union**
Category: Social Club, Music Venues
Address: Queens Road
Bristol BS8 1LN, UK
Phone: +44 117 954 5800

#165
Redland Park
Category: Park
Address: 1-2 Redland Green Road
Bristol BS6 7HE, UK
Phone: +44 117 924 8112

#166
Kingsdown Sport Centre
Category: Leisure Centre, Gym, Yoga
Address: Portland Street
Bristol BS2 8HL, UK
Phone: +44 117 903 1633

#167
Hush Hush
Category: Wine Bar, Music Venues
Address: 233 Cheltenham Road
Bristol BS6 5QP, UK
Phone: +44 117 942 2700

#168
Bristol School Of Gymnastics
Category: Leisure Centre
Address: 245 Gloucester Road
Bristol BS7 8NY, UK
Phone: +44 117 942 9620

#169
Cube Gallery
Category: Art Gallery
Address: 12 Perry Road
Bristol BS1 5BG, UK
Phone: +44 117 377 1470

#170
Vue Cinemas
Category: Cinema
Address: Aspects Leisure Park
Bristol BS30 9AS, UK
Phone: +44 871 224 0240

#171
**Bristol Lawn Tennis
& Squash Club**
Category: Tennis, Social Club
Address: Redland Green
Bristol BS6 7HF, UK
Phone: +44 117 973 1139

#172
Vue Bristol Longwell Green
Category: Cinema
Address: Aspects Leisure Park
Bristol BS15 9LA, UK
Phone: +44 871 224 0240

Shops, Restaurants, Attractions & Nightlife/ Bristol Guidebook 2020

#173
Create Centre
Category: Art Gallery
Address: Smeaton Road
Bristol BS1 6XN, UK
Phone: +44 117 925 0505

#174
The Mothers Ruin
Category: Pub, Music Venues
Address: 7-9 St Nicholas Market
Bristol BS1 1UE, UK
Phone: +44 117 329 2141

#175
Head 4 Heights
Category: Climbing
Address: Guthrie Road
Bristol BS8 3HA, UK
Phone: +44 117 974 7300

#176
Centrespace Gallery
Category: Art Gallery
Address: 6 Leonard Lane
Bristol BS1 1EA, UK
Phone: +44 117 929 1234

#177
Victoria Park Bowling Club
Category: Bowling
Address: Nutgrove Avenue
Bristol BS3 4QF, UK
Phone: +44 117 966 3083

#178
Snap
Category: Art Gallery
Address: 20-21 Lower Park Row
Bristol BS1 5BN, UK
Phone: +44 117 376 3564

#179
Diamonds Massage Studio
Category: Gym
Address: 363 Bath Road
Bristol BS4 3EW, UK
Phone: +44 117 977 4659

#180
Ardagh Sports Club
Category: Sports Club, Dog Park
Address: Kellaway Avenue
Bristol BS6 7YL, UK
Phone: +44 117 924 9880

#181
The Grant Bradley Gallery
Category: Art Gallery, Framing
Address: 1 St Peters Court
Bristol BS3 4AQ, UK
Phone: +44 117 963 7673

#182
Alexander Gallery
Category: Art Gallery
Address: 122 Whiteladies Road
Bristol BS8 2RP, UK
Phone: +44 117 973 9582

#183
Ashton Bowls Club
Category: Bowling
Address: Grevllive Smyth Park
Bristol BS3, UK
Phone: +44 117 964 9562

#184
Bristol Industrial Museum
Category: Museum, Art Gallery
Address: Princes Wharf
Bristol BS1 4RN, UK
Phone: +44 117 925 1470

#185
Badock Hall Tennis Courts
Category: Tennis
Address: Stoke Park Rd
Bristol BS9 1JQ, UK
Phone: +44 117 903 2480

#186
Glass Designs
Category: Art Gallery, Home Decor
Address: 261 North St
Bristol BS3 1JN, UK
Phone: +44 117 378 9227

#187
Bristol Balloons
Category: Active Life
Address: 23 - 51 Winterstoke Road
Bristol BS3 2NP, UK
Phone: +44 117 963 7858

#188
Reckless Engineer
Category: Pub, Music Venues
Address: Temple Gate
Bristol BS1 6PL, UK
Phone: +44 117 922 0487

#189
University of Bristol Botanical Garden
Category: Park, University
Address: Stoke Park Road
Bristol BS9 1JB, UK
Phone: +44 117 331 4906

#190
The Childrens Scrapstore
Category: Children's Charity
Address: The Proving House
Bristol BS2 9QX, UK
Phone: +44 117 908 2090

#191
Henleaze Lake
Category: Swimming Pool
Address: Lake Road Bristol BS10, UK
Phone: +44 117 962 0696

#192
Ents 24
Category: Music Events
Address: 16-18 Whiteladies Road
Bristol BS8 2LG, UK
Phone: +44 117 973 0548

#193
Bristol Rugby Club
Category: Sports Club
Address: The Memorial Stadium Filton Avenue Bristol BS7 0QA, UK
Phone: +44 871 208 2234

#194
Coexist
Category: Cultural Centre
Address: 80 Hamilton House
Bristol BS1 3QY, UK
Phone: +44 117 924 9599

#195
St. Pauls Community Sports Academy
Category: Leisure Centre
Address: Newfoundland Road
Bristol BS2 9NH, UK
Phone: +44 117 377 3405

#196
Bristol Blue Glass
Category: Glass Works
Address: 14 The Arcade
Bristol BS1 3JA, UK
Phone: +44 117 922 6833

#197
Bailey Balloons
Category: Hot Air Balloon Ride
Address: 44 Ham Green
Bristol BS20 0HA, UK
Phone: +44 1275 375300

#198
Stokes Croft Museum
Category: Art Gallery
Address: Stokes Croft
Bristol BS1 3, UK
Phone: +44 7866 627052

#199
South Bristol Sports Centre
Category: Trainers, Soccer, Leisure Centre
Address: West Town Lane
Bristol BS14 9EA, UK
Phone: +44 117 903 8681

#200
Kings Weston Roman Villa
Category: Active Life
Address: Long Cross
Bristol BS11 0LP, UK
Phone: +44 117 950 6789

#201
Planetarium
Category: Science Centre
Address: Millennium Square
Bristol BS1 5DB, UK
Phone: +44 845 345 1235

#202
Coombe Dingle Sports Complex
Category: Sports Club
Address: Coombe Lane
Bristol BS9 2BJ, UK
Phone: +44 117 962 6718

#203
Colston Hall 2
Category: Bar, Music Venues
Address: Colston Street
Bristol BS1 5AR, UK
Phone: +44 117 922 3686

#204
Skizm @ Basement 45
Category: Music Venues
Address: 8 Frogmore Street
Bristol BS1 5NA, UK
Phone: +44 117 929 3554

Shops, Restaurants, Attractions & Nightlife/ Bristol Guidebook 2020

#205
Goals
Category: Soccer
Address: Broomhill Road
Bristol BS4 5RG, UK
Phone: +44 117 977 4455

#206
Noahs Ark Play Centre
Category: Kids Activities
Address: 828 Bath Road
Bristol BS4 5LQ, UK
Phone: +44 117 971 2599

#207
Golden Hill Training Centre
Category: Stadium, Fitness, Soccer
Address: Lime Trees Road
Bristol BS6 7XW, UK
Phone: +44 117 942 1912

#208
Holmes Place Health Club
Category: Gym
Address: Beggar Bush Lane
Bristol BS8 3TG, UK
Phone: +44 870 120 1999

#209
Guerrilla Gallery
Category: Art Gallery
Address: 140 Gloucester Road
Bristol BS7 8NT, UK
Phone: +44 7766 138333

#210
Hengrove Park Leisure Centre
Category: Leisure Centre
Address: Hengrove Promenade
Bristol BS14 0JZ, UK
Phone: +44 117 937 0200

#211
South Bank Studio
Category: Music Venues, Jazz & Blues
Address: 31 Dean Ln
Bristol BS3 1DB, UK
Phone: +44 117 966 5552

#212
Calon Personal Training
Category: Trainers
Address: Oldmead Walk
Bristol BS13 7, UK
Phone: +44 7974 792066

#213
Aces Bar
Category: Social Club, Music Venues
Address: 29-31 ST Pauls Road
Bristol BS8 1LX, UK
Phone: +44 117 973 4866

#214
Riverside Leisure Club
Category: Gym
Address: Station Road
Bristol BS34 6HW, UK
Phone: +44 1454 888666

#215
Snappa
Category: Performing Arts, Local Flavor
Address: Bristol BS1, UK
Phone: +44 7890 149661

#216
Henbury Golf Club
Category: Golf
Address: Henbury Road
Bristol BS10 7QB, UK
Phone: +44 117 950 0660

#217
Pro 5 Soccer
Category: Leisure Centre
Address: Broomhill Road
Bristol BS4 5RG, UK
Phone: +44 117 977 4455

#218
St Bonaventures Social Club
Category: Social Club
Address: Egerton Road
Bristol BS7 8HR, UK
Phone: +44 1452 411466

#219
Adventurous Activity Company
Category: Recreation Centre
Address: 18 Heath Ridge
Bristol BS41 9EW, UK
Phone: +44 1275 394558

#220
Redgrave Theatre
Category: Performing Arts
Address: Percival Road
Bristol BS8 3LE, UK
Phone: +44 117 907 8079

Shops, Restaurants, Attractions & Nightlife/ Bristol Guidebook 2020

#221
Hambrook Golf Range
Category: Golf
Address: Commonmead Lane
Bristol BS16 1QQ, UK
Phone: +44 117 970 1116

#222
The Brewery
Category: Performing Arts
Address: Raleigh Road
Bristol BS3 1JU, UK
Phone: +44 117 902 0344

#223
Henbury Secondary School
Category: Fitness & Instruction
Address: Station Road
Bristol BS10 7QH, UK
Phone: +44 117 903 0100

#224
Tobacco Factory Theatre
Category: Performing Arts
Address: Raleigh Road
Bristol BS3 1TF, UK
Phone: +44 117 902 0344

#225
The Upfest Gallery
Category: Art Gallery
Address: 198 North Road
Bristol BS3 1, UK
Phone: +44 7725 231878

#226
Power Station
Category: Gym
Address: 107 Wells Rd
Bristol BS4 2BS, UK
Phone: +44 117 940 5808

#227
Coral
Category: Casino
Address: 3/5 New Station Rd
Bristol BS16 3, UK
Phone: +44 117 959 0762

#228
Start The Bus
Category: Music Venues, Lounge
Address: 7-9 Baldwin Street
Bristol BS1 1RU, UK
Phone: +44 117 930 4370

#229
The Cycle Hub
Category: Bike Rental
Address: Temple Meads Station
Bristol BS1 6Q, UK
Phone: +44 7824 776923

#230
Alphabet Zoo
Category: Landmark, Historical Building
Address: 28 Winterstoke Road
Bristol BS3 2NQ, UK
Phone: +44 117 966 3366

#231
Max Events
Category: Stag & Hen Adventure
Address: Berwick Drive
Bristol BS10 7TD, UK
Phone: +44 117 950 8080

#232
Imax Theatre Bristol
Category: Cinema
Address: Anchor Road
Bristol BS1 5DB, UK
Phone: +44 117 915 5000

#233
Clifton College Sports Centre
Category: Gym
Address: Guthrie Road
Bristol BS8 3, UK
Phone: +44 117 315 7678

#234
River Reeds
Category: Performing Arts
Address: Bristol, UK
Phone: +44 117 962 1138

#235
Henleaze Tennis Club
Category: Tennis
Address: Tennessee Grove
Bristol BS6 7XH, UK
Phone: +44 117 950 5862

#236
Bristol Academy 2
Category: Bar, Music Venues
Address: Frogmore Street
Bristol BS1 5NA, UK
Phone: +44 117 927 9227

#237
Bristol Orienteering Klub
Category: Active Life
Address: Bristol, UK
Phone: +44 7907 778865

#238
Hillsfield Park
Category: Playground, Dog Park
Address: Thicket Ave
Bristol BS16 4EH, UK
Phone: +44 117 922 3719

#239
Action Indoor Sport
Category: Leisure Centre
Address: Bamfield
Bristol BS14 0XA, UK
Phone: +44 117 903 1434

#240
Kingswood Leisure Centre
Category: Leisure Centre
Address: Church Road
Bristol BS16 4RH, UK
Phone: +44 30 0333 0300

#241
Vue Cinemas
Category: Cinema
Address: Cribbs Causeway
Bristol BS10 7TU, UK
Phone: +44 871 224 0240

#242
Spirit Health & Fitness Club
Category: Gym
Address: Filton Road
Bristol BS16 1QX, UK
Phone: +44 117 970 1462

#243
View Art Gallery
Category: Art Gallery
Address: 159-161 Hotwell Rd
Bristol BS8 4RY, UK
Phone: +44 56 0311 6753

#244
British Military Fitness
Category: Trainers
Address: Various Park
Bristol BS1, UK
Phone: +44 20 7751 9742

#245
Sea Mills Boys & Girls Club
Category: Social Club
Address: Woodleaze
Bristol BS9 2HX, UK
Phone: +44 117 968 5167

#246
Bikram Yoga Bristol
Category: Fitness & Instruction
Address: 38 High Street
Bristol BS1 2AW, UK
Phone: +44 117 930 0454

#247
Castle Gallery
Category: Art Gallery
Address: Pegasus Road
Bristol BS34 5UR, UK
Phone: +44 117 959 4647

#248
Henbury Social Club
Category: Social Club
Address: Tormarton Crescent
Bristol BS10 7LN, UK
Phone: +44 117 950 6325

#249
BS7 Sports & Fitness Club
Category: Gym, Sports Club
Address: Nevil Road
Bristol BS7 9EG, UK
Phone: +44 117 910 8000

#250
Pirate Walks
Category: Local Flavor
Address: Bristol BS1, UK
Phone: +44 7950 56683

#251
Bristol Sports Centre
Category: Gym, Martial Arts
Address: Dean Street
Bristol BS9 1QX, UK
Phone: +44 7590 383287

#252
The Bristol Gallery
Category: Art Gallery
Address: Unit 2 Bldg 8
Bristol BS1 5TY, UK
Phone: +44 117 930 0005

Shops, Restaurants, Attractions & Nightlife/ Bristol Guidebook 2020

#253
Bristol City Shorinji Kempo Dojo
Category: Martial Arts
Address: 15-29 Union Street
Bristol BS1 2DF, UK
Phone: +44 7972 815064

#254
Salsa Souls
Bristol Latin Dance School
Category: Dance Studio, Music Venues
Address: 26 - 28 St Nicholas Street
Bristol BS1 1UB, UK
Phone: +44 7982 241923

#255
John Wesleys New Room Chapel
Category: Art Gallery, Church
Address: 36 The Horsefair
Bristol BS1 3JE, UK
Phone: +44 117 926 4740

#256
Bubalu
Category: Gym, Sports Club
Address: 79 / 81 Gloucester Road
Bristol BS7 8AS, UK
Phone: +44 117 924 5381

#257
360 Pole Dancing
Category: Dance Studio
Address: 37 Philip Street
Bristol BS3 4EA, UK
Phone: +44 7928 523824

#258
The Albany Centre
Category: Performing Arts
Address: Shaftesbury Avenue
Bristol BS6 5LT, UK
Phone: +44 117 330 5038

#259
Delta Force Paintball
Category: Paintball
Address: Gloucester Road
Bristol GL12 8EA, UK
Phone: +44 844 477 5115

#260
Clara Lemon Yoga
Category: Beauty &Spa, Yoga
Address: 4 North View
Bristol BS6 7QB, UK
Phone: +44 7759 131009

#261
Luckys Cinema
Category: Comedy Club, Cinema
Address: St John's Steep
Bristol BS1 2LE, UK
Phone: +44 117 329 1979

#262
Workout
Category: Active Life
Address: Brewery Court North Street
Bristol BS3 1JS, UK
Phone: +44 117 963 3070

#263
Coral
Category: Bookmakers
Address: 101 Whiteladies Rd
Bristol BS8 2PB, UK
Phone: +44 800 328 4273

#264
Bristol Rugby Shop
Category: Active Life
Address: 28 The Arcade
Bristol BS1 3JD, UK
Phone: +44 871 208 2234

#265
Myawareness
Category: Yoga
Address: 8A Picton Lane
Bristol BS6 5PX, UK
Phone: +44 4477 1349 0401

#266
R S Studio
Category: Rehearsal & Recording Studio
Address: 47-57 Feeder Road
Bristol BS2 0SE, UK
Phone: +44 117 971 1495

#267
Artemis BJJ | Central Bristol
Category: Sports Club
Address: Dean Street
Bristol BS2 8SF, UK
Phone: +44 7787 476499

#268
Bristol Boxing Gym
Category: Sports Club
Address: 40 Thomas St
Bristol BS2 9LL, UK
Phone: +44 117 908 6655

Shops, Restaurants, Attractions & Nightlife/ Bristol Guidebook 2020

#269
Turtle Tots
Category: Swimming Pool
Address: Bristol, UK
Phone: +44 1275 857805

#270
Cineworld
Category: Cinema
Address: Hengrove Way
Bristol BS14 0HR, UK
Phone: +44 871 200 2000

#271
St James Personal Training Studio
Category: Weight Loss Centre, Gym
Address: Victoria Street
Bristol BS1, UK
Phone: +44 7817 034610

#272
Innocent Fine Art
Category: Art Gallery
Address: 7a Boyces Avenue
Bristol BS8 4AA, UK
Phone: +44 117 973 2614

#273
Bex Personal Training
Category: Trainers, Gym, Nutritionists
Address: Philadelphia Street
Bristol BS1 3DU, UK
Phone: +44 7906 158663

#274
Nicholas
Category: Wineries
Address: 116 Coldharbour Road
Bristol BS6 7SL, UK
Phone: +44 117 924 8423

#275
Krav Maga Bristol
Category: Martial Arts
Address: Horley Road
Bristol BS2 9TJ, UK
Phone: +44 7545 876249

#276
Bristol Story Cafe
Category: Storytelling
Address: Gloucester Rd
Bristol BS7 8AS, UK
Phone: +44 117 952 0070

#277
Absolute Health
Category: Gym
Address: 21-23 Oxford Street
Bristol BS2 0QT, UK
Phone: +44 117 955 5258

#278
Jean Jones Gallery
Category: Art Gallery
Address: 13 Clifton Arcade
Bristol BS8 4AA, UK
Phone: +44 7926 196978

#279
The Outside Element
Category: Kayaking & Canoeing
Address: Bristol BS1 2BD, UK
Phone: +44 7974 703129

#280
Gallery 2C
Category: Art Gallery
Address: 23 The Mall
Bristol BS8 4JG, UK
Phone: +44 117 904 7216

#281
The Joy of Hooping
Category: Weight Loss Centre, Dance Studio, Performing Arts
Address: 108 Redland Road
Bristol BS6 6, UK
Phone: +44 7989 411573

#282
Clifton Suspension Bridge Visitor Centre
Category: Hotel, Museum
Address: Sion Place
Bristol BS8 4HA, UK
Phone: +44 117 974 4664

#283
Lets Sk8
Category: Trainers, Skate Hire
Address: Bristol BS2 9XL, UK
Phone: +44 7766 335799

#284
Triple-S
Category: Art Gallery
Address: 200 North Street
Bristol BS3 1TF, UK
Phone: +44 7773 370698

#285
Oakfields Personal Training
Category: Trainers, Gym
Address: 26 Oakfield Road
Bristol BS8, UK
Phone: +44 117 973 8121

#286
Broad Plain Rugby & Social Club
Category: Social Club
Address: Off St Johns Lane
Bristol BS3 5AZ, UK
Phone: +44 117 966 5050

#287
Yogawest
Category: Yoga
Address: Denmark Place
Bristol BS7 8NW, UK
Phone: +44 117 924 3330

#288
Eqpix
Category: Horseback Riding
Address: Bristol BS1 5UH, UK
Phone: +44 7769 675474

#289
Anytime Fitness
Category: Gym
Address: 48 Queens Road
Bristol BS8 1RE, UK
Phone: +44 117 927 7225

#290
Water Babies
Category: Swimming Pool, Kids Activities
Address: 31-33 Alma Vale Road
Bristol BS8 2HL, UK
Phone: +44 117 946 6919

#291
Stone House
Category: Bar, Music Venues
Address: 28 Baldwin Street
Bristol BS1 1NG, UK
Phone: +44 117 946 8160

#292
Subaquaholics
Category: Diving
Address: 1 Albert Cresent
Bristol BS2, UK
Phone: +44 117 977 6227

#293
Kuumba
Category: Performing Arts
Address: 20-23 Hepburn Rd
Bristol BS2 8UD, UK
Phone: +44 117 942 1870

#294
Sheer Adventure
Category: Climbing
Address: 48 William Street
Bristol BS3 4TY, UK
Phone: +44 7900 335832

#295
Krav Maga Bristol - Fishponds
Category: Martial Arts
Address: Bristol Metropolitan Academy Snowdon Road Bristol BS16 2HD, UK
Phone: +44 7813 347795

#296
Mint Casino
Category: Casino, British
Address: 1-2 Portwall Ln
Bristol BS1 6NB, UK
Phone: +44 117 926 2753

#297
Vital Pilates
Category: Pilates
Address: 123 Pembroke Road
Bristol BS8 3EU, UK
Phone: +44 7732 246866

#298
Pot Stop
Category: Potstop Pottery
Address: 42 The Grove
Bristol BS1 4RB, UK
Phone: +44 117 923 1818

#299
Goldstrike
Category: Casino
Address: 67 East Street
Bristol BS3 4HB, UK
Phone: +44 117 963 3703

#300
Bristol Balloons
Category: Hot Air Balloon Ride
Address: Coronation Road
Bristol BS3 1RE, UK
Phone: +44 845 077 0730

Shops, Restaurants, Attractions & Nightlife/ Bristol Guidebook 2020

#301
Gala Casino
Category: Casino, Steakhouse
Address: Explore Lane
Bristol BS1 5TY, UK
Phone: +44 117 906 9970

#302
GH Fitness
Category: Gym
Address: 184 Hotwell Road
Bristol BS8 4RP, UK
Phone: +44 7973 683539

#303
Cotham Gallery
Category: Art Gallery
Address: 25 North View
Bristol BS6 7PT, UK
Phone: +44 117 973 6026

#304
KapapBristol
Category: Martial Arts
Address: 83a East street
Bristol BS3 4EX, UK
Phone: +44 7927 175552

#305
The Good Cook School
Category: Venues & Event Space, Kids Activities, Cooking School
Address: 37 Milford Street
Bristol BS3 1EE, UK
Phone: +44 7769 665020

#306
Bristol Kettlebell Club
Category: Trainers
Address: 69 Princess Victoria St
Bristol BS8 4, UK
Phone: +44 7800 542416

#307
Bawa
Category: Venues & Event Space
Address: 589 Southmead Road
Bristol BS34 7RG, UK
Phone: +44 117 976 8066

#308
iFit Active
Category: Trainers, Sports Club, Summer Camp
Address: Lewis Road
Bristol BS13 7JB, UK
Phone: +44 7544 275851

#309
Theatek
Category: Performing Arts, Party & Event Planning
Address: Unit 1 95 Church Road
Bristol BS13 8JU, UK
Phone: +44 117 978 2360

#310
International Soccer School
Category: Kids Activities
Address: Badminton School
Bristol BS9 3BA, UK
Phone: +44 845 643 5272

#311
Hengrove Leisure Park
Category: Arcade
Address: Hengrove Way
Bristol BS14 0HR, UK
Phone: +44 1275 892100

#312
Kings Camp
Category: Kids Activities
Address: Badminton School
Bristol BS9 3BA, UK
Phone: +44 845 643 5272

#313
Grosvenor Casino
Category: Casino
Address: 266 Anchor Rd
Bristol BS1 5TT, UK
Phone: +44 117 929 2932

#314
Bristol City Yoga
Category: Yoga, Venues & Event Space
Address: 16 Backfields Lane
Bristol BS2 8QW, UK
Phone: +44 117 924 4414

#315
William Hill
Category: Arcade
Address: Oxford St
Bristol BS3 4RQ, UK
Phone: +44 870 518 1715

#316
Golden Nugget Amusements
Category: Amusement Park
Address: 30 Stokes Croft
Bristol BS1 3QD, UK
Phone: +44 117 924 6912

Shops, Restaurants, Attractions & Nightlife/ Bristol Guidebook 2020

#317
The Stone House
Category: Pub, Music Venues
Address: 28 Baldwin Street
Bristol BS1 1NG, UK
Phone: +44 117 946 8160

#318
Coexist CIC
Category: Recreation Centre
Address: Hamilton House 80 Stokes Croft
Bristol BS1 3QY, UK
Phone: +44 117 924 9599

#319
Beyond Limits Training
Category: Vocational,
Technical School, Sailing
Address: Harbury Road
Bristol BS9 4PN, UK
Phone: +44 117 244 3589

#320
Easton Community Centre
Category: Cultural Centre
Address: Kilburn St
Bristol BS5 6AW, UK
Phone: +44 117 954 1409

#321
**Tenderfoot Gifts,Craft
and WorkShop**
Category: Kids Activities, Art Gallery
Address: 100 Wick Road
Bristol BS4 4HF, UK
Phone: +44 117 971 7138

#322
Fitness4Less Avon
Category: Gym
Address: 15-29 Union Street
Bristol BS1 2DF, UK
Phone: +44 117 000000

#323
**The Art Warehouse
& Framing Factory**
Category: Art Gallery
Address: Wapping Wharf
Bristol BS1 6JP, UK
Phone: +44 117 929 8089

#324
Fitness4Less Avon
Category: Gym
Address: 15-29 Union Street
Bristol BS1 2DF, UK
Phone: +44 7507 556659

#325
Westbury Art Club
Category: Local Flavor
Address: The Greenway Centre
Bristol BS10 5PY, UK
Phone: +44 117 962 9799

#326
Art Original
Category: Art Gallery, Framing
Address: 5 Union Street
Bristol BS1 2DD, UK
Phone: +44 117 927 3646

#327
Thekla
Category: Pub, Music Venues
Address: The Grove
Bristol BS1 4RB, UK
Phone: +44 117 929 3301

#328
Lolly Lollipop
Category: Kids Activities
Address: Bristol BS1 2BD, UK
Phone: +44 117 902 8136

#329
Potters
Category: Art Gallery
Address: 9 Perry Rd
Bristol BS1 5BQ, UK
Phone: +44 117 330 8445

#330
**Puddle Ducks Baby
and Toddler Swimming**
Category: Kids Activities
Address: 9 Kensington Park Road
Bristol BS4 3HP, UK
Phone: +44 117 971 7165

#331
Centurys Club
Category: Social Club
Address: 322-324 Two Mile Hill Road
Bristol BS15 1AJ, UK
Phone: +44 117 907 7773

Shops, Restaurants, Attractions & Nightlife/ Bristol Guidebook 2020

#332
Ginger Gallery
Category: Art Gallery
Address: 86 Hotwell Road
Bristol BS8 4UB, UK
Phone: +44 117 929 2527

#333
Mr Picture Fixer
Category: Photography Store
Address: Bristol BS1 2BD, UK
Phone: +44 7952 980873

#334
Admiral Gaming Lounge
Category: Casino
Address: 164/166 Regent Street
Kingswood BS15 8, UK
Phone: +44 117 960 0631

#335
Bannatynes Health Club
Category: Gym, Swimming Pool
Address: 80 Redland Close
Bristol BS6 6AG, UK
Phone: +44 117 942 8122

#336
1Loveart
Category: Art Gallery
Address: 80 Stokes Croft
Bristol BS1 3QY, UK
Phone: +44 117 942 7180

#337
Zumba Fitness with Amy Louise
Category: Dance Studio
Address: St Werburghs Community Centre
Bristol BS2 9TJ, UK
Phone: +44 7854 778323

#338
Krav Maga in Bristol
Category: Martial Arts
Address: St Werburghs Community Centre
Bristol BS2 9TJ, UK
Phone: +44 7545 876249

#339
Easton
Category: Social Club
Address: 5 Stapleton Road
Bristol BS5 0QR, UK
Phone: +44 7817 435073

#340
SunYogaBristol
Category: Yoga
Address: 1 Cleave Street
Bristol BS2 9UD, UK
Phone: +44 7583 147726

#341
Anns Taylored Art
Category: Gift Shop, Wedding Planning
Address: 23 aylesbury crescent
Bristol BS3 5NW, UK
Phone: +44 7804 792385

#342
Sakya Buddhist Meditation Centre
Category: Meditation Centre
Address: 121 Sommerville Road
Bristol BS6 5BX, UK
Phone: +44 117 924 4424

#343
PR4Books
Category: Public Relations Consultants
Address: 10 Park street
Bristol BS1 5HX, UK
Phone: +44 117 908 4630

#344
4Yourwall
Category: Home Decor
Address: 131 Gloucester Road
Bristol BS7 8AX, UK
Phone: +44 117 942 5355

#345
Aro Ling Buddhist Centre
Category: Yoga, Buddhist Temple
Address: 127 Gloucester Road
Bristol BS7 8AX, UK
Phone: +44 117 239 8505

#346
Inspiring Fitness
Category: Trainers
Address: Bristol, UK
Phone: +44 7966 494459

#347
Kundalini Yoga Bristol
Category: Yoga
Address: 27-29 Wilder Street
Bristol BS2 8, UK
Phone: +44 7726 892631

Shops, Restaurants, Attractions & Nightlife/ Bristol Guidebook 2020

#348
Rob James: Close up Magician
Category: Contemporary Magician
Address: 66 Egerton Rd
Bristol BS7 8, UK
Phone: +44 7748 830644

#349
Do a Wheelie
Category: Cycle Shop and Repair
Address: Bristol BS1 1YL, UK
Phone: +44 7786 643732

#350
Vu Guide
Category: Newspapers & Magazines
Address: 40 Liberty Gardens
Bristol BS1, UK
Phone: +44 117 330 9293

#351
Nuffield Health Club
Category: Gym
Address: Pavillion Queens Road
Bristol BS8 1QS, UK
Phone: +44 870 120 1999

#352
T-Junction Function Band
Category: Entertainment for Weddings
Address: 7 Seymour Rd
Bristol BS7 9HR, UK
Phone: +44 7789 174223

#353
NewRoots Central
Category: Kids Activities
Address: 126 Hampton Road
Bristol BS6 6JE, UK
Phone: +44 7980 765947

#354
Julian Cox - Artist
Category: West Bristol Art
Address: Phoenix Grove
Bristol BS6, UK
Phone: +44 7814 556936

#355
City Academy Sports Centre
Category: Leisure Centre
Address: Russell Town Avenue
Bristol BS5 9JH, UK
Phone: +44 117 954 2811

#356
Avh Slideshows
Category: Video/Film Production
Address: Passage Road
Bristol BS9 3LF, UK
Phone: +44 7789 083722

#357
Tonic Pilates
Category: Pilates
Address: 39 Alma Vale Rd
Bristol BS8 2HL, UK
Phone: +44 117 973 4729

#358
St.Annes Mediums
Category: Psychic & Clairvoyant
Address: 44 Langton Court Road
Bristol BS4 4EJ, UK
Phone: +44 7575 910164

#359
Origami Events Limited
Category: Event Organiser
Address: Harbury road
Bristol BS9 4PN, UK
Phone: +44 117 989 8211

#360
360 Pole Dancing At The Spring Garden Tavern
Category: Dance Studio
Address: 37 Philip Street
Bristol BS3 4EA, UK
Phone: +44 7928 523824

#361
Redpoint Bristol Climbing Centre
Category: Social Club
Address: 40 Winterstoke Rd
Bristol BS3 2NW, UK
Phone: +44 117 332 2222

#362
Personal Space
Category: Trainers
Address: 187 Redland Road
Bristol BS6 6XP, UK
Phone: +44 117 974 4422

#363
Flat Earth Scenery & Staging
Category: Design Services
Address: Unit A White Street
Bristol BS5 0TS, UK
Phone: +44 117 954 1102

Shops, Restaurants, Attractions & Nightlife/ Bristol Guidebook 2020

#364
Pirate Attack
Category: Kids Activities
Address: 34 Osborne Road
Bristol BS3 1PW, UK
Phone: +44 117 939 4311

#365
Song-Bird
Category: Books, Mags, Gift Shop
Address: Bristol BS1 2BD, UK
Phone: +44 7794 010518

#366
Krav Maga Bristol
Category: Martial Arts
Address: Gutherie Rd
Bristol BS8 3EZ, UK
Phone: +44 7812 346025

#367
Paper Artist
Category: Art & Craft
Address: 33 Victoria Street
Bristol BS1 6AS, UK
Phone: +44 117 934 6683

#368
Karma Active
Category: Martial Arts
Address: Portland street Bristol, UK
Phone: +44 117 328 1482

#369
Country Studio
Category: Professional Services
Address: 33 Victoria Street
Bristol BS1 6AS, UK
Phone: +44 7883 903400

#370
The Outside Element
Category: Rafting/Kayaking
Address: Bristol BS9 4UG, UK
Phone: +44 7974 703129

#371
Asian Arts Agency
Category: Arcade
Address: Royal Oak Avenue
Bristol BS1 4GB, UK
Phone: +44 117 929 1110

#372
Clara Lemon Yoga
Category: Yoga
Address: 4 North View
Bristol BS6 7QB, UK
Phone: +44 7530 053543

#373
Pilates Moves
Category: Pilates
Address: 31-33 Myrtle St
Bristol BS3, UK
Phone: +44 117 977 9897

#374
Yoho Media
Category: 4k Video Production
Address: 26 Berkeley Square
Bristol BS8, UK
Phone: +44 7710 070159

#375
Go Faster Food
Category: Active Life
Address: 10 Freeland Place
Bristol BS8 4NP, UK
Phone: +44 7968 716503

#376
Platinum Angels Bristol
Category: Event Performers & Models
Address: 9 Tottenham Place
Bristol BS8 1AJ, UK
Phone: +44 7730 434199

#377
Stick or Twist - Fun Casino Hire
Category: Casino,
Party & Event Planning
Address: 66 Egerton Rd
Bristol BS7 8HP, UK
Phone: +44 117 914 3650

#378
Fun French and Spanish - LCFClub - Athanase Vouha **Category:** Kids Activities
Address: Bristol BS5 7AU, UK
Phone: +44 117 951 9760

#379
KidSing Time
Category: Arts & Entertainment
Address: 7 Seymour Rd
Bristol BS7 9HR, UK
Phone: +44 7789 174223

Shops, Restaurants, Attractions & Nightlife/ Bristol Guidebook 2020

#380
Super Camp
Category: Kids Activities
Address: Colston's School Bell Hill
Bristol BS16, UK
Phone: +44 1235 832222

#381
Tannith Perry Ballroom & Latin Dancing
Category: Dance Studio
Address: Eastgate Road
Bristol BS5 6XX, UK
Phone: +44 7929 774631

#382
Mushin Martial Arts
Category: Martial Arts, Tai Chi
Address: Two Mile Hill Road
Bristol BS15 1BG, UK
Phone: +44 1454 885114

#383
RDF Media
Category: TV Production
Address: Regent House Regent St
Bristol BS8 4HG, UK
Phone: +44 117 970 7627

#384
Push Bikewear
Category: Active Life
Address: PO Box 319
Bristol BS16 0BN, UK
Phone: +44 7879 335047

#385
Courtyard Gallery
Category: Art Gallery
Address: 4 22 Paintworks
Bristol BS4 3EH, UK
Phone: +44 7977 219037

#386
Zoe Rayne Pilates
Category: Pilates
Address: Westbury on Trym
Bristol BS9 3AZ, UK
Phone: +44 7747 696938

#387
Clifton Art House
Category: Art Gallery
Address: 23 The Mall
Bristol BS8 4JG, UK
Phone: +44 117 909 3846

#388
JW Fitness Solutions
Category: Trainers
Address: Abbots Leigh Road
Bristol BS8 3QD, UK
Phone: +44 7876 684602

#389
Sirius B - Bristol Salsa Band
Category: Performing Arts
Address: 46 Ash Road
Bristol BS7 8RN, UK
Phone: +44 33 3400 8162

#390
Motiv8 Personal Training
Category: Trainers
Address: Bristol, UK
Phone: +44 7929 593598

#391
Kidstime Childrens Parties
Category: Children's Entertainers
Address: 453 Speedwell Rd
Bristol BS15 1ER, UK
Phone: +44 117 904 5907

#392
Bishop Of Clifton
Category: Religious Organisation
Address: St Ambrose
Bristol BS8 3PW, UK
Phone: +44 117 973 3072

#393
Swim4All
Category: Swimming School
Address: Bristol BS4 2LP, UK
Phone: +44 117 329 5013

#394
Ballooning Network
Category: Arts & Entertainment
Address: 23 - 51 Winterstoke Road
Bristol BS3 2NP, UK
Phone: +44 845 077 0729

#395
Dedicated Fisherman
Category: Fishing
Address: 105 Newquay Road
Bristol BS4 1EE, UK
Phone: +44 117 977 3574

Shops, Restaurants, Attractions & Nightlife/ Bristol Guidebook 2020

#396
Alejandro Velasco
Category: Dance School
Address: Raleigh Road
Bristol BS3 1, UK
Phone: +44 4477 6656 2990

#397
Salsa Da Capo Loco
Category: Dance Studio
Address: Frenchay Park Road
Bristol BS16 1HY, UK
Phone: +44 7906 381464

#398
R A F A Club
Category: Social Club
Address: Eastfield
Bristol BS9 4BE, UK
Phone: +44 117 962 8720

#399
Maree Rice Pilates
Category: Physical Therapy, Pilates
Address: 3 Greenfield Ave
Bristol BS10 5LN, UK
Phone: +44 117 950 2411

#400
Lenastrol - Leonard Fleets Astrology Services
Category: Psychic & Astrologer
Address: 3 Bristol Hill
Bristol BS4 5AA, UK
Phone: +44 7951 517688

#401
Bristol Titans Krav Maga Academy
Category: Martial Arts
Address: Bristol Brunel Academy
Bristol BS15 1NU, UK
Phone: +44 7813 347795

#402
Tristan Body Magic
Category: Recreation Centre
Address: 334 Speedwell Road
Bristol BS5 7SZ, UK
Phone: +44 117 907 1760

#403
Salsa Bristol
Category: Dance School
Address: West Town Lane
Bristol, UK
Phone: +44 7985 609912

#404
Whitchurch Dance Studio
Category: Kids Activities
Address: 88 Hengrove Lane
Bristol BS14 9DQ, UK
Phone: +44 7766 755734

#405
Arnolfini Gallery
Category: Art Gallery, Cinema
Address: 16 Narrow Quay
Bristol BS1 4QA, UK
Phone: +44 117 917 2300

#406
Bristol Martial Arts Academy
Category: Martial Arts
Address: 252 Central Park
Bristol BS14 9BZ, UK
Phone: +44 845 643 4074

#407
Fishponds Conservative Club
Category: Social Club
Address: 761 Fishponds Road
Bristol BS16 3UP, UK
Phone: +44 117 965 3975

#408
Long Ashton Golf Club
Category: Golf
Address: Clarken Coombe
Bristol BS41 9DW, UK
Phone: +44 1275 392229

#409
Elizabeth English
Category: Psychic & Astrologer
Address: 2 Perrymans Close
Bristol BS16 2JN, UK
Phone: +44 117 370 6338

#410
Vue Cinemas
Category: Active Life
Address: Merlin Road
Almondsbury BS10 7SR, UK
Phone: +44 871 224 0240

#411
Bristol Tiles
Category: Performing Arts
Address: 104 Sylvan Way
Bristol BS9 2LZ, UK
Phone: +44 117 968 3130

Shops, Restaurants, Attractions & Nightlife/ Bristol Guidebook 2020

#412
Mma Club
Category: Gym
Address: Pen Park Road
Bristol BS10 6, UK
Phone: +44 7403 412937

#413
Royal British Legion
Category: Social Club
Address: Kendall Road
Bristol BS16 4NB, UK
Phone: +44 117 956 8129

#414
Bristol North & Bristol South TaeKwon-Do
Category: Martial Arts
Address: Whitchurch Community Centre
Bristol BS14 9AL, UK
Phone: +44 117 339 0069

#415
C-Pem
Category: Performing Arts
Address: 77 Albert Road
Bristol BS31 1AE, UK
Phone: +44 117 914 8774

#416
Knowle Golf Club
Category: Golf
Address: Fairway
Bristol BS4 5DF, UK
Phone: +44 117 977 0660

#417
Attic Attack Studio
Category: Recording Studio
Address: 25 Portland Square
Bristol BS2 8NN, UK
Phone: +44 117 989 2642

#418
Bristol & Clifton Golf Club
Category: Golf
Address: Beggar Bush Lane
Bristol BS8 3TH, UK
Phone: +44 1275 394575

#419
Toybox Studio
Category: Recording Studio
Address: 25 Portland Square
Bristol BS2 8NN, UK
Phone: +44 117 989 2642

#420
Bristol Harlequins Rugby Football Club
Category: Amateur Sport Team
Address: Broomhill Road
Bristol BS4, UK
Phone: +44 117 972 1650

#421
Blu Inc.
Category: Performing Arts
Address: 8 Brunswick Square
Bristol BS2 8PE, UK
Phone: +44 117 942 2684

#422
Greenway Training & Enterprise Centre
Category: Gym, Sports Club
Address: Doncaster Road
Bristol BS10 5PY, UK
Phone: +44 117 907 3351

#423
Brunswick Club & Institute
Category: Social Club
Address: 15-16 Brunswick Square
Bristol BS2 8NX, UK
Phone: +44 117 924 6977

#424
Sheer Adventure
Category: Outdoor Activities
Address: 11 Norton Farm Road
Bristol BS10 7DE, UK
Phone: +44 7900 335832

#425
Bwerani Project
Category: Music Venues
Address: 20-22 Hepburn Road
Bristol BS2 8UD, UK
Phone: +44 117 915 9805

#426
Willis Newson
Category: Performing Arts
Address: 10-12 Picton Street
Bristol BS6 5QA, UK
Phone: +44 117 924 7617

#427
Woodspring Golf & Country Club
Category: Golf
Address: Yanley Lane
Bristol BS41 9LR, UK
Phone: +44 1275 394378

#428
Severn Jazz Men
Category: Music Band
Address: 4 Cotham Side
Bristol BS6 5TP, UK
Phone: +44 117 924 0081

#429
Fitness World Bristol
Category: Trainers
Address: Cater Road
Bristol BS13 7, UK
Phone: +44 117 902 2022

#430
Hands Up Theatre Company of Avon
Category: Performing Arts
Address: City Road
Bristol BS2 8YQ, UK
Phone: +44 117 942 3236

#431
Its Leisure
Category: Gym
Address: 23 Wood Road
Bristol BS15 8DT, UK
Phone: +44 117 961 3191

#432
Gee Baby I Love You
Category: Music Band
Address: 38 Cotham Road
Bristol BS6 6DP, UK
Phone: +44 117 942 2415

#433
Shirehampton Park Golf Club
Category: Golf
Address: Parkhill Shirehampton
Bristol BS11 0UH, UK
Phone: +44 117 982 2083

#434
Avon Chinese Association
Category: Social Club
Address: 9-15 Lower Ashley Road
Bristol BS2 9QA, UK
Phone: +44 117 955 5225

#435
Spirit Health & Fitness Club
Category: Gym
Address: Filton Road
Bristol BS16 1QX, UK
Phone: +44 870 120 1999

#436
Kinneir Dufort Design
Category: Performing Arts
Address: 5 Host Street
Bristol BS1 5BU, UK
Phone: +44 117 901 4000

#437
Sea Cadet Corps Avonmouth & Shirehampton Unit
Category: Kids Activities
Address: TS Enterprise Station Road
Bristol BS11 9TU, UK
Phone: +44 117 982 3938

#438
Blueblood Records
Category: Record Company
Address: 33 Perry Street
Bristol BS5 0SY, UK
Phone: +44 117 907 9358

#439
Black Belt Academy
Category: Martial Arts
Address: 1st Floor Page Park Pavillion
Bristol BS16 5LD, UK
Phone: +44 7598 505299

#440
Jacqueline East Illustration
Category: Performing Arts
Address: 6 Leonard Lane
Bristol BS1 1EA, UK
Phone: +44 117 904 8226

#441
Kyoto Shotokan Karate Club
Category: Martial Arts
Address: Avonmouth Rfc
Bristol BS11 9NG, UK
Phone: +44 7890 396276

#442
Lohlein
Category: Performing Arts
Address: 6 Leonard Lane
Bristol BS1 1EA, UK
Phone: +44 117 929 9077

Shops, Restaurants, Attractions & Nightlife/ Bristol Guidebook 2020

#443
Team Sport
Category: Leisure Centre, Go Karts
Address: Avonmouth Way
Bristol BS11 8DE, UK
Phone: +44 844 998 0000

#444
Bti UK Hogg Robinson
Category: Corporate Entertainment
Address: Bond Street
Bristol BS1 3AE, UK
Phone: +44 117 917 2100

#445
Bristol Therapy Rooms
Category: Yoga
Address: 16 Backfields Lane
Bristol BS2 8QW, UK
Phone: +44 7582 425237

#446
David Simon
Category: Art Gallery
Address: 17 Lower Park Row
Bristol BS1 5BN, UK
Phone: +44 117 929 2444

#447
Murder By Design
Category: Arts & Entertainment
Address: Elmgrove Road
Bristol BS6 6AH, UK
Phone: +44 117 942 0377

#448
Bristol Boxing Gym
Category: Boxing, Gym
Address: 40 Thomas Street
Bristol BS2 9LL, UK
Phone: +44 117 949 6699

#449
Bristol County Sports Club
Category: Social Club
Address: 40 Colston Street
Bristol BS1 5AE, UK
Phone: +44 117 927 3534

#450
Empire Sports Club
Category: Sports Club
Address: 223 Newfoundland Road
Bristol BS2 9NX, UK
Phone: +44 117 955 8478

#451
Photographique
Category: Art Gallery, Photography Store & Services, Framing
Address: 27 Clare Street
Bristol BS1 1XA, UK
Phone: +44 117 930 0622

#452
Essential Massage
Category: Gym
Address: 54 Old Market Street
Bristol BS2 0ER, UK
Phone: +44 117 922 6944

#453
West Of England Bridge Club
Category: Social Club
Address: Cheltenham Road
Bristol BS6 5RR, UK
Phone: +44 117 924 4199

#454
Southwest Wingtsun
Category: Martial Arts
Address: Wilson Place
Bristol BS2 9HJ, UK
Phone: +44 117 955 7156

#455
O2 Academy Bristol
Category: Music Venues
Address: 1 Trenchard Street
Bristol BS1, UK
Phone: +44 117 927 9227

#456
Wingtsun
Category: Martial Arts
Address: Wilson Place
Bristol BS2 9HJ, UK
Phone: +44 1275 846604

#457
South West Casting
Category: Performing Arts
Address: 2 Clare Street
Bristol BS1 1XR, UK
Phone: +44 117 927 5980

#458
Yun Jung Do International
Category: Martial Arts
Address: 38 Cotham Road
Bristol BS6 6DP, UK
Phone: +44 117 944 2469

Shops, Restaurants, Attractions & Nightlife/ Bristol Guidebook 2020

#459
Metropolis Music
Category: Performing Arts
Address: 7 Zetland Road
Bristol BS6 7AG, UK
Phone: +44 117 907 5350

#460
Unison
Category: Amusement Park
Address: Fairfax Street
Bristol BS1 3BN, UK
Phone: +44 117 940 5002

#461
Cucumber Street
Category: Performing Arts
Address: 42a Ravenswood Road
Bristol BS6 6BT, UK
Phone: +44 117 942 4256

#462
Fujian White Crane Kung Fu
Category: Martial Arts
Address: All Saints Street
Bristol BS1 2LZ, UK
Phone: +44 7957 261417

#463
King Street Studio
Category: Art Gallery
Address: 35 King Street
Bristol BS1 4DZ, UK
Phone: +44 117 903 0504

#464
The Club
Category: Gym
Address: 32-34 Midland Road
Bristol BS2 0JY, UK
Phone: +44 117 927 3207

#465
Jolly Serious Events
Category: Corporate Entertainment
Address: Colston Street
Bristol BS1 5AE, UK
Phone: +44 117 934 0616

#466
St. Pauls Adventure Playground
Category: Leisure Centre
Address: Thomas Street
Bristol BS2 9LL, UK
Phone: +44 117 954 2145

#467
Alastair Currie
Category: Event Management
Address: Colston Avenue
Bristol BS1 4TR, UK
Phone: +44 117 317 8140

#468
Trogen Gym & Fitness Centre
Category: Sports Club
Address: 216-220 Cheltenham Road
Bristol BS6 5QU, UK
Phone: +44 117 983 0555

#469
David Poore Music
Category: Film & TV Composer
Address: 4 Unity Street
Bristol BS1 5HH, UK
Phone: +44 117 925 7685

#470
Living Well
Category: Gym
Address: 80 Redland Road
Bristol BS6 6AG, UK
Phone: +44 117 942 5805

#471
Freemasons Hall
Category: Social Club
Address: 31 Park Street
Bristol BS1 5NH, UK
Phone: +44 117 926 5254

#472
L A Gym
Category: Leisure Centre
Address: 7 Lawrence Hill
Bristol BS5 0BY, UK
Phone: +44 117 954 2146

#473
Stanley Annabelle Casino
Category: Casino
Address: 1-2 Portwall Lane
Bristol BS1 6NB, UK
Phone: +44 117 926 2753

#474
Millennium Fitness Centre
Category: Gym
Address: Portland Street
Bristol BS2 8HL, UK
Phone: +44 117 915 2000

#475
K Anderson
Category: Psychic & Astrologer
Address: 21 Carnarvon Road
Bristol BS6 7DT, UK
Phone: +44 117 924 7825

#476
Bristol Community Sport
Category: Leisure Centre
Address: Portland Street
Bristol BS2 8HL, UK
Phone: +44 117 942 6582

#477
Roc International
Category: Social Club
Address: 104 Park Street
Bristol BS1 5HX, UK
Phone: +44 117 907 4778

#478
Ace Of Diamonds Leisure
Category: Amusement Park
Address: 35 Gloucester Road
Bristol BS7 8AD, UK
Phone: +44 117 942 6649

#479
Bristol Telephones Recreation Association
Category: Social Club
Address: Telephone House
Bristol BS1 4HQ, UK
Phone: +44 117 920 6401

#480
Bristol North Swimming Pool
Category: Swimming Pool
Address: 98 Gloucester Road
Bristol BS7 8AT, UK
Phone: +44 117 924 3548

#481
Wickham Theatre
Category: Music Venues
Address: Cantocks Close
Bristol BS8 1UP, UK
Phone: +44 117 928 7834

#482
Top Notch
Category: Gym
Address: The Pithayall Saints Street
Bristol BS1 2LZ, UK
Phone: +44 117 929 7311

#483
Odd Fellows Friendly Society
Category: Social Club
Address: 20 West Park
Bristol BS8 2LT, UK
Phone: +44 117 974 1073

#484
Exercere Club One
Category: Gym
Address: Welsh Back Squash & Health Club
Bristol BS1 4SB, UK
Phone: +44 117 921 4450

#485
Art & Power
Category: Art Gallery
Address: Horley Road
Bristol BS2 9TJ, UK
Phone: +44 117 908 9859

#486
World Snooker
Category: Sports Club
Address: 111-117 Victoria Street
Bristol BS1 6AX, UK
Phone: +44 117 317 8200

#487
University Literary Club
Category: Social Club
Address: 20 Berkeley Square
Bristol BS8 1HP, UK
Phone: +44 117 929 1881

#488
The Elite Retreat
Category: Gym
Address: Alfred Street
Bristol BS2 0RF, UK
Phone: +44 117 955 3655

#489
The Bristol Improv Network
Category: Festival, Performing Arts
Address: Chaplin Road
Bristol BS5 0JT, UK
Phone: +44 7811 184209

#490
Anytime Fitness
Category: Gym
Address: 48 Queens Road
Bristol BS8 1RE, UK
Phone: +44 117 927 7225

Shops, Restaurants, Attractions & Nightlife/ Bristol Guidebook 2020

#491
Wounded Buffalo Sound Studio
Category: Sound Studio
Address: 19 Hampton Lane
Bristol BS6 6LE, UK
Phone: +44 117 946 7348

#492
John Nike Leisuresport
Category: Skating Rink
Address: Frogmore Street
Bristol BS1 5NA, UK
Phone: +44 117 929 2148

#493
Event Management Co
Category: Event Management
Address: 10 Triangle South
Bristol BS8 1EY, UK
Phone: +44 117 929 4500

#494
Bristol Commonwealth Society
Category: Social Club
Address: 14 Whiteladies Road
Bristol BS8 1PD, UK
Phone: +44 117 973 4720

#495
Triangle Casino
Category: Casino
Address: 7-12 Triangle South
Bristol BS8 1EY, UK
Phone: +44 117 929 1515

#496
Cycle the City
Category: Bike Rental
Address: 1 Canons Road
Bristol BS1 5UH, UK
Phone: +44 7525 467186

#497
Way Art West
Category: Performing Arts
Address: 14 Westbourne Road
Bristol BS5 0RP, UK
Phone: +44 117 955 2396

#498
Personal Trainers Bristol
Category: Trainers
Address: 4a Byron Place
Bristol BS8 1JT, UK
Phone: +44 7500 333205

#499
Mecca Social Club
Category: Social Club
Address: Barrow Road
Bristol BS5 0AE, UK
Phone: +44 117 955 1006

#500
Undercover Rock
Category: Bristol Climbing Centre
Address: 73 Saint Werburgh's Park
Bristol BS2 9YX, UK
Phone: +44 117 908 3491

TOP 500 NIGHTLIFE
Recommended by Locals & Trevelers
(From #1 to #500)

#1
Cube Cinema
Category: Music Venues
Average price: Inexpensive
Address: 4 Princess Row
Bristol BS2 8NQ, UK
Phone: +44 117 907 4190

#2
Thekla
Category: Dance Club, Pub
Average price: Modest
Address: The Grove
Bristol BS1 4RB, UK
Phone: +44 117 929 3301

#3
The Old Duke
Category: Pub, Jazz & Blues
Average price: Inexpensive
Address: 45 King Street
Bristol BS1 4ER, UK
Phone: +44 117 927 7137

#4
Bristol Folk House
Category: Music Venues
Average price: Inexpensive
Address: 40a Park Street
Bristol BS1 5JG, UK
Phone: +44 117 926 2987

#5
The Cambridge Arms
Category: Pub, British
Average price: Modest
Address: Coldharbour Road
Bristol BS6 7JS, UK
Phone: +44 117 973 9786

#6
The Apple
Category: Pub, British
Average price: Modest
Address: The Apple
Bristol BS1 4SB, UK
Phone: +44 117 925 3500

#7
Duke Of York
Category: Pub
Average price: Inexpensive
Address: 2 Jubilee Road
Bristol BS2 9RS, UK
Phone: +44 117 941 3677

#8
The Farm
Category: Pub, Music Venues
Average price: Modest
Address: Hopetoun Road
Bristol BS2 9YL, UK
Phone: +44 117 944 2384

#9
Amoeba Lounge Bar
Category: Cocktail Bar, Lounge
Average price: Modest
Address: 10 Kings Road
Bristol BS8 4AB, UK
Phone: +44 117 946 6461

#10
The Louisiana
Category: Pub, Music Venues, British
Average price: Modest
Address: Bathurst Terrace
Bristol BS1 6UA, UK
Phone: +44 117 936 3615

#11
The Victoria
Category: Pub
Average price: Modest
Address: 2 Southleigh Road
Bristol BS8 2BH, UK
Phone: +44 117 974 5675

#12
Start The Bus
Category: Music Venues, Lounge
Average price: Modest
Address: 7-9 Baldwin Street
Bristol BS1 1RU, UK
Phone: +44 117 930 4370

#13
King William Ale House
Category: Pub
Address: 20 King Street
Bristol BS1 4EF, UK
Phone: +44 117 926 8672

#14
The Bell
Category: Pub
Average price: Modest
Address: Hillgrove Street
Bristol BS2 8JT, UK
Phone: +44 117 909 6612

Shops, Restaurants, Attractions & Nightlife/ Bristol Guidebook 2020

#15
Grain Barge
Category: Bar, European, Music Venues
Average price: Modest
Address: Hotwells Road
Bristol BS8 4RU, UK
Phone: +44 117 929 9347

#16
The Windmill
Category: Pub
Average price: Modest
Address: 14 Windmill Hill
Bristol BS3 4LU, UK
Phone: +44 117 963 5440

#17
The Cornubia
Category: Pub
Average price: Modest
Address: 142 Temple Street
Bristol BS1 6EN, UK
Phone: +44 117 925 4415

#18
Renatos
Category: Pizza, Bar
Average price: Inexpensive
Address: 19 King Street
Bristol BS1 4EF, UK
Phone: +44 117 929 7712

#19
Clifton Sausage
Category: Pub, British
Average price: Expensive
Address: 7-9 Portland Street
Bristol BS8 4JA, UK
Phone: +44 117 973 1192

#20
Coronation Tap
Category: Pub, Music Venues
Average price: Modest
Address: 8 Sion Place
Bristol BS8 4AX, UK
Phone: +44 117 973 9617

#21
Tinto lounge
Category: Lounge
Average price: Inexpensive
Address: 344-346 Gloucester Road
Bristol BS7 8TP, UK
Phone: +44 117 942 0526

#22
The Hillgrove Porter Stores
Category: Pub
Average price: Modest
Address: 53 Hillgrove Street North
Bristol BS2 8LT, UK
Phone: +44 117 924 8234

#23
Hope & Anchor
Category: Pub, British
Average price: Modest
Address: 38 Jacobs Wells Road
Bristol BS8 1DR, UK
Phone: +44 117 929 2987

#24
Tobacco Factory
Category: Music Venues, Mediterranean, Performing Arts
Average price: Modest
Address: Raleigh Road
Bristol BS3 1TF, UK
Phone: +44 117 902 0344

#25
Robin Hoods Retreat
Category: Pub, British
Average price: Modest
Address: 197 Gloucester Road
Bristol BS7 8BG, UK
Phone: +44 117 924 8639

#26
Cafe Kino
Category: Music Venues
Average price: Inexpensive
Address: 108 Stokes Croft
Bristol BS1 3RU, UK
Phone: +44 117 924 9200

#27
The Golden Lion
Category: Pub, Music Venues
Average price: Modest
Address: 244 Gloucester Road
Bristol BS7 8NZ, UK
Phone: +44 117 924 6449

#28
Kings Head
Category: Pub
Average price: Inexpensive
Address: 60 Victoria Street
Bristol BS1 6DE, UK
Phone: +44 117 929 2338

#29
The Clifton
Category: Pub, GastroPub
Average price: Expensive
Address: 16 Regent Street
Bristol BS8 4HG, UK
Phone: +44 117 974 1967

#30
Bristol Old Vic
Category: Performing Arts, Music Venues
Address: 36 King Street
Bristol BS1 4DZ, UK
Phone: +44 117 987 7877

#31
Hausbar
Category: Cocktail Bar
Average price: Expensive
Address: 52 Upper Belgrave Road
Bristol BS8 2XP, UK
Phone: +44 117 946 6081

#32
Llandoger Trow
Category: Bar
Average price: Modest
Address: King St
Bristol BS1 4ER, UK
Phone: +44 117 926 1650

#33
St George's Bristol
Category: Music Venues
Average price: Modest
Address: Bristol BS1 5RR, UK
Phone: +44 845 402 4001

#34
Mr Wolfs
Category: Music Venues
Average price: Inexpensive
Address: 33 St Stephens Street
Bristol BS1 1JX, UK
Phone: +44 117 927 3221

#35
Prince Of Wales
Category: Pub
Average price: Modest
Address: 5 Gloucester Road
Bristol BS7 8AA, UK
Phone: +44 117 924 5552

#36
Zerodegrees
Category: Italian, Bar
Average price: Modest
Address: 53 Colston Street
Bristol BS1 5BA, UK
Phone: +44 117 925 2706

#37
The Big Chill Bar
Category: Lounge, Pub, Tapas Bar
Average price: Modest
Address: 15 Small Street
Bristol BS1 1DE, UK
Phone: +44 117 930 4217

#38
The Apple Cider Co.
Category: Bar
Average price: Modest
Address: Welsh Back
Bristol BS1 4SL, UK
Phone: +44 117 925 3500

#39
The Vittoria
Category: Pub
Average price: Modest
Address: 57 Whiteladies Road
Bristol BS8 2LY, UK
Phone: +44 117 329 1282

#40
The Old Fish Market
Category: Pub
Average price: Modest
Address: 59-63 Baldwin Street
Bristol BS1 1QZ, UK
Phone: +44 117 921 1515

#41
Rummer Hotel
Category: British, Cocktail Bar
Average price: Expensive
Address: All Saints Lane
Bristol BS1 1JH, UK
Phone: +44 117 929 0111

#42
Hyde & Co.
Category: Lounge
Average price: Modest
Address: 2 The Basement
Bristol BS8 1JY, UK
Phone: +44 117 929 7007

#43
Hare On The Hill
Category: Pub, British
Average price: Modest
Address: 41 Thomas Street North
Bristol BS2 8LX, UK
Phone: +44 117 908 1982

#44
The White Lion
Category: Pub
Average price: Modest
Address: Colston Avenue
Bristol BS1 1EB, UK
Phone: +44 117 925 4819

#45
Showcase Cinema de Lux
Category: Cinema, Lounge
Average price: Modest
Address: Glass House
Bristol BS1 3BX, UK
Phone: +44 871 220 1000

#46
Severnshed Restaurant
Category: Lounge
Average price: Modest
Address: Severn Shed
Bristol BS1 4RB, UK
Phone: +44 117 925 1212

#47
The Fleece
Category: Pub, Dance Club
Average price: Modest
Address: 12 St Thomas Street
Bristol BS1 6JJ, UK
Phone: +44 117 945 0996

#48
Miners Arms
Category: Pub
Average price: Modest
Address: 136 Mina Road
Bristol BS2 9YQ, UK
Phone: +44 117 907 9874

#49
The White Bear
Category: Pub, British
Average price: Modest
Address: 133 St Michaels Hill
Bristol BS2 8BS, UK
Phone: +44 117 904 9054

#50
The Bierkeller
Category: Dance Club, Music Venues
Average price: Modest
Address: All Saints Street
Bristol BS1 2NA, UK
Phone: +44 117 926 8514

#51
The Penny Farthing
Category: Pub
Average price: Modest
Address: 115 Whiteladies Road
Bristol BS8 2PB, UK
Phone: +44 117 973 3539

#52
Mr Wolfs
Category: Music Venues, Dance Club
Average price: Expensive
Address: 33 Saint Stephens Street
Bristol BS1 1JX, UK
Phone: +44 117 927 3221

#53
Cosies Wine Bar
Category: Dance Club, GastroPub
Average price: Modest
Address: 34 Portland Square
Bristol BS2 8RG, UK
Phone: +44 117 942 4110

#54
Rajpoot
Category: Indian, Bar, Pakistani
Address: 52 Upper Belgrave Road
Bristol BS8 2XP, UK
Phone: +44 117 973 3515

#55
The Woods
Category: Pub
Average price: Modest
Address: 1 Park Street Avenue
Bristol BS1 5LQ, UK
Phone: +44 117 925 0890

#56
Colston Hall
Category: Music Venues
Average price: Expensive
Address: Colston Street
Bristol BS1 5AR, UK
Phone: +44 117 922 3686

#57
Alterego
Category: Sports Bar, Lounge
Average price: Modest
Address: 77 Whiteladies Rd
Bristol BS8 2NT, UK
Phone: +44 7789 968053

#58
Black Swan
Category: Dance Club, Music Venues
Average price: Modest
Address: 438 Stapleton Road
Bristol BS5 6NR, UK
Phone: +44 117 902 9984

#59
The Lansdown
Category: Pub
Average price: Modest
Address: 8 Clifton Road
Bristol BS8 1AF, UK
Phone: +44 117 973 4949

#60
Small Bar
Category: Pub
Average price: Modest
Address: 31/32 King Street
Bristol BS1 4DZ, UK
Phone: +44 7709 449708

#61
Bristol Flyer
Category: Pub, British, Music Venues
Average price: Expensive
Address: 96 Gloucester Road
Bristol BS7 8BN, UK
Phone: +44 117 944 1658

#62
Papajis
Category: Cocktail Bar
Address: 109 Whiteladies Road
Bristol BS8 2PB, UK
Phone: +44 117 946 6144

#63
Colston Hall Foyer
Category: Bar, Performing Arts
Average price: Modest
Address: 13 Colston Street
Bristol BS1 5AR, UK
Phone: +44 117 922 3682

#64
The Portcullis
Category: Pub
Average price: Modest
Address: 3 Wellington Ter
Bristol BS8 4LE, UK
Phone: +44 117 908 5536

#65
Bristol Ticket Shop
Category: Music Venues
Average price: Modest
Address: 26 Union Street
Bristol BS1 2DP, UK
Phone: +44 117 929 9008

#66
The Cadbury
Category: Pub
Average price: Modest
Address: 68 Richmond Road
Bristol BS6 5EW, UK
Phone: +44 117 924 7874

#67
The Pipe & Slippers
Category: Pub
Average price: Modest
Address: 118 Cheltenham Rd
Bristol BS6 5RW, UK
Phone: +44 117 942 7711

#68
Halo
Category: British, Bar
Average price: Modest
Address: 141 Gloucester Road
Bristol BS7 8BA, UK
Phone: +44 117 944 2504

#69
Banco Lounge
Category: Lounge
Average price: Modest
Address: 107 Wells Rd
Bristol BS4 2BS, UK
Phone: +44 117 908 6010

#70
The Bunker
Category: Dance Club
Average price: Inexpensive
Address: 78 Queens Road
Bristol BS8 1QU, UK
Phone: +44 117 930 4604

Shops, Restaurants, Attractions & Nightlife/ Bristol Guidebook 2020

#71
Browns
Category: Wine Bar, British, Lounge
Average price: Modest
Address: 38 Queens Road
Bristol BS8 1RE, UK
Phone: +44 117 930 4777

#72
Goldbrick House
Category: Champagne Bar
Average price: Expensive
Address: 69 Park St
Bristol BS1 5PB, UK
Phone: +44 117 945 1950

#73
Roo Bar
Category: Pub
Average price: Exclusive
Address: Whiteladies Road
Bristol BS8 2PN, UK
Phone: +44 117 923 7204

#74
The Quadrant
Category: Pub, Champagne Bar
Average price: Modest
Address: 2 Princess Victoria Street
Bristol BS8 4BP, UK
Phone: +44 117 974 1025

#75
Lab
Category: Dance Club, Music Venues
Average price: Modest
Address: 27 Broad Street
Bristol BS1 2HG, UK
Phone: +44 117 922 6456

#76
Volunteer Tavern
Category: Pub
Average price: Modest
Address: 9 New Street
Bristol BS2 9DX, UK
Phone: +44 117 955 8498

#77
The Kings Arms
Category: Pub
Average price: Modest
Address: 168 Whiteladies Road
Bristol BS8 2XZ, UK
Phone: +44 117 973 5922

#78
The Hill
Category: Pub, Pizza, Wine Bar
Average price: Modest
Address: 33-35 Cotham Hill
Bristol BS6 6JY, UK
Phone: +44 117 973 3793

#79
Yia Mass
Category: Bar, Mediterranean
Average price: Expensive
Address: 67 Park Street
Bristol BS1 5PB, UK
Phone: +44 117 929 9530

#80
The Ostrich Inn
Category: Pub
Average price: Expensive
Address: Lower Guinea St
Bristol BS1 6TJ, UK
Phone: +44 117 927 3774

#81
White Lion Bar and Terrace
Category: Pub
Average price: Expensive
Address: Sion Hill
Bristol BS8 4LD, UK
Phone: +44 117 973 8955

#82
The Spotted Cow
Category: Pub
Average price: Expensive
Address: 139 North Street
Bristol BS3 2EZ, UK
Phone: +44 117 963 4433

#83
Deco Lounge
Category: Lounge, European
Average price: Modest
Address: 50 Cotham Hill
Bristol BS6 6JX, UK
Phone: +44 117 373 2688

#84
Coach & Horses
Category: Pub
Average price: Modest
Address: 2 Highland Square
Bristol BS8 2YB, UK
Phone: +44 117 974 5176

Shops, Restaurants, Attractions & Nightlife/ Bristol Guidebook 2020

#85
The Hatchet Inn
Category: Pub, Dance Club
Average price: Modest
Address: 27-29 Frogmore Street
Bristol BS1 5NA, UK
Phone: +44 117 929 4118

#86
Beeses Bar & Tea Gardens
Category: Pub
Average price: Modest
Address: Wyndham Crescent
Bristol BS4 4SX, UK
Phone: +44 117 977 7412

#87
The Bishops
Category: Pub
Average price: Modest
Address: 225-229 Cheltenham Rd
Bristol BS6 5QP, UK
Phone: +44 117 944 5169

#88
The Lion
Category: Pub
Average price: Modest
Address: 19 Church Ln
Bristol BS8 4TX, UK
Phone: +44 117 926 8492

#89
Star & Garter
Category: Pub
Average price: Inexpensive
Address: 33 Brook Road
Bristol BS6 5LR, UK
Phone: +44 117 940 5552

#90
The Junction
Category: Pub, Dance Club
Average price: Modest
Address: 51 Stokes Croft
Bristol BS1 3QP, UK
Phone: +44 117 942 4470

#91
The Kingsdown Wine Vaults
Category: Wine & Spirits, Pub
Average price: Expensive
Address: 29-31 Kingsdown Parade
Bristol BS6 5UE, UK
Phone: +44 117 924 9134

#92
The Crown
Category: Pub
Average price: Inexpensive
Address: 10 All Saints Lane
Bristol BS1 1JH, UK
Phone: +44 117 934 9996

#93
Cotham Porter Stores
Category: Pub
Average price: Modest
Address: 15 Cotham Road S
Bristol BS6 5TZ, UK
Phone: +44 117 903 0689

#94
The Kensington Arms
Category: Pub, GastroPub, British
Average price: Expensive
Address: 35-37 Stanley Road
Bristol BS6 6NP, UK
Phone: +44 117 944 6444

#95
Joe Publics
Category: Dance Club
Average price: Expensive
Address: 3 Queens Avenue
Bristol BS8 1QU, UK
Phone: +44 117 973 1249

#96
The Albion
Category: Pub, British
Average price: Expensive
Address: Boyces Ave
Bristol BS8 4AA, UK
Phone: +44 117 973 3522

#97
The Bag Of Nails
Category: Pub
Average price: Modest
Address: 141 St. Georges Road
Bristol BS1 5UW, UK
Phone: +44 117 940 6776

#98
Fiddlers
Category: Music Venues
Average price: Modest
Address: Willway Street
Bristol BS3 4BG, UK
Phone: +44 117 987 3403

Shops, Restaurants, Attractions & Nightlife/ Bristol Guidebook 2020

#99
The Wellington
Category: Pub
Average price: Inexpensive
Address: Gloucester Road
Bristol BS7 8UR, UK
Phone: +44 117 951 3022

#100
The Blue Lagoon Cafe & Bar
Category: Pub, Music Venues
Average price: Modest
Address: 20 Gloucester Road
Bristol BS7 8AE, UK
Phone: +44 117 942 7471

#101
Hen & Chicken
Category: Pub, Comedy Club
Average price: Modest
Address: 210 North Street
Bristol BS3 1JF, UK
Phone: +44 117 966 3143

#102
Old Market Tavern
Category: Pub, Gay Bar, British
Average price: Inexpensive
Address: 29-30 Old Market Street
Bristol BS2 0HB, UK
Phone: +44 117 922 6123

#103
The Seven Stars
Category: Music Venues, Pub
Average price: Modest
Address: Thomas Lane
Bristol BS1 6JG, UK
Phone: +44 117 927 2845

#104
The Bank
Category: Pub
Average price: Modest
Address: 8 John Street
Bristol BS1 2HR, UK
Phone: +44 117 930 4691

#105
Leftbank Centre
Category: Bar
Average price: Modest
Address: 128 Cheltenham Rd
Bristol BS6 5RW, UK
Phone: +44 117 944 4433

#106
The Slug and Lettuce
Category: Bar
Average price: Modest
Address: 26-28 St Nicholas Street
Bristol BS1 1UB, UK
Phone: +44 117 952 9900

#107
Graze Bar and Chophouse
Category: Lounge, British
Average price: Modest
Address: 63 Queen Square
Bristol BS1 4JZ, UK
Phone: +44 117 927 6706

#108
Cottage Inn
Category: Pub, British
Average price: Modest
Address: Cumberland Road
Bristol BS1 6XG, UK
Phone: +44 117 921 5256

#109
O2 Academy
Category: Bar, Dance Club
Average price: Expensive
Address: Frogmore Street
Bristol BS1 5NA, UK
Phone: +44 117 927 9227

#110
The Star & Dove
Category: Pub, British
Average price: Modest
Address: 75-78 St Lukes Road
Bristol BS3 4RY, UK
Phone: +44 117 933 2892

#111
The Royal Oak
Category: Pub
Address: 50 The Mall
Bristol BS8 4JG, UK
Phone: +44 117 973 8846

#112
Mbargo
Category: Bar, Music Venues
Average price: Inexpensive
Address: 38-40 Triangle West
Bristol BS8 1ER, UK
Phone: +44 117 925 3256

#113
The White Harte
Category: Pub, British, Pool Hall
Average price: Inexpensive
Address: 54-58 Park Row
Bristol BS1 5LH, UK
Phone: +44 117 929 2490

#114
Ashton Court Mansion
Category: Music Venues
Address: Ashton Court
Bristol BS41 9JN, UK
Phone: +44 117 963 3438

#115
Hole in the Wall
Category: British, Pub
Average price: Modest
Address: 2 The Grove
Bristol BS1 4QZ, UK
Phone: +44 117 926 5967

#116
BrewDog
Category: Burgers, Pub
Average price: Expensive
Address: 58 Baldwin Street
Bristol BS1 1QW, UK
Phone: +44 117 927 9258

#117
Illusions Magic Bar
Category: Bar
Average price: Modest
Address: 2 Byron Place
Bristol BS8 1JT, UK
Phone: +44 117 909 3405

#118
The Milk Thistle
Category: Bar
Address: Colston Avenue
Bristol BS1 1EB, UK
Phone: +44 117 929 4429

#119
Po Na Na
Category: Dance Club, Bar
Address: 67a Queens Road
Bristol BS8 1QL, UK
Phone: +44 117 925 6225

#120
Revolution
Category: Lounge, Pub, Pizza
Average price: Modest
Address: St Nicholas Street
Bristol BS1 1UA, UK
Phone: +44 117 930 4335

#121
The Hare
Category: Pub
Average price: Modest
Address: 51 North Street
Bristol BS3 1EN, UK
Phone: +44 117 966 5740

#122
Timbuk2
Category: Dance Club
Average price: Modest
Address: 22 Small Street
Bristol BS1 1DW, UK
Phone: +44 117 945 8459

#123
Racks Bar & Kitchen
Category: GastroPub, British
Average price: Modest
Address: St Pauls Road
Bristol BS8 1LX, UK
Phone: +44 117 974 1626

#124
Bunch Of Grapes
Category: Pub
Average price: Modest
Address: 8 Denmark Street
Bristol BS1 5DQ, UK
Phone: +44 117 987 0500

#125
The Commercial Rooms
Category: Pub
Average price: Inexpensive
Address: 43-45 Corn Street
Bristol BS1 1HT, UK
Phone: +44 117 927 9681

#126
The Ship Inn
Category: Pub
Average price: Modest
Address: 10 Lower Park Row
Bristol BS1 5BJ, UK
Phone: +44 117 929 4390

Shops, Restaurants, Attractions & Nightlife/ Bristol Guidebook 2020

#127
The Scotchman & His Pack
Category: Pub, British
Average price: Modest
Address: 20 St Michaels Hill
Bristol BS2 8DX, UK
Phone: +44 117 373 0138

#128
Cadbury House
Category: Pub
Average price: Modest
Address: 68 Richmond Road
Bristol BS6 5EW, UK
Phone: +44 117 924 7874

#129
The Green Man
Category: Pub, British
Average price: Expensive
Address: 21 Alfred Place
Bristol BS2 8HD, UK
Phone: +44 117 930 4824

#130
The Love Inn
Category: Bar, Music Venues
Address: 84 Stokes Croft
Bristol BS1 3QY, UK
Phone: +44 117 923 2565

#131
Beerd
Category: Bar, Tapas Bar
Address: 155 St Michael's Hill
Bristol BS2 8DB, UK
Phone: +44 845 202 5837

#132
The Barley Mow
Category: Pub
Address: 39 Barton Road
Bristol BS2 0LF, UK
Phone: +44 117 929 8202

#133
The Chimp House
Category: Lounge
Average price: Inexpensive
Address: 232 Gloucester Rd
Bristol BS7 8NZ, UK
Phone: +44 7903 068686

#134
The Tunnels
Category: Dance Club, Music Venues
Address: Arches 31-32 Lower Approach
Road Bristol BS1 6QS, UK
Phone: +44 845 605 0255

#135
The Thunderbolt
Category: Pub, Music Venues
Average price: Modest
Address: 124 Bath Road
Bristol BS4 3ED, UK
Phone: +44 117 373 8947

#136
Blue Mountain
Category: Dance Club
Average price: Modest
Address: 2 Stokes Croft
Bristol BS1 3PR, UK
Phone: +44 117 924 6666

#137
Metropolis
Category: Comedy Club
Average price: Modest
Address: 135 - 137 Cheltenham Road
Bristol BS6 5RR, UK
Phone: +44 117 909 6655

#138
Number 10
Category: Bar
Average price: Modest
Address: 10 Zetland Road
Bristol BS6 7AD, UK
Phone: +44 117 924 1301

#139
Zest
Category: Lounge
Average price: Exclusive
Address: 408 Gloucester Road
Bristol BS7 8TR, UK
Phone: +44 117 949 0142

#140
The Hobgoblin
Category: Pub, American
Average price: Modest
Address: 69-71 Gloucester Road
Bristol BS7 8AS, UK
Phone: +44 117 942 9534

#141
The Royal Oak
Category: Pub, European
Average price: Modest
Address: 385 Gloucester Road
Bristol BS7 8TN, UK
Phone: +44 117 989 2522

#142
Port Of Call
Category: Pub
Average price: Modest
Address: 3 York Street
Bristol BS8 2YE, UK
Phone: +44 117 973 3600

#143
The Pump House
Category: Pub, British, European
Average price: Expensive
Address: Merchants Road
Bristol BS8 4PZ, UK
Phone: +44 117 927 2229

#144
The Adam & Eve
Category: Pub
Average price: Modest
Address: 7 Hope Chapel Hill
Bristol BS8 4ND, UK
Phone: +44 117 329 2025

#145
Rose Of Denmark
Category: Pub
Average price: Modest
Address: 6 Dowry Place
Bristol BS8 4QL, UK
Phone: +44 117 940 5866

#146
Bristol Ram
Category: Pub, GastroPub
Average price: Modest
Address: 32 Park Street
Bristol BS1 5JA, UK
Phone: +44 117 926 8654

#147
Clifton Wine Bar
Category: Wine Bar
Address: 4 Richmond Terrace
Bristol BS8 1AB, UK
Phone: +44 117 973 2069

#148
Totos Wine Bar & Restaurant
Category: Pub, British
Average price: Modest
Address: 125 Redcliff Street
Bristol BS1 6HU, UK
Phone: +44 117 930 0231

#149
The Rising Sun
Category: Pub
Average price: Modest
Address: 86 - 90 Gloucester Road
Bristol BS7 8BN, UK
Phone: +44 117 989 2471

#150
Basement 45
Category: Dance Club, Music Venues
Average price: Expensive
Address: 8 Frogmore Street
Bristol BS1 5NA, UK
Phone: +44 117 929 3554

#151
Elbow Room
Category: Bar, Pool Hall
Average price: Modest
Address: 64 Park St
Bristol BS1 5JN, UK
Phone: +44 117 930 0242

#152
Bocabar
Category: Pub
Average price: Modest
Address: Unit 3 1 Paintworks
Bristol BS4 3EH, UK
Phone: +44 117 972 8838

#153
Cat & Wheel
Category: Pub, Music Venues
Average price: Inexpensive
Address: 207 Cheltenham Rd
Bristol BS6 5QX, UK
Phone: +44 117 942 7862

#154
The Mardyke
Category: Pub
Average price: Inexpensive
Address: 126 Hotwell Road
Bristol BS8 4UB, UK
Phone: +44 117 907 7499

Shops, Restaurants, Attractions & Nightlife/ Bristol Guidebook 2020

#155
Snuff Mill Harvester
Category: British, Pub
Average price: Expensive
Address: 207 Frenchay Park Road
Bristol BS16 1LF, UK
Phone: +44 117 956 6560

#156
Toby Carvery
Category: Pub, British
Average price: Modest
Address: 189 Henbury Road
Bristol BS10 7AD, UK
Phone: +44 117 950 0144

#157
Watershed Café and Bar
Category: Lounge
Average price: Modest
Address: Watershed Media Centre 1
Canon's Rd Bristol BS1 5TX, UK
Phone: +44 117 927 5100

#158
The Shakespeare
Category: Pub
Average price: Modest
Address: Lower Redland Road
Bristol BS6 6SS, UK
Phone: +44 117 973 3909

#159
The River
Category: British, Pub
Address: Canons Road
Bristol BS1 5UH, UK
Phone: +44 117 930 0498

#160
The Shakespeare
Category: Pub
Average price: Modest
Address: 1 Henry Street
Bristol BS3 4UD, UK
Phone: +44 117 907 8818

#161
The Cooler
Category: Dance Club, Music Venues
Average price: Modest
Address: 48 Park Street
Bristol BS1 5JG, UK
Phone: +44 117 945 0999

#162
Day + Night
Category: Dance Club, Music Venues
Average price: Inexpensive
Address: 10 St Nicholas Street
Bristol BS1 1UQ, UK
Phone: +44 7765 208690

#163
Kensington Arms
Category: Pub
Address: 35 Stanley Road
Bristol BS6 6NP, UK
Phone: +44 117 942 4394

#164
Penfold's
Category: Wine Bar, Tapas Bar
Address: 85 Whiteladies Road
Bristol BS8 2NT, UK
Phone: +44 117 909 4383

#165
Jersey Lily
Category: Pub, British
Average price: Modest
Address: 193 Whiteladies Rd
Bristol BS8 2SB, UK
Phone: +44 117 973 9037

#166
Bristol Cider House
Category: Pub
Address: 8-9 Surrey Street
Bristol BS2 8PS, UK
Phone: +44 117 942 8196

#167
Take 5 Cafe
Category: Dance Club
Address: 72 Stokes Croft
Bristol BS1 3QY, UK
Phone: +44 117 907 7502

#168
Famous Royal Navy Volunteer
Category: Pub
Address: 17-18 King Street
Bristol BS1 4EF, UK
Phone: +44 117 929 1763

#169
Blowpop
Category: Dance Club
Address: 24 Park Street
Bristol BS1 5JA, UK
Phone: +44 117 925 5002

#170
Nova Scotia
Category: Pub
Average price: Modest
Address: Nova Scotia Place
Bristol BS1 6XJ, UK
Phone: +44 117 929 7994

#171
The Brunel
Category: British, Pub
Address: 315 St John's Lane
Bristol BS3 5AZ, UK
Phone: +44 117 966 3339

#172
The Shakespeare Tavern
Category: Pub
Address: 68 Prince Street
Bristol BS1 4QD, UK
Phone: +44 117 929 7695

#173
The Sugar Loaf
Category: Pub
Address: 51, St Mark's Road
Bristol BS5 6HX, UK
Phone: +44 117 939 4498

#174
Polish Ex Servicemen's Club
Category: Bar, Music Venues
Address: 50 St Pauls Road
Bristol BS8 1LP, UK
Phone: +44 117 973 6244

#175
The Syndicate Superclub
Category: Dance Club
Average price: Modest
Address: 15 Nelson Street
Bristol BS1 2JY, UK
Phone: +44 117 945 0325

#176
Whitehall Tavern
Category: Pub
Average price: Inexpensive
Address: 30 Devon Road
Bristol BS5 9AD, UK
Phone: +44 117 955 6798

#177
Old Lock & Weir
Category: Pub, British
Average price: Modest
Address: Hanham Mills
Bristol BS15 3NU, UK
Phone: +44 117 967 3793

#178
Rileys Sports Bar & Bingo Club
Category: Pool Hall, Sports Bar
Average price: Modest
Address: 15-19 Queens Road
Bristol BS8 1QE, UK
Phone: +44 117 929 4295

#179
Lakota
Category: Dance Club, Music Venues
Average price: Expensive
Address: 6 Upper York Street
Bristol BS2 8QN, UK
Phone: +44 117 942 6208

#180
The Kellaway
Category: British, Pub
Average price: Modest
Address: 138-140 Kellaway Avenue
Bristol BS6 7YQ, UK
Phone: +44 117 942 6210

#181
Lloyds No.1 Bar
Category: Dance Club
Average price: Modest
Address: V Shed Canons Road
Bristol BS1 5TX, UK
Phone: +44 117 952 9950

#182
Alma Tavern
Category: Pub, British
Average price: Modest
Address: 18-20 Alma Vale Road
Bristol BS8 2HY, UK
Phone: +44 117 973 5171

#183
The Dovecote
Category: Pub
Address: Ashton Road
Bristol BS41 9LX, UK
Phone: +44 1275 392245

#184
Java
Category: Lounge, Dance Club
Average price: Modest
Address: 9 Park St
Bristol BS1 5NF, UK
Phone: +44 117 930 4561

#185
The Prince Of Wales
Category: Pub
Average price: Modest
Address: 84 Stoke Lane
Bristol BS9 3SP, UK
Phone: +44 117 962 3715

#186
Channings Hotel
Category: Pub
Average price: Modest
Address: 20 Pembroke Rd
Bristol BS8 3BB, UK
Phone: +44 117 973 3970

#187
Horts City Tavern
Category: Pub, British
Average price: Modest
Address: 49 Broad Street
Bristol BS1 2EP, UK
Phone: +44 117 925 2520

#188
The Berkeley
Category: Pub
Average price: Inexpensive
Address: 15-19 Queens Road
Bristol BS8 1QE, UK
Phone: +44 117 927 9550

#189
Cross Hands
Category: Pub
Average price: Inexpensive
Address: 85 Down Road
Bristol BS36 1BZ, UK
Phone: +44 1454 850077

#190
Red Lion
Category: Pub, British
Average price: Modest
Address: 26 Worrall Road
Bristol BS8 2UE, UK
Phone: +44 117 903 0773

#191
University Of Bristol Student Union
Category: Social Club, Music Venues
Average price: Modest
Address: Queens Road
Bristol BS8 1LN, UK
Phone: +44 117 954 5800

#192
Greenhouse
Category: Pub, British
Average price: Inexpensive
Address: 37 College Green
Bristol BS1 5SP, UK
Phone: +44 117 927 6426

#193
Punch Bowl
Category: Pub
Average price: Modest
Address: 23 Old Market Street
Bristol BS2 0HB, UK
Phone: +44 117 930 4967

#194
Hush Hush
Category: Dance Club, Music Venues
Average price: Modest
Address: 233 Cheltenham Road
Bristol BS6 5QP, UK
Phone: +44 117 942 2700

#195
The H Bar
Category: Bar, Mediterranean, Spanish
Average price: Modest
Address: Colston Street
Bristol BS1 5AR, UK
Phone: +44 117 204 7130

#196
Eldon House
Category: Pub
Average price: Modest
Address: 6 Lower Clifton Hill
Bristol BS8 1BT, UK
Phone: +44 117 922 1271

#197
Wetherspoons
Category: Pub
Average price: Inexpensive
Address: 94-96 Regent Street
Bristol BS15 8HP, UK
Phone: +44 117 967 2247

Shops, Restaurants, Attractions & Nightlife/ Bristol Guidebook 2020

#198
Robert Fitzharding
Category: Pub
Address: 24 Cannon Street
Bristol BS3 1BN, UK
Phone: +44 117 966 2757

#199
The Mothers Ruin
Category: Pub, Music Venues
Average price: Inexpensive
Address: 7-9 St Nicholas Market
Bristol BS1 1UE, UK
Phone: +44 117 329 2141

#200
ONeills
Category: Irish, Bar
Average price: Inexpensive
Address: 16-24 Baldwin Street
Bristol BS1 1SE, UK
Phone: +44 117 945 8891

#201
Inn On The Green
Category: Pub
Average price: Modest
Address: 2 Filton Road
Bristol BS7 0PA, UK
Phone: +44 117 952 1391

#202
White Hart
Category: Pub
Average price: Inexpensive
Address: Lower Maudlin Street
Bristol BS1 2LU, UK
Phone: +44 117 926 8747

#203
QueenShilling
Category: Pub, Dance Club, Gay Bar
Address: 9 Frogmore Street
Bristol BS1 5NA, UK
Phone: +44 117 927 7070

#204
The Foresters
Category: Pub
Average price: Inexpensive
Address: 99 Gloucester Rd
Bristol BS7 8AT, UK
Phone: +44 117 940 1848

#205
The Old Fox
Category: Pub
Address: 310 Gloucester Road
Bristol BS7 8PE, UK
Phone: +44 117 940 1145

#206
The Greyhound
Category: Pub
Address: 32 Princess Victoria Street
Bristol BS8 4BZ, UK
Phone: +44 117 973 4187

#207
Antix
Category: British, Lounge
Average price: Modest
Address: 44 Park St
Bristol BS1 5JG, UK
Phone: +44 117 925 1139

#208
Propaganda
Category: Dance Club
Average price: Modest
Address: 15 Nelson Street
Bristol BS1 2JY, UK
Phone: +44 117 945 0325

#209
Pitcher & Piano
Category: British, Bar
Average price: Modest
Address: Cannon's Road
Bristol BS1 5UH, UK
Phone: +44 117 929 9652

#210
Surrey Wine Vaults
Category: Pub
Address: 8-9 Surrey Street
Bristol BS2 8PS, UK
Phone: +44 117 942 8196

#211
The Bridge Inn
Category: Pub
Average price: Modest
Address: 16 Passage Street
Bristol BS2 0JF, UK
Phone: +44 117 949 9967

#212
Level 1
Category: Gay Bar
Address: 41 Colston St
Bristol BS1 5AP, UK
Phone: +44 117 930 0444

#213
Zoom+
Category: Bar
Address: 41-43 Baldwin St
Bristol BS1 1RB, UK
Phone: +44 117 929 7328

#214
Reckless Engineer
Category: Pub, Music Venues
Average price: Inexpensive
Address: Temple Gate
Bristol BS1 6PL, UK
Phone: +44 117 922 0487

#215
The Priory
Category: Pub
Address: Station Road
Bristol BS20 7TN, UK
Phone: +44 1275 378411

#216
The Sandringham Public House
Category: Pub
Average price: Expensive
Address: Quakers Road
Bristol BS16 6NH, UK
Phone: +44 117 970 9060

#217
Phoenix Restaurant and Bar
Category: British, Bar
Address: The Mercure Hotel
Bristol BS1 6SQ, UK
Phone: +44 117 968 9900

#218
Bristol Bear Bar
Category: Gay Bar, Pub
Average price: Inexpensive
Address: 2-4 West Street
Bristol BS2 0BH, UK
Phone: +44 117 955 1967

#219
Colston Hall 2
Category: Bar, Music Venues
Address: Colston Street
Bristol BS1 5AR, UK
Phone: +44 117 922 3686

#220
The Social
Category: Bar, British
Address: 130 Cheltenham Road
Bristol BS6 5RW, UK
Phone: +44 117 924 4500

#221
The Stag & Hounds
Category: Pub
Average price: Modest
Address: 74 Old Market Street
Bristol BS2 0EJ, UK
Phone: +44 117 929 1407

#222
Skizm @ Basement 45
Category: Music Venues
Address: 8 Frogmore Street
Bristol BS1 5NA, UK
Phone: +44 117 929 3554

#223
The Robin Hood
Category: Pub
Address: 56 Saint Michael's Hill
Bristol BS2 8DX, UK
Phone: +44 117 929 4915

#224
South Bank Studios
Category: Music Venues, Jazz & Blues
Average price: Exclusive
Address: 31 Dean Ln
Bristol BS3 1DB, UK
Phone: +44 117 966 5552

#225
Aces Bar
Category: Social Club, Music Venues
Average price: Modest
Address: 29-31 ST Pauls Road
Bristol BS8 1LX, UK
Phone: +44 117 973 4866

#226
The Parkway
Category: Pub
Average price: Inexpensive
Address: 43 North Road
Bristol BS34 8PB, UK
Phone: +44 117 969 0329

#227
Shore Cafe Bar
Category: Pub
Average price: Modest
Address: Prince Street
Bristol BS1 4QF, UK
Phone: +44 117 923 0333

#228
Brunel Wine Bar
Category: Wine Bar, Tapas Bar
Average price: Modest
Address: 38 The Mall
Bristol BS8 4DS, UK
Phone: +44 117 973 4443

#229
Winford Arms
Category: Pub
Average price: Modest
Address: Bridgwater Road
Bristol BS41 8JP, UK
Phone: +44 1275 392178

#230
Fire Engine
Category: Pub
Address: 188 Church Road
Bristol BS5 9HX, UK
Phone: +44 7521 974070

#231
The Anchor
Category: Pub, British
Average price: Inexpensive
Address: 323 Gloucester Road
Bristol BS7 8PE, UK
Phone: +44 117 924 1769

#232
Lizard Lounge
Category: Dance Club
Average price: Inexpensive
Address: 66 Queens Road
Bristol BS8 1QU, UK
Phone: +44 117 949 7778

#233
The Albert Inn
Category: Pub
Average price: Inexpensive
Address: 1 West Street
Bristol BS3 3NN, UK
Phone: +44 872 107 7077

#234
Dundry Inn
Category: Pub
Average price: Inexpensive
Address: Church Road
Bristol BS41 8LH, UK
Phone: +44 117 964 1722

#235
Eastfield Inn
Category: Pub, Food
Average price: Modest
Address: 219 Henleaze Road
Bristol BS9 4NQ, UK
Phone: +44 117 239 1466

#236
Niko's
Category: Hookah Bar
Average price: Modest
Address: 72 Park St
Bristol BS1 5JX, UK
Phone: +44 117 929 1166

#237
Golden Lion
Category: Pub
Average price: Modest
Address: 641 Fishponds Road
Bristol BS16 3BA, UK
Phone: +44 117 958 6446

#238
The Sportsman
Category: Pub, Sports Bar, Pool Hall
Address: Nevil Road
Bristol BS7 9EQ, UK
Phone: +44 117 942 7525

#239
Victoria Inn
Category: Pub
Address: 20 Chock Lane
Bristol BS9 3EX, UK
Phone: +44 117 950 0441

Shops, Restaurants, Attractions & Nightlife/ Bristol Guidebook 2020

#240
Ye Shakespeare
Category: Pub
Average price: Inexpensive
Address: 78 Victoria Street
Bristol BS1 6DR, UK
Phone: +44 117 929 4755

#241
Bristol Academy 2
Category: Bar, Music Venues
Average price: Modest
Address: Frogmore Street
Bristol BS1 5NA, UK
Phone: +44 117 927 9227

#242
Tikka Flame
Category: Wine Bar, Indian
Average price: Modest
Address: Anchor Road
Bristol BS1 5DB, UK
Phone: +44 117 316 9393

#243
Lock Keeper
Category: Pub, British
Average price: Modest
Address: Keynsham Road
Bristol BS31 2DD, UK
Phone: +44 117 986 2383

#244
Agora
Category: Dance Club, Bar
Average price: Modest
Address: 55 Park Street
Bristol BS1 5NT, UK
Phone: +44 117 929 4888

#245
Seamus O'Donnells
Category: Pub
Average price: Modest
Address: 13 St Nicholas Street
Bristol BS1 1UE, UK
Phone: +44 117 925 1283

#246
Three Tuns
Category: Pub
Average price: Modest
Address: 78 ST. Georges Road
Bristol BS1 5UR, UK
Phone: +44 117 926 8434

#247
The Coronation
Category: Pub
Address: 18 Dean Lane
Bristol BS3 1DD, UK
Phone: +44 117 940 9044

#248
The Hophouse
Category: Pub
Average price: Expensive
Address: 16 Kings Road
Bristol BS8 4AB, UK
Phone: +44 117 923 7390

#249
The Assembly
Category: Pub, British
Address: 110-112 East Street
Bristol BS3 4EY, UK
Phone: +44 117 966 6506

#250
Kings Head
Category: Pub
Address: 91 Bridgwater Road
Bristol BS13 8AE, UK
Phone: +44 117 964 3582

#251
George Inn
Category: Pub
Address: Manor Road
Bristol BS8 3RP, UK
Phone: +44 1275 372467

#252
All Bar One
Category: Wine Bar
Address: 45-47 Corn Street
Bristol BS1 1HT, UK
Phone: +44 117 946 8751

#253
Slug & Lettuce
Category: Pub, British, Lounge
Average price: Modest
Address: 41 Corn Street
Bristol BS1 1HT, UK
Phone: +44 117 930 0909

#254
The Oxford
Category: Pub
Average price: Modest
Address: 120-122 Oxford St
Bristol BS3 4RH, UK
Phone: +44 117 972 8028

#255
The Somerset House
Category: Pub
Average price: Modest
Address: 11 Princess Victoria St
Bristol BS8 4BX, UK
Phone: +44 117 973 6831

#256
The Cross Hands
Category: Pub
Average price: Expensive
Address: 1 Staple Hill Road
Bristol BS16 5AA, UK
Phone: +44 117 965 4684

#257
Prince of Wales
Category: Bar
Address: 130 Ashley Rd
Bristol BS6 5PA, UK
Phone: +44 117 908 0855

#258
Karaoke-Me!
Category: Karaoke
Average price: Inexpensive
Address: 12 St. Stephens St
Bristol BS1 1EL, UK
Phone: +44 117 376 3100

#259
Under the Stars
Category: Coffee & Tea, Bar
Average price: Modest
Address: Narrow Quay
Bristol BS1 4QA, UK
Phone: +44 117 929 8392

#260
The Myrtle Tree
Category: Pub
Address: 127 St George's Road
Bristol BS1 5UW, UK
Phone: +44 117 971 9455

#261
Jack's Brasserie
Category: Bar, British
Address: 1 Hannover Quay
Bristol BS1 5JE, UK
Phone: +44 117 945 3990

#262
The Black Bear
Category: Pub
Address: 168 Whiteladies Road
Bristol BS8 2XZ, UK
Phone: +44 117 973 3993

#263
Orchard Inn
Category: Pub
Average price: Inexpensive
Address: Hanover Place
Bristol BS1 6XT, UK
Phone: +44 117 926 2678

#264
The Pumphouse
Category: Pub
Average price: Expensive
Address: Merchants Rd
Bristol BS8 4PZ, UK
Phone: +44 117 927 2229

#265
The Queen Vic
Category: Pub
Address: 426 Gloucester Road
Bristol BS7 8TX, UK
Phone: +44 117 987 3725

#266
Westbury Park Tavern
Category: Pub
Average price: Modest
Address: Northumbria Drive
Bristol BS9 4HP, UK
Phone: +44 117 962 4235

#267
Clyde Arms
Category: Pub
Address: 129 Hampton Road
Bristol BS6 6JE, UK
Phone: +44 117 923 7936

Shops, Restaurants, Attractions & Nightlife/ Bristol Guidebook 2020

#268
La Rocca
Category: Dance Club
Average price: Inexpensive
Address: 7-9 Triangle S
Bristol BS8 1EY, UK
Phone: +44 117 926 0924

#269
Jolly Collier
Category: Pub
Average price: Inexpensive
Address: 57 West Street
Bristol BS3 3NU, UK
Phone: +44 117 940 6068

#270
Queens Head
Category: Pub
Average price: Modest
Address: 286 Fishponds Road
Bristol BS5 6PY, UK
Phone: +44 117 951 8457

#271
Cock O The North
Category: Pub
Average price: Modest
Address: Northumbria Drive
Bristol BS9 4HP, UK
Phone: +44 117 962 4235

#272
Princes Motto
Category: Pub
Average price: Modest
Address: Barrow Street
Bristol BS48 3RY, UK
Phone: +44 1275 472282

#273
Fox & Goose
Category: Pub
Address: Bridgwater Rd
Bristol BS48 3SL, UK
Phone: +44 1275 472202

#274
The Knights Templar
Category: British, Pub
Average price: Inexpensive
Address: 1 The Square
Bristol BS1 6DG, UK
Phone: +44 117 925 4439

#275
The Yeoman
Category: Pub
Address: Wells Road
Bristol BS14 9HX, UK
Phone: +44 1275 890041

#276
Walkabout
Category: Pub, Sports Bar, British
Average price: Modest
Address: 40 Corn Street
Bristol BS1 1HQ, UK
Phone: +44 117 930 0181

#277
The Coronation Tap
Category: Pub
Average price: Exclusive
Address: 8 Sion Pl
Bristol BS8 4AX, UK
Phone: +44 117 973 9617

#278
White Horse
Category: Pub
Address: 24 High Street
Bristol BS9 3DZ, UK
Phone: +44 117 950 7622

#279
The Van Dyke Forum
Category: Pub
Address: 748-756 Fishponds Road
Bristol BS16 3UA, UK
Phone: +44 117 965 1337

#280
The Black Castle
Category: Pub
Average price: Inexpensive
Address: Castle Ct
Bristol BS4 3BD, UK
Phone: +44 117 977 8720

#281
The Tao Bar
Category: Bar
Address: 128 Cheltenham Road
Bristol BS6 5RW, UK
Phone: +44 117 924 7733

Shops, Restaurants, Attractions & Nightlife/ Bristol Guidebook 2020

#282
The Beaufort
Category: Pub
Address: 21 York Road
Bristol BS6 5QB, UK
Phone: +44 117 955 5216

#283
Colston Arms
Category: Pub
Address: 24 St Michael's Hill
Bristol BS2 8DX, UK
Phone: +44 117 9264 5004

#284
Rewind
Category: Dance Club
Average price: Modest
Address: 40 Corn Street
Bristol BS1 1HQ, UK
Phone: +44 117 930 0181

#285
Central Chambers
Category: Adult Entertainment
Address: 9-11 St Stephens Street
Bristol BS1 1EE, UK
Phone: +44 117 934 9348

#286
Circoteque
Category: Bar
Address: 31 Corn street
Bristol BS1 1HT, UK
Phone: +44 117 929 0118

#287
Clockwork Club
Category: Dance Club
Address: Bristol BS1 3PR, UK
Phone: +44 870 444 4400

#288
Horn & Trumpet
Category: Pub
Address: 14-16 St Augustines Parade
Bristol BS1 4UT, UK
Phone: +44 117 929 8391

#289
Luckys Cinema
Category: Comedy Club
Address: St John's Steep
Bristol BS1 2LE, UK
Phone: +44 117 329 1979

#290
Oppo Harmonic Fusion
Category: British, Bar
Address: 72 Park Street
Bristol BS1 5JX, UK
Phone: +44 117 929 1166

#291
Quinton House
Category: Pub
Address: 2 Park Place
Bristol BS8 1JW, UK
Phone: +44 117 907 7858

#292
The Bear Inn Public House
Category: Pub
Address: 261 Hotwell Road
Bristol BS8 4SF, UK
Phone: +44 117 987 7796

#293
The Grapes
Category: Pub
Address: 2 Sion Pl
Bristol BS8 4AX, UK
Phone: +44 117 946 7123

#294
The Victoria Park
Category: Pub
Address: 66 Raymend Rd
Bristol BS3 4QW, UK
Phone: +44 117 330 6043

#295
Bar Salt
Category: Pub
Average price: Modest
Address: 4-6 North Street
Bristol BS3 1HT, UK
Phone: +44 117 953 1446

#296
Langton Court Hotel
Category: Pub
Address: Langton Court Road
Bristol BS4 4EG, UK
Phone: +44 117 987 2528

#297
Merchants Arms
Category: Pub
Address: Bell Hill
Bristol BS16 1BQ, UK
Phone: +44 117 951 8771

Shops, Restaurants, Attractions & Nightlife/ Bristol Guidebook 2020

#298
King William IV
Category: Pub
Address: 62 Broad Street
Bristol BS16 5NP, UK
Phone: +44 117 983 1183

#299
Baileys Court Pub
Category: Pub
Address: Baileys Court Road
Bristol BS32 8BH, UK
Phone: +44 117 923 6486

#300
Stone House
Category: Bar, Music Venues
Average price: Modest
Address: 28 Baldwin Street
Bristol BS1 1NG, UK
Phone: +44 117 946 8160

#301
The Kings Arms
Category: Pub
Average price: Inexpensive
Address: Little Paul St
Bristol BS2 8HG, UK
Phone: +44 872 107 7077

#302
The Platinum Club
Category: Adult Entertainment
Address: Denmark Street
Bristol BS1 5DQ, UK
Phone: +44 7961 012208

#303
Old Tavern, Bristol
Category: Pub
Address: Blackberry Hill
Bristol BS16 1DB, UK
Phone: +44 117 965 7309

#304
Portwall Tavern
Category: Pub, British
Average price: Inexpensive
Address: Portwall Lane
Bristol BS1 6NB, UK
Phone: +44 117 922 0442

#305
Wetherspoon
Category: Pub
Address: 84 High Street
Bristol BS16 5HN, UK
Phone: +44 117 956 8543

#306
The Mezza Bar
Category: Hookah Bar
Address: 145 St Michael's Hill
Bristol BS2 8DB, UK
Phone: +44 117 973 7620

#307
The Berkeley - J.
Category: Pub
Average price: Modest
Address: 15 - 19 Queens Road
Bristol BS8 1QE, UK
Phone: +44 117 927 9550

#308
Blackboy Inn
Category: Pub
Address: 171 Whiteladies Road
Bristol BS8 2RY, UK
Phone: +44 117 973 5233

#309
The Pack Horse
Category: Pub
Average price: Inexpensive
Address: 166-168 Lawrence Hill
Bristol BS5 0DN, UK
Phone: +44 117 940 5877

#310
Grupo Lounge
Category: Lounge
Average price: Expensive
Address: 8 Canford Lane
Bristol BS9 3DH, UK
Phone: +44 117 950 0279

#311
Gala Casino
Category: Casino
Average price: Modest
Address: Explore Lane
Bristol BS1 5TY, UK
Phone: +44 117 906 9970

#312
Swan Inn
Category: Pub
Address: Conham Hill
Bristol BS15 3AP, UK
Phone: +44 117 967 3947

#313
The Old Stillage
Category: Pub
Average price: Modest
Address: 145-147 Church Rd
Bristol BS5 9LA, UK
Phone: +44 117 939 4079

#314
The Old Globe
Category: Pub
Average price: Inexpensive
Address: 117 East Street
Bristol BS3 4EX, UK
Phone: +44 117 963 4378

#315
Railway Tavern
Category: Pub
Address: Station Road
Bristol BS16 3SG, UK
Phone: +44 117 965 8774

#316
The Crown Inn Harvester
Category: British, Pub
Average price: Inexpensive
Address: 126 Bath Road
Bristol BS30 9DE, UK
Phone: +44 117 932 2846

#317
The Limo People
Category: Limousine Hire
Address: 90 Hungerford Road
Bristol BS4 5HG, UK
Phone: +44 117 370 6485

#318
Old Post Office
Category: Pub
Address: 786 Fishponds Road
Bristol BS16 3TT, UK
Phone: +44 117 965 5730

#319
Bar BS3
Category: Pub, Sports Bar
Average price: Inexpensive
Address: 21 Ashton Road
Bristol BS3 2EA, UK
Phone: +44 117 966 9777

#320
Bawa
Category: Music Venues
Address: 589 Southmead Road
Bristol BS34 7RG, UK
Phone: +44 117 976 8066

#321
Jongleurs Comedy Club
Category: Comedy Club
Address: 28 Baldwin Street
Bristol BS1 1NG, UK
Phone: +44 870 111960

#322
The George, Abbots Leigh
Category: Pub
Address: the George Inn Manor Road
Bristol BS8 3RP, UK
Phone: +44 1275 376985

#323
V-Shed
Category: Pub
Average price: Inexpensive
Address: Canons Rd
Bristol BS1 5UH, UK
Phone: +44 117 952 9950

#324
St. Georges Hall
Category: Pub
Average price: Inexpensive
Address: 203 Church Road
Bristol BS5 9HL, UK
Phone: +44 117 955 1488

#325
Jolly Sailor
Category: Pub
Address: High Street
Bristol BS15 3DQ, UK
Phone: +44 117 960 0834

Shops, Restaurants, Attractions & Nightlife/ Bristol Guidebook 2020

#326
Cross Hands
Category: Pub
Average price: Expensive
Address: 1 Bridgwater Road
Bristol BS13 7AQ, UK
Phone: +44 117 966 0894

#327
Jesters Comedy Club
Category: Comedy Club
Average price: Expensive
Address: 140-142 Cheltenham Rd
Bristol BS6 5RL, UK
Phone: +44 117 909 6655

#328
Elm Tree Inn
Category: Pub
Address: 74 Abbots Road
Bristol BS15 3NR, UK
Phone: +44 117 967 5193

#329
Bay Horse
Category: Pub
Average price: Modest
Address: Lewins Mead
Bristol BS1 2LJ, UK
Phone: +44 117 925 8287

#330
King William IV
Category: Pub
Address: 62 Broad Street
Bristol BS16 5NP, UK
Phone: +44 117 956 5471

#331
Mackies Bar
Category: Pub, Dance Club
Address: 84 Stokes Croft
Bristol BS1 3QY, UK
Phone: +44 117 924 9995

#332
Mackenzies Cafe Bar
Category: Lounge
Average price: Modest
Address: 1 Canons Road
Bristol BS1 5UH, UK
Phone: +44 117 922 5496

#333
The ship
Category: Pub
Address: 93 Temple Street
Bristol BS31 1EP, UK
Phone: +44 117 986 9841

#334
The Anchor
Category: Pub
Address: 60 Ham Green
Bristol BS20 0HB, UK
Phone: +44 1275 372253

#335
The Bush
Category: Pub
Average price: Inexpensive
Address: Wells Road
Bristol BS4 2BA, UK
Phone: +44 117 908 6805

#336
The Sandringham
Category: Pub
Average price: Modest
Address: 8 Sandy Park Road
Bristol BS4 3PE, UK
Phone: +44 117 983 0383

#337
The Horseshoe
Category: Pub
Address: 41 Siston Common
Bristol BS15 4PA, UK
Phone: +44 117 967 1435

#338
Castro
Category: Dance Club
Address: 72-73 Old Market Street
Bristol BS2 0EJ, UK
Phone: +44 117 922 0774

#339
The Colosseum
Category: Pub
Address: Redcliff Hill
Bristol BS1 6SJ, UK
Phone: +44 117 987 0070

#340
Platform 1
Category: Dance Club
Address: Whiteladies road
Bristol BS8 2PN, UK
Phone: +44 117 973 4388

#341
Pressure @ Thekla
Category: Dance Club
Average price: Inexpensive
Address: The Grove
Bristol BS1 4RB, UK
Phone: +44 117 929 3301

#342
The Hop House
Category: Pub, British
Address: 16 King's Rd
Bristol BS8 4AB, UK
Phone: +44 117 923 7390

#343
Avon Packet
Category: Pub
Average price: Inexpensive
Address: 185-187 Coronation Road
Bristol BS3 1RF, UK
Phone: +44 117 987 2431

#344
The Masonic
Category: Pub
Average price: Inexpensive
Address: 110 North St
Bristol BS3 1HF, UK
Phone: +44 117 902 0132

#345
Lamb Inn
Category: Pub
Average price: Inexpensive
Address: 36 Windsor Place
Bristol BS16 9DD, UK
Phone: +44 117 970 9081

#346
Wackum Inn
Category: Pub
Average price: Inexpensive
Address: 533 Whitehall Rd
Bristol BS5 7DA, UK
Phone: +44 117 951 7277

#347
Second Floor Bar
Category: Champagne Bar
Address: Philadelphia St
Bristol BS1 3BZ, UK
Phone: +44 117 916 8898

#348
The Stone House
Category: Pub, Music Venues
Address: 28 Baldwin Street
Bristol BS1 1NG, UK
Phone: +44 117 946 8160

#349
Antix
Category: Bar, British
Address: 44 Park Street
Bristol BS1 5JG, UK
Phone: +44 117 925 1140

#350
Omg
Category: Gay Bar
Average price: Modest
Address: 1-2 Frog Lane
Bristol BS1 5UX, UK
Phone: +44 7970 189600

#351
The Bar
Category: Bar
Address: Broad Quay
Bristol BS1 4BY, UK
Phone: +44 117 934 9500

#352
The Drawbridge
Category: Pub
Average price: Modest
Address: 14-15 St. Augustines Parade
Bristol BS1 4, UK
Phone: +44 117 929 8391

#353
The Ropewalk
Category: Pub
Average price: Inexpensive
Address: 5 Nelson Parade
Bristol BS3 4JA, UK
Phone: +44 117 923 1300

#354
Venus Bar
Category: Bar
Address: 198 Gloucester Rd
Bristol BS7 8NU, UK
Phone: +44 117 942 5849

#355
The Jersey Lilly
Category: Pub
Address: 193 Whiteladies Road
Bristol BS8 2SB, UK
Phone: +44 117 973 9037

#356
Horseshoe Inn
Category: Pub
Average price: Expensive
Address: Downend Road
Bristol BS16 6BA, UK
Phone: +44 117 956 0471

#357
Post Office Tavern
Category: Pub
Address: 17 Westbury Hill
Bristol BS9 3AG, UK
Phone: +44 117 940 1233

#358
Lloyds TSB Bank
Category: Bar, Banks & Credit Unions
Address: 145 East Street
Bristol BS3 4EJ, UK
Phone: +44 845 072 3333

#359
The Merchants Arms
Category: Pub
Address: 5 Merchants Road
Bristol BS8 4PZ, UK
Phone: +44 117 904 0037

#360
The George
Category: Pub
Average price: Inexpensive
Address: 228 Wells Road
Bristol BS4 2AX, UK
Phone: +44 117 949 3314

#361
Engineers Arms
Category: Pub
Address: St Johns Lane
Bristol BS3 5AZ, UK
Phone: +44 117 966 3339

#362
Coopers Arms
Category: Pub
Average price: Inexpensive
Address: 12-13 Ashton Road
Bristol BS3 2EA, UK
Phone: +44 117 902 0359

#363
Three Lions
Category: Pub
Average price: Inexpensive
Address: 206 West Street
Bristol BS3 3NB, UK
Phone: +44 117 902 0056

#364
Bijou
Category: Dance Club, Bar
Address: 135 Whiteladies Rd
Bristol BS8 2PL, UK
Phone: +44 117 970 6589

#365
Newman Hall Booking Line
Category: Bar
Average price: Modest
Address: Grange Court Road
Bristol BS9 4DR, UK
Phone: +44 117 909 4780

#366
Millhouse
Category: Pub
Address: 94 Shirehampton Rd
Bristol BS9 2DS, UK
Phone: +44 117 968 2913

#367
Princess of Wales
Category: Pub
Address: 1 Westbourne Grove
Bristol BS3 3LQ, UK
Phone: +44 117 949 3008

#368
Tantric Jazz
Category: Bar, Jazz & Blues
Average price: Modest
Address: 39-41 ST Nicholas St
Bristol BS1 1TP, UK
Phone: +44 117 940 2304

#369
Black Swan
Category: Pub
Address: 92 Stoke Lane
Bristol BS9 3SP, UK
Phone: +44 117 962 5111

#370
The Spotted Cow
Category: Pub
Address: 120 Lodge Causeway
Bristol BS16 3JP, UK
Phone: +44 117 965 8772

#371
White Hart
Category: Pub
Address: Brislington Hill
Bristol BS4 5BD, UK
Phone: +44 117 977 7148

#372
Foresters At Westbury
Category: Pub
Address: Westbury Hill
Bristol BS9 3AD, UK
Phone: +44 117 962 4881

#373
Long Bar
Category: Pub
Average price: Modest
Address: 70 Old Market Street
Bristol BS2 0EJ, UK
Phone: +44 117 927 6785

#374
Queens Head
Category: Pub
Address: 29 Lower Hanham Road
Bristol BS15 8QP, UK
Phone: +44 117 967 4995

#375
Fishponds Tavern
Category: Pub
Average price: Inexpensive
Address: 47 Lewington Road
Bristol BS16 4AB, UK
Phone: +44 117 949 8972

#376
Bonapartes
Category: Pub
Average price: Expensive
Address: Temple Meads Station
Bristol BS1 6QG, UK
Phone: +44 117 925 2953

#377
Planet Venus
Category: Pub
Average price: Modest
Address: 198 Gloucester Road
Bristol BS7 8NU, UK
Phone: +44 117 942 5849

#378
White Hart
Category: Pub
Average price: Modest
Address: 84 Bedminster Parade
Bristol BS3 4HL, UK
Phone: +44 117 966 3623

#379
Tap & Barrel
Category: Sports Bar
Average price: Inexpensive
Address: 43 Dean Lane
Bristol BS3 1BS, UK
Phone: +44 117 966 7385

#380
The Shant
Category: Pub
Average price: Modest
Address: Crown Road
Bristol BS15 1PR, UK
Phone: +44 117 967 3693

#381
The Turnpike
Category: Pub
Address: 169 Soundwell Road
Bristol BS16 4RP, UK
Phone: +44 117 970 9071

#382
BSB Whiteladies
Category: Bar
Address: 93-95 Whiteladies Rd
Bristol BS8 2NT, UK
Phone: +44 117 911 4950

Shops, Restaurants, Attractions & Nightlife/ Bristol Guidebook 2020

#383
The Barley Mow
Category: Pub, British
Address: 1-3 East St
Bristol BS3 4HH, UK
Phone: +44 117 983 0386

#384
Downend Tavern
Category: Pub
Average price: Inexpensive
Address: 125 Downend Road
Bristol BS16 5BE, UK
Phone: +44 117 956 1277

#385
Black Horse
Category: Pub
Address: 172-174 Church Road
Bristol BS5 9HX, UK
Phone: +44 117 939 4494

#386
Reflex
Category: Dance Club, Lounge
Average price: Inexpensive
Address: 16-24 Baldwin Street
Bristol BS1 1SE, UK
Phone: +44 117 945 8891

#387
Chequers Inn
Category: Pub
Address: Hanham Mills
Bristol BS15 3NU, UK
Phone: +44 117 967 4242

#388
The Crofters Rights
Category: Pub
Average price: Modest
Address: 117 - 119 Stokes Croft
Bristol BS1 3RW, UK
Phone: +44 117 231 0079

#389
The Old England
Category: Pub
Average price: Modest
Address: 43 Bath Buildings
Bristol BS6 5PT, UK
Phone: +44 117 944 1037

#390
Native
Category: Dance Club
Address: 15 Small St
Bristol BS1 1, UK
Phone: +44 117 930 4217

#391
Circotheque
Category: Dance Club, Wine Bar
Address: 31 Corn St
Bristol BS1 1, UK
Phone: +44 117 929 0118

#392
Vanilla Bar
Category: Dance Club, Lounge
Address: 30 Clare Street
Bristol BS1 1YH, UK
Phone: +44 117 929 7997

#393
Sports Cafe
Category: Bar
Address: 13-21 Baldwin St
Bristol BS1 1NA, UK
Phone: +44 117 917 5520

#394
Bed bar
Category: Pub
Address: King Street
Bristol BS1 4ER, UK
Phone: +44 117 926 1650

#395
Knights Templer
Category: Pub
Average price: Inexpensive
Address: 1 The Square
Bristol BS1 6DG, UK
Phone: +44 117 930 8710

#396
Baja Bar
Category: Pub, Dance Club
Address: Canons Road
Bristol BS1 5UH, UK
Phone: +44 117 929 4276

#397
Bar Pam Pam
Category: Pub
Address: Queens Avenue
Bristol BS8 1QU, UK
Phone: +44 117 973 1249

Shops, Restaurants, Attractions & Nightlife/ Bristol Guidebook 2020

#398
Beaufort Arms
Category: Pub
Average price: Modest
Address: 55 North Road
Bristol BS34 8PB, UK
Phone: +44 117 974 9131

#399
Rope Walk
Category: Pub
Average price: Modest
Address: 5 Nelson Parade
Bristol BS3 4JA, UK
Phone: +44 117 985 0067

#400
Bar 100
Category: Sports Bar, Lounge
Address: Queens Road Bristol, UK
Phone: +44 117 954 5800

#401
Wessex Flyer
Category: Pub
Average price: Modest
Address: Hengrove Way
Bristol BS14 0HR, UK
Phone: +44 1275 834340

#402
BSB Corn Street
Category: Bar, British
Address: 41 Corn St
Bristol BS1 1HT, UK
Phone: +44 117 911 4950

#403
The Slug & Lettuce
Category: Pub
Average price: Modest
Address: 41 Corn Street
Bristol BS1 1HS, UK
Phone: +44 117 930 0909

#404
Star Inn
Category: Pub
Address: 539 Fishponds Road
Bristol BS16 3AF, UK
Phone: +44 117 965 4685

#405
The Fellowship
Category: Pub
Address: 390 Filton Avenue
Bristol BS7 0LJ, UK
Phone: +44 117 909 9567

#406
White Lion
Category: Pub, British
Average price: Inexpensive
Address: Passage Road
Bristol BS9 3HN, UK
Phone: +44 117 941 9460

#407
Evolution
Category: Dance Club
Average price: Modest
Address: U Shed Canons Road
Bristol BS1 5UH, UK
Phone: +44 117 922 0330

#408
Chicago Rock Cafe
Category: American, Bar
Address: Canons Road
Bristol BS1 5UH, UK
Phone: +44 117 929 1361

#409
Funky Greek Bar Taverna Club
Category: Wine Bar
Average price: Modest
Address: 30 Clare Street
Bristol BS1 1YH, UK
Phone: +44 117 945 7777

#410
BSB Waterside
Category: Pub
Address: Canons Road
Bristol BS1 5UH, UK
Phone: +44 117 922 0382

#411
Trout Tavern
Category: Pub
Address: 46 Temple Street
Bristol BS31 1EH, UK
Phone: +44 117 986 2754

Shops, Restaurants, Attractions & Nightlife/ Bristol Guidebook 2020

#412
The Brass Pig
Category: Bar, British
Address: 1 Clifton Heights
Bristol BS8 1EJ, UK
Phone: +44 117 329 4471

#413
Friendship Inn
Category: Pub
Address: Axbridge Road
Bristol BS4 2RU, UK
Phone: +44 117 977 6926

#414
Mechanics Arms
Category: Pub
Address: 123 Clouds Hill Road
Bristol BS5 7LH, UK
Phone: +44 117 955 6915

#415
The Portcullis
Category: Pub
Address: 130 High Street
Bristol BS16 5HH, UK
Phone: +44 117 907 7302

#416
Koh Thai Tapas
Category: Dance Club, Thai
Address: 7-8 Triangle S
Bristol BS8 1EY, UK
Phone: +44 117 922 6699

#417
Bristol Tantric
Category: Adult Entertainment
Address: 28 waterloo Road
Bristol BS2 0PN, UK
Phone: +44 7584 624712

#418
Salsa Souls
Bristol Latin Dance School
Category: Music Venues
Average price: Inexpensive
Address: 26 - 28 St Nicholas Street
Bristol BS1 1UB, UK
Phone: +44 7982 241923

#419
The Elephant
Category: Pub, British
Address: 20 St Nicholas St
Bristol BS1 1UB, UK
Phone: +44 117 929 3561

#420
Chin! Chin! Bar & Kitchen
Category: Wine Bar, British, Pub
Average price: Modest
Address: 155 Saint Michael's Hill
Bristol BS2 8DB, UK
Phone: +44 117 973 9393

#421
The Richmond
Public House and Kitchen
Category: Pub
Address: 33-37 Gordon Rd
Bristol BS5 7, UK
Phone: +44 117 923 7542

#422
Stokers Public House
Category: Pub
Average price: Modest
Address: Gipsy Patch Lane
Bristol BS34 8LU, UK
Phone: +44 117 940 5495

#423
Chasers
Category: Dance Club
Average price: Expensive
Address: 63-65 Regent Street
Bristol BS15 8LD, UK
Phone: +44 117 960 8191

#424
The Phoenix
Category: Pub
Average price: Modest
Address: 15 Wellington Road
Bristol BS2 9DA, UK
Phone: +44 117 955 8327

#425
Copper Jacks
Category: Cocktail Bar, British
Address: Clare Street
Bristol BS1 1YH, UK
Phone: +44 117 927 6762

#426
The Kitchen
Category: Bar
Address: Zetland Road
Bristol BS6 7AH, UK
Phone: +44 117 942 2299

#427
Bibas Lounge Bar & Restaurant
Category: Cocktail Bar
Address: 51 Welsh Back
Bristol BS1 4AN, UK
Phone: +44 117 376 3636

#428
La Tomatina
Category: Lounge, Tapas Bar
Address: 2 Park Street
Bristol BS1 5PW, UK
Phone: +44 117 302 0008

#429
Abanico Salsa Bristol Clifton
Category: Dance Club
Address: 20 West Park
Bristol BS8 2LT, UK
Phone: +44 7771 666119

#430
Project Apocalypse
Category: Dance Club, DJs
Address: 57 Prince Street
Bristol BS1, UK
Phone: +44 7806 432533

#431
Salsa Sabrosa
Category: Dance Club
Address: 59 Whiteladies Road
Bristol BS8 2LY, UK
Phone: +44 7946 577141

#432
K2
Category: Dance Club
Address: Whiteladies Gate
Bristol BS8 2PH, UK
Phone: +44 117 973 4388

#433
Riproar Comedy
Category: Comedy Club
Address: The Cresswell Centre College Square Bristol BS1 5TT, UK
Phone: +44 117 914 0910

#434
The Surrey Vaults
Category: Pub
Address: 8-9 Surrey Street
Bristol BS2 8PS, UK
Phone: +44 117 942 6476

#435
The Inkerman
Category: Pub
Address: 2-4 Grosvenor Road
Bristol BS2 8XW, UK
Phone: +44 117 924 1104

#436
Club Creme
Category: Adult Entertainment
Average price: Modest
Address: 46 West Street
Bristol BS2 0BH, UK
Phone: +44 117 914 6624

#437
Vault Room
Category: Pub
Address: 47 Corn Street
Bristol BS1 1HT, UK
Phone: +44 117 946 8751

#438
Pranj's Bar
Category: Sports Bar
Address: 41 Corn Street
Bristol BS1 1HT, UK
Phone: +44 7779 985443

#439
Lounge at 30
Category: Adult Entertainment
Address: 30 Clare St
Bristol BS1 1YH, UK
Phone: +44 7532 488458

#440
Urban Tiger
Category: Adult Entertainment
Address: 4 Broad Quay
Bristol BS1 4DA, UK
Phone: +44 117 927 2181

#441
Dial a Drink 4u
Category: Bar
Address: 131 Easton Road
Bristol BS5 0EX, UK
Phone: +44 7407 688155

Shops, Restaurants, Attractions & Nightlife/ Bristol Guidebook 2020

#442
The Rock Playground
Category: Dance Club
Address: 57 Prince Street
Bristol BS1, UK
Phone: +44 7740 366921

#443
Horse & Groom
Category: Pub
Address: 17 St Georges Road
Bristol BS1 5UU, UK
Phone: +44 117 927 3641

#444
Its A Scream
Category: Pub
Address: 86-90 Gloucester Road
Bristol BS7 8BN, UK
Phone: +44 117 989 2471

#445
Golden Guinea
Category: Pub
Address: 19 Guinea Street
Bristol BS1 6SX, UK
Phone: +44 117 987 2034

#446
Dristis
Category: Bar
Address: 40 - 44 St Pauls Road
Bristol BS8 1LR, UK
Phone: +44 117 923 8788

#447
Coach House
Category: Pub
Address: 380 Stapleton Road
Bristol BS5 6NQ, UK
Phone: +44 117 939 3324

#448
Zazus Kitchen
Category: Bar, British
Address: 225 Gloucester Road
Bristol BS7 8NR, UK
Phone: +44 117 944 5500

#449
Rhubarb Tavern
Category: Pub
Average price: Modest
Address: 30 Queen Ann Road
Bristol BS5 9TX, UK
Phone: +44 117 955 0584

#450
Express Shisha
Category: Hookah Bar
Address: 7 Eastpark Drive
Bristol BS5 6YL, UK
Phone: +44 7773 904068

#451
The Hauliers Arms
Category: Pub
Address: Hauliers Arms
Bristol BS5 9NT, UK
Phone: +44 117 955 4756

#452
Houkara
Category: Hookah Bar
Average price: Modest
Address: 417 Gloucester Rd
Bristol BS7 8TZ, UK
Phone: +44 117 951 1930

#453
Trinity
Category: Music Venues
Average price: Modest
Address: Trinity Road
Bristol BS2 0NW, UK
Phone: +44 117 935 1200

#454
New Inn
Category: Pub
Address: 90 Bath Hill
Bristol BS31 1HN, UK
Phone: +44 117 986 5335

#455
Gloucester Arms
Category: Pub
Average price: Inexpensive
Address: 635 Gloucester Road
Bristol BS7 0BJ, UK
Phone: +44 117 951 4925

#456
Alcorunner
Category: Alcohol Delivery Service
Average price: Modest
Address: 123 Westbury Road
Bristol BS9, UK
Phone: +44 117 962 4602

#457
Miners Arms
Category: Pub
Address: 70 Bedminster Down Road
Bristol BS13 7AD, UK
Phone: +44 117 902 0062

#458
The Black Horse
Category: Pub
Address: 372 Two Mile Hill Road
Bristol BS15 1AH, UK
Phone: +44 117 967 3132

#459
Horse & Jockey
Category: Pub
Address: 56 Nags Head Hill
Bristol BS5 8LW, UK
Phone: +44 117 909 4417

#460
The Trooper
Category: Pub
Average price: Modest
Address: 90 Bryants Hill
Bristol BS5 8QT, UK
Phone: +44 117 967 3326

#461
Full Moon
Category: Pub
Address: 780 Fishponds Road
Bristol BS16 3TT, UK
Phone: +44 117 965 1853

#462
Maytree Public House
Category: Pub
Address: St Peters Rise
Bristol BS13 7QT, UK
Phone: +44 117 978 3732

#463
The Wayfarer
Category: Pub
Address: Pen Park Road
Bristol BS10 6BY, UK
Phone: +44 117 975 3620

#464
Wishing Well
Category: Pub
Address: Kingswood Aspects Leisure Park
Bristol BS15 9LA, UK
Phone: +44 117 947 5341

#465
Star Inn
Category: Pub
Address: 13 Bank Place
Bristol BS20 0AQ, UK
Phone: +44 1275 375562

#466
Jolly Cobbler
Category: Pub
Address: Chiphouse Road
Bristol BS15 4TS, UK
Phone: +44 117 960 2109

#467
Masons Arms
Category: Pub
Address: Lawrence Weston Road
Bristol BS11 0PP, UK
Phone: +44 117 982 1032

#468
The Lifeboat
Category: Pub
Address: 25 High Street
Bristol BS11 0DX, UK
Phone: +44 117 987 3781

#469
Blankety Quiz
Category: Comedy Club
Address: 51 Stokes Croft
Bristol BS1 3QP, UK
Phone: +44 117 914 8048

#470
Bwerani Project
Category: Music Venues
Address: 20-22 Hepburn Road
Bristol BS2 8UD, UK
Phone: +44 117 915 9805

#471
King Charles
Category: Pub
Address: 11 King Square Avenue
Bristol BS2 8HU, UK
Phone: +44 117 904 0034

#472
Tavern Holdings
Category: Pub
Address: 118 Cheltenham Road
Bristol BS6 5RW, UK
Phone: +44 117 923 2823

#473
St. Nicholas House
Category: Pub
Address: 19 ST. Nicholas Road
Bristol BS2 9JX, UK
Phone: +44 117 955 4395

#474
The Works
Category: Dance Club
Address: 15 Nelson Street
Bristol BS1 2JY, UK
Phone: +44 117 929 2658

#475
Preview Bar
Category: Wine Bar
Address: 50 Fairfax Street
Bristol BS1 2DF, UK
Phone: +44 7887 644598

#476
Arisona Leisure
Category: Pub
Address: 50 Fairfax Street
Bristol BS1 3BL, UK
Phone: +44 117 930 0276

#477
Crown Tavern
Category: Pub
Address: 17 Lawfords Gate
Bristol BS2 0DY, UK
Phone: +44 117 941 1085

#478
The Lanes Bristol
Category: Bar
Address: 22 Nelson Street
Bristol BS1 2LE, UK
Phone: +44 117 370 0625

#479
Bristol Karaoke Co
Category: Karaoke
Address: 50 Old Market Street
Bristol BS2 0ER, UK
Phone: +44 117 904 0400

#480
Bristol Comedy Pub
Category: Pub
Address: Stokes Croft
Bristol BS1 3RW, UK
Phone: +44 117 903 0796

#481
Chophouse and Jazz
Category: American, Lounge
Address: Future Inns
Bristol BS1 3EN, UK
Phone: +44 117 304 1020

#482
Helen Farley
Category: Massage, Pub
Address: 15 Cotham Road South
Bristol BS6 5TZ, UK
Phone: +44 7803 505949

#483
Justwins
Category: Dance Club
Address: 25 West Street
Bristol BS2 0DF, UK
Phone: +44 117 955 9269

#484
The Mall
Category: Pub, British
Average price: Modest
Address: 66 The Mall Clifton BS8 3, UK
Phone: +44 117 974 5318

#485
The Canteen
Category: Music Venues, Bar
Average price: Modest
Address: 80 Stokes Croft
Bristol BS1 3QY, UK
Phone: +44 117 923 2017

#486
Highbury Vaults
Category: Pub
Average price: Modest
Address: 164 St Michaels Hill
Bristol BS2 8DE, UK
Phone: +44 117 973 3203

#487
The Fox Den
Category: Pub, British
Average price: Expensive
Address: New Road
Stoke Gifford BS34 8TJ, UK
Phone: +44 117 979 1861

Shops, Restaurants, Attractions & Nightlife/ Bristol Guidebook 2020

#488
Miners Rest
Category: Pub
Average price: Inexpensive
Address: 42 Providence Lane Long Ashton BS41 9DJ, UK
Phone: +44 1275 393449

#489
King George VI
Category: Pub
Average price: Modest
Address: Filton Avenue Bristol BS34, UK
Phone: +44 117 969 1526

#490
The Wine Bar
Category: Wine Bar
Average price: Modest
Address: 19 High Street Keynsham BS31 1DP, UK
Phone: +44 117 914 3153

#491
The Old Bank
Category: Pub
Average price: Inexpensive
Address: 20 High Street Keynsham BS31 1DQ, UK
Phone: +44 117 986 4766

#492
The Air Balloon
Category: Pub
Average price: Inexpensive
Address: 115 Gloucester Road North Filton BS34 7PY, UK
Phone: +44 117 931 2706

#493
Red Lion
Category: Pub
Average price: Inexpensive
Address: 19 St James Street Bristol BS16 9HD, UK
Phone: +44 845 230 1986

#494
Hooters
Category: Sports Bar
Average price: Modest
Address: Unit 2, Building 11, Harborside England BS1 5SZ, UK
Phone: +44 114 41179 300750

#495
The Crown Inn
Category: Pub
Average price: Modest
Address: 63 Bristol Road Keynsham BS31 2WA, UK
Phone: +44 117 986 2150

#496
Eton
Category: Bar
Average price: Modest
Address: 28 Baldwin Street Bristol BS1 1NG, UK
Phone: +44 117 927 9813

#497
The Lanes
Category: Bowling, Dance Club
Average price: Modest
Address: 22 Nelson Street Bristol BS1 2LE, UK
Phone: +44 117 325 1979

#498
The Full Moon
Category: Pub, Music Venues
Average price: Modest
Address: Stokes Croft Bristol BS1 3PR, UK
Phone: +44 117 924 5007

#499
Bar Humbug
Category: Pub, British, Lounge
Average price: Modest
Address: 89 Whiteladies Road Bristol BS8 2NT, UK
Phone: +44 117 904 0061

#500
The Park
Category: Pub
Average price: Expensive
Address: 37 Triangle West Bristol BS8 1ER, UK
Phone: +44 117 940 6101

Printed in Great Britain
by Amazon